# Public Office, Private Interest

# Public Office, Private Interest
## Bureaucracy and Corruption in India

S. K. Das

OXFORD
UNIVERSITY PRESS

# OXFORD
UNIVERSITY PRESS

YMCA Library Building, Jai Singh Road, New Delhi 110001

Oxford University Press is a department of the University of Oxford. It furthers the
University's objective of excellence in research, scholarship, and education
by publishing worldwide in

Oxford   New York

Athens   Auckland   Bangkok   Bogota   Buenos Aires   Calcutta
Cape Town   Chennai   Dar es Salaam   Delhi   Florence   Hong Kong   Istanbul
Karachi   Kuala Lumpur   Madrid   Melbourne   Mexico City   Mumbai
Nairobi   Paris   Sao Paolo   Shanghai   Singapore   Taipei   Tokyo   Toronto   Warsaw

with associated companies in   Berlin   Ibadan

Oxford is a registered trade mark of Oxford University Press
in the UK and in certain other countries

Published in India
By Oxford University Press, New Delhi

ISBN 019 565382 3

Typeset in Palatino
By Urvashi Press, 75 Gandhi Nagar, Meerut
Printed in India at Karan Press, New Delhi 110020
and published by Manzar Khan, Oxford University Press
YMCA Library Building, Jai Singh Road, New Delhi 110001

* Just as it is not possible not to taste honey or poison placed on the surface of the tongue, even so it is not possible for one dealing with the money of the king not to taste the money in however small a quantity.

* Just as fish moving inside water cannot be known when drinking water, even so officers appointed for carrying out works cannot be known when appropriating money.

* It is possible to know even the path of birds flying in the sky, but not the ways of officers moving with their intentions concealed.

* And he should make those who have amassed (money wrongfully) yield it up and should change them in (their) works, so that they do not consume (the king's) property or disgorge what is consumed.

* But those who do not consume (the king's) goods and increase them in just ways, should be made permanent in their offices, being devoted to what is agreeable and permanent to the king.

*The Kautiliya Arthasastra*
2.9.32–36

# Acknowledgements

I am indebted, to a number of people for support in writing this book. An overwhelmingly large number of them are from the civil service; they will remain nameless because they prefer it that way, but I welcome the opportunity to acknowledge their generous support.

I am grateful to Sudha Krishnan who took time off her engagements to go through the draft and offer very valuable suggestions; the book owes its present form to her creative comments. I owe a deep debt to Sridevi for her assistance with the book.

It gives me great pleasure to acknowledge the support of Manzar Khan, Gaurav Ghose, and Nitasha Devasar. They have been good to me in countless ways, and this despite the fact that it must be particularly trying to put up with a civil servant writing a book on the civil service.

My most profound thanks to my wonderful family—my sons Rohit and Siddharth, and my wife, Malati—for their support. My sons were very supportive and Malati was the epitome of patience while I was working on this book.

# Contents

# Tables

# 1

# Introduction

Paradigms often get lost and are replaced by new ones. Thomas Kuhn tells us how.[1] Paradigms are universally recognized worldviews which, for a time, provide model solutions. Conditions are considered to be normal when a paradigm finds acceptance. The acceptance provides the necessary consensus for a common field of practice. There may be puzzles, but so long as they do not threaten the consensus, they are not seriously considered.

But when these puzzles are not solved over a period of time, there is a crisis and a loss of faith in the paradigm, leaving the way open to alternatives. The paradigm is in ferment, and a revolution occurs when the older paradigm is replaced by a new one. Then, there ensues a normal era of the new paradigm.

This book is substantially about a paradigm now in ferment, and less extensively about an alternative paradigm. Both the paradigms relate to public bureaucracies, specifically, to how they should be structured so that bureaucratic office is not used for private gain. The older paradigm is in ferment, because it has failed to solve the puzzle. The new paradigm offers those solutions.

The older paradigm gained acceptance in the nineteenth century when many states replaced their patronage bureaucracies with merit-based ones. In a patronage bureaucracy, bureaucrats are appointed to public office on the basis of loyalty to the ruler, and they use their public office for private gain. In essence, a patronage bureaucracy makes no distinction between public interest and private interest.

The nineteenth century paradigm challenged the premises of patronage by positing the concept of a merit system. It suggested the virtues of merit and expertise as the foundations of administration. By the logic of this paradigm, private means of entry to a public bureaucracy is ruled out. If rules are the sole basis of administration, whoever learned these rules could apply their expertise to particular cases uniformly. Expertise, like merit, is public; and when expertise and merit are made the basis of administration, they would exclude private interest from administration.

Incentives and punishment were critical components of this paradigm. Incentives were important because the idea of a career in civil service was proposed on the principle of life-time employment. It called for early commitment, foregoing other career opportunities. Given the opportunity costs involved for individuals of merit, early commitment demanded attractive incentives.

The paradigm contemplated some punitive measures, as well. Mechanisms were put in place to punish bureaucrats using public office for private gain.

*Esprit de corps* was nurtured so that bureaucrats would be loyal to their organization. The idea was that because of *esprit de corps*, bureaucrats would identify with the government organization, and would promote the interests of that organization. It was assumed that these measures would insulate public bureaucracies from politics.

The question is: did the paradigm succeed in what it set out to do? This book looks at the Indian experience for an answer. The Indian patronage bureaucracy was rationalized in the middle of the nineteenth century to create a merit-based civil service system. The rationalization put in place the essential sources of motivation—meritocratic recruitment, a reward structure, control systems and conditions to enable identification of the civil servants with the organization. That was in colonial India; but when the country became independent, the basic structure of the rationalized system was retained, although liberties were taken with the individual sources of motivation.

Has the paradigm succeeded in separating the civil servants

from the pursuit of their private interests as it intended to do? The book finds that the answer is in the negative. The public bureaucracy in India is rated as one of the most corrupt in the world. What is disturbing is that corruption in India is now entrenched—it is pervasive, organized and monopolistic. Even more disturbing is how patrimonial politics has colonized the entire public bureaucracy.

The paradigm has obviously failed to solve the puzzle. Its failure, it would seem, can be attributed to the fact that it did not construct boundaries between the public bureaucracy and its environs, notably politics. The assumptions that the paradigm had made, have been belied. Merit as the criterion of selecting incumbents has not kept politics out. Reliance on expertise has not removed political considerations from administration.

In evaluating this paradigm the peculiar circumstances which prevailed in the nineteenth century, need to be put in perspective. At the time the assumptions were made, the public bureaucracy was used to serve the narrow ends of patrimonial politics. In such a scenario, merit and expertise were viewed as the foundations of a good government as opposed to the one provided by politics. In fact, politics was the evil that was sought to be exorcised from administration. Political considerations were regarded as particularistic considerations, and it was assumed that such considerations in the selection of civil servants or in the manner of their functioning would be detrimental.

Politics, obviously, had to be kept out. But where the paradigm fails, is in its refusal to see that merit and expertise are not sufficient to depoliticize administration. The process of keeping politics out involves a lot more than putting in place a merit-based civil service system. At a minimum, it calls for a restructuring of the relations between a public bureaucracy and the ruling politicians.

This, in essence, is the conundrum. Merit and expertise are expected to offset the evil of patrimonial politics, and at the same time, respond to its legitimate authority. There is a dilemma here. Politics, even if patrimonial in nature, means popular participation in government through elections. The bottom line, therefore, is that the civil service system has to be made responsive to political direction. But patrimonial politics has an unrelenting urge to be self-serving. So the essential question is: how can we include politics in the system of administration so that there is popular participation in the government, and yet, exclude it so that it does not use the administration to further its partisan ends?[2]

The new paradigm offers a solution. What the new paradigm does is to separate the roles and functions of both the actors—the ruling politicians and the civil servants. Once this is done, the areas of functioning are delimited and kept distinct by recourse to contractual arrangements to which both the politicians and civil servants agree. The new paradigm is the 'new public management' or 'new managerialism', and it has already been implemented in New Zealand, Australia, the United Kingdom, and Sweden.

The new paradigm recognizes that opportunities for corruption arise because people do not have information. It emphasizes that corruption is best fought when systematic efforts are made to inform citizens about their rights and entitlements and empower them to resist corruption. In other words, the new paradigm gives the people the leading role in anti-corruption efforts.

The book is about these two paradigms: the older paradigm which is in ferment, and the new one which offers a solution to the paradigmatic puzzle. After a general introduction (Chapter 1), Chapter 2 lays down the framework for subsequent discussion. It looks at the conditions which led to the rationalization of the patronage bureaucracies and creation of the modern merit-based civil service systems. It defines the sources of motivation which such systems put in place—meritocratic recruitment, reward structure, control systems and organizational identification.

Chapter 3 looks at the history of public bureaucracies in India. It is a study of specific historical periods—the Maurya, the Delhi Sultanate, the Mughal and the East India Company. Chapter 4 looks at the conditions leading to the rationalization of the public bureaucracy in India and examines the nature of the civil service system that the rationalization put in place.

The next four chapters are about the four sources of motivation. Chapter 5 discusses the system of recruiting civil servants in India on the basis of merit; it evaluates the extent of effective meritocracy in the civil service. Chapter 6 is an assessment of the reward structure. Chapter 7 looks at the control systems. Chapter 8 is about organizational identification—the extent to which the civil servants in India identify with the organizations in which they work.

The last chapter (9), the conclusion, analyses why the present paradigm is in ferment. It also looks at the new paradigm which offers a solution to the puzzle, and it assesses to what extent the new paradigm has the credentials to succeed.

## NOTES

1. Thomas S. Kuhn, *The Structure of Scientific Revolutions* (Chicago: University of Chicago Press, Phoenix Edition, 1964), p. 91.
2. For a discussion on this point, see Patricia Wallace Ingraham, *The Foundation of Merit: Public Service in American Democracy* (Baltimore: The Johns Hopkins University Press, 1995).

# 2

# The Paradigm

A bureaucracy is not quite the most efficient way of organizing things, Weber's claim notwithstanding. What Weber did was to suggest certain basic features that a system of administration should have for it to qualify as a bureaucracy.[1]

First, systematic division of labour defined such an organization. Weber suggested that administration should be broken down into repetitive tasks, each the jurisdiction of a particular office. It was, therefore, necessary to define the tasks given to every link in the organization.

Second, such an organization follows the principle of hierarchy with lower offices being supervised by the higher office. Within a continuous chain of subsumption of authority, every node in the hierarchy was accountable to its immediately superordinate authority not only for its own actions but also for the actions of those subordinate to it.

Third, the management of an office should follow general rules, capable of being learned, which defined the responsibility of every member of the organization. The rule-bound nature of administration enabled it to deal uniformly with a large number of tasks, irrespective of the number of people engaged in fulfilling them.

Fourth, Weber postulated the principle of impersonality. In Weber's own words.

Its specific nature, which is welcomed by capitalism, develops the more perfectly the more bureaucracy is 'dehumanised', the more completely it succeeds in eliminating from official business love, hatred, and all purely personal, irrational, and emotional elements which escape calculation. This is the specific nature of bureaucracy and it is appraised as its special virtue.

Fifth, office-holders were selected on the basis of merit. The office was a full-time salaried occupation, with a predictable career structure which offered prospects of regular progression.

Sixth, a public bureaucracy based on meritocratic recruitment, and with assured career progression, developed *esprit de corps* among employees and inculcated in them staunch loyalty to the organization.

Seventh, holders of office were given expert training in the rules to be followed. The management of the office, according to Weber, was to be based on written documents (files) which were to be preserved and accessed only by incumbents.

Eighth, office was separated from ownership of the means of administration. This ensured that the administration was freed from the financial limitations of the private household, and the office became dependent on the government for its existence, and hence was amenable to its discipline. It also meant that those holding office were discouraged from using their official position for private gain.

Weber's definitional model of bureaucracy found ready acceptance. There could possibly be no objection to such a model; after all, all that Weber was doing was to identify the basic features common to modern systems of large-scale administration and use them to build a definitional model. What was problematic, however, was Weber's claim that a bureaucracy with these features, was also the most efficient form of administration.

## THE EFFICIENCY CLAIM

Weber's efficiency claim has been widely critiqued, and with good reason. Yet, in fairness to Weber, his claim deserves to be put in perspective. When Weber claimed that bureaucracy was the most efficient form of administration, his referent was not some absolute ideal, but forms of administration such as kinship networks or the rule of local notables. As Weber himself pointed out, the internal combustion engine may appear wasteful when compared with some ideal of maximum energy utilization, but is vastly superior to a horse.

Weber used the efficiency argument in a relative sense. He was inviting attention to the inefficiency of the earlier forms of administration because they failed to exclude personal interest from the execution of official tasks. To Weber, the efficiency of an organization increased only to the extent that it was able to depersonalize the execution of official tasks.

Weber's efficiency argument was premised on his concept of impersonality or *sina ira et studio*, that is, without hatred or passion. Weber developed his argument in two ways. First, he constructed depersonalized roles for bureaucrats selected on merit. Second, he argued that behaviour governed by rules forced bureaucrats to be separated from their private interests. Weber's essential proposition was that rules governing the selection, appointment, advancement, and range of discretion of bureaucrats while making decisions are also the rules which restrain pursuit of private interest.[2] The idea of separating the office-holder from his personal or private interest is central to the Weberian paradigm.

## RATIONALIZING PUBLIC BUREAUCRACIES

It is unlikely to be a coincidence that the nineteenth-century states which rationalized their public bureaucracies were not in search of efficiency goals although the outcome of the process resembled Weber's definitional model of bureaucracy. The early leaders were France, Prussia and England. The French bureaucracy's Napoleonic rationalization was not driven by reasons of efficiency. Nor was the mandarin-like rationalization of the Prussian bureaucracy.

Likewise, it was not the demand for efficiency that brought about the rationalization of the English bureaucracy. Until the early nineteenth century, the affairs of the state in England were administered by bureaucrats who owed their positions to patronage. There was no common system of pay. Bribes augmented uneven salaries of officials. The public offices were viewed as private property, which, like any other asset, could be sold or used for making money.

The English bureaucracy was rationalized in the second half of the nineteenth century. The blueprint for rationalization was the Northcote–Trevelyan Report of 1854. The Report proposed the creation of a merit-based bureaucracy based on the idea of a career civil service. Drawing on similar ideas advanced for the Indian civil service by the Macaulay Report, presented to the House of Commons earlier that year, Northcote and Trevelyan recommended competitive entry examination and the creation of 'a career service, *immune from nepotism and political jobbery* and, by the same token, attractive for its total security as well as for the intellectual achievement and social status that success in the entry examination implied'.[3]

The recommendations of the Northcote–Trevelyan Report provoked considerable debate and opposition and its implementation took time. Although the Civil Service Commission was established in 1855, many departments continued to recruit their staff on the basis of patronage. It was not until 1870 that patronage was finally abolished, and selection of civil servants on the basis of merit was made compulsory for all the departments of the government.

In Japan too, it was not the search for efficiency which drove the rationalization of the bureaucracy in the nineteenth century. The Japanese bureaucracy was rationalized in the 1880s, after the Meiji Restoration. With the Imperial Ordinance of 1871, which dissolved the old feudal structure of Japan, *samurai* officials lost their ranks and positions as the hereditary bureaucratic class of Japan.

Even after this, the Meiji government continued the old practice of appointing bureaucrats on the basis of loyalty. Persons who had been part of the Meiji Restoration and were loyal to the new government were rewarded with office. But it had become clear by the early 1880s that this practice could not be defended rationally. It invited the opprobrium that private rather than public interest was being furthered in the Meiji administration.

This prompted the Meiji dispensation to search for a system of recruitment and functioning that was self-evidently in the public interest. Hirobumi Ito, a front-ranking leader of the Meiji Restoration, visited Europe to study the systems there and find a model. Ito returned with a blueprint for creating a public bureaucracy on the Prussian model. Bureaucrats were selected on the basis of merit, given extensive training in law, and made to function in an environment where all official acts were regulated by a strict rule of law.

It was only in the United States of America that there was a big outcry about the way the bureaucracy functioned, but the outcry was directed at the venality of the patronage system. In the second half of the nineteenth century, Boss Tweed and his contemporaries ran the administration like a personal fiefdom, and bureaucratic administration was an unabashed exercise in patronage. The Progressive movement under the leadership of Theodore Roosevelt, Woodrow Wilson, and Louis Brandeis sought to end such patronage. The passage of the Pendleton Act (1883) was the first step in providing for a merit-based system in place of patronage. In due course, the Progressives created a civil service system based on written examinations, fixed pay scales, and protection from arbitrary recruitment and dismissal.

In essence, the process of rationalization of public bureaucracies in the nineteenth century was meant to replace patronage with merit as the basis for selection, on the assumption that the pursuit of private interest by bureaucrats would be eliminated. In other words, the *publicness* of the public bureaucracies was sought to be achieved.

The rationalization of public bureaucracies by nineteenth-century states was the culmination of a larger historical process which had started several centuries before. The process spanned the change-over from the purely personal service of the ruler to patronage bureaucracies and ultimately to the concept of public service. The transition from the personal to the public was but a part of the whole gamut of social change from feudalism to bureaucratic absolutism to capitalism and political democracy.

## PATRIMONIAL BUREAUCRACIES

Initially, all office-holders were the servants of the ruler. Starting with Egypt—the historical model of all later bureaucracies—where officials were slaves of the Pharaoh, office was held on the patronage of the ruler. Much later, in England, all major offices were held on the King's discretion. In the days of Charles I, civil servants were 'his own, and not yet those of some institutional abstraction, the Crown or State'.[4]

Weber's work on patrimonial states provides interesting insights.[5] The ruler in a patrimonial state governs on the basis of personal, traditional authority, and the model is that of a patriarchal family. Obedience is to the ruler and not to an office, and therefore, it is limited only by the ruler's discretion. The patrimonial kingdom is small in size, and in its organization and functioning is similar to a patriarchal family.

Patrimonial-bureaucratic empires came about when the rulers of the patriarchal kingdoms expanded the boundaries of their kingdoms. Consequently, the nature of authority changed from the patriarchal, which was personal, to the purely political, which had to be administered by officials who were extra-patrimonial.

There was no change in the style of administration, however. The ruler continued to exercise power in the same personal way as had been done in the patriarchal kingdom. But the empires were now larger in size, and so, rulers had to evolve a strategy enabling them to exercise power in the same personal, patriarchal way as before, despite the increase in the number of subjects and area of rule.

The strategy was to have a bureaucracy which partook of the patrimonial nature of the political organization. In the patrimonial kingdom, administration was personalized, and there was no difference between the officials of the state and officials of the ruler's household. In patrimonial-bureaucratic empires, there was a difference between these two categories. Since the area of rule was larger extra-patrimonial officials had to be part of the administration.

In patrimonial kingdom, officials were compensated for their services directly from the ruler's household. This was not possible in patrimonial-bureaucratic empires. So rulers temporarily assigned large tracts of lands or villages to officials. However, since the area of patrimonial-bureaucratic empires was large and officials had to work away from the royal seat of power, the personal nature of patrimonial authority, hitherto the instrument of control over officials, no longer worked. Rulers started losing control over their officials, and officials asserted their independence by assuming hereditary ownership of assigned lands.

Rulers now reasserted their authority by travelling extensively, compelling the regular court attendance of officials and effecting periodic transfer of officials. Intelligence networks reported on the activities of officials. Offices with overlapping responsibilities were established to create a system of checks and balances.

Above all, rulers enforced the temporariness of land grants to officials.

This, then, is a patrimonial bureaucracy. As Weber says, 'Patrimonialism, and in the extreme case, sultanism tend to arise whenever traditional domination develops and administration and a military force which are the personal instruments of the master.'[6]

Patrimonial domination, however, had to contend with various local, autonomous and centrifugal forces. Rulers had to confront and overcome these forces by using personal resources such as landed property and loyal officials. As Weber puts it, 'The continuous struggle of the central power with the various centrifugal local powers creates a specific problem for patrimonialism when the patrimonial ruler, with his personal power resources—his landed property, other sources of revenue, and personal loyal officers and soldiers—confronts not a mere mass of subjects differentiated only according to sibs and vocations, but when he stands as one landlord over other landlords, who as local honaritiores wield autonomous authority of their own.'[7]

A patrimonial bureaucracy differs from a modern bureaucracy in several ways. While in a modern bureaucracy, the incumbents are recruited on the basis of merit, those in a patrimonial bureaucracy are selected on the basis of loyalty. The officers in a modern bureaucracy are paid regular salaries, while those in a patrimonial bureaucracy are assigned prebends or benefices which consists of appropriation of fees, taxes or goods that are otherwise due to the state. In a modern bureaucracy a job is a career and is the only occupation of the official, while in a patrimonial bureaucracy the officials serve at the pleasure of the ruler and often perform tasks unrelated to their appointment. In a modern bureaucracy, the officers are subject to an official-impersonal authority, but in a patrimonial bureaucracy, personal loyalty and allegiance are demanded of the officials.

The most important difference, however, is in the nature of the distinction which these two types of bureaucracies make between the public and private, or the official and the personal. The patrimonial bureaucracy makes no such distinction, while such a distinction is crucial to how a modern bureaucracy functions.

The patrimonial bureaucracy's indifference to the distinction between the private and the public or the official and the personal, derives from the very nature of patrimonialism. In a modern bureaucracy, there is a hierarchy of precisely circumscribed offices, while the officials in a patrimonial bureaucracy fill positions that are loosely defined.[8] The conception of office in a patrimonial bureaucracy is purely economic. Rulers assign to officials rent payments for life, payments which are fixed to objects or which are essentially economic usufruct from land or other sources. These are compensations for the discharge of official duties—goods permanently set aside for the economic assurance of office. The office is a source of rent, and no distinction is made between the use of the office for public or private purpose. Official duties and compensation are interrelated in such a way that the official does not transfer to the ruler any yield gained from the objects left to him, but, in turn, he renders to the ruler services of a personal, military or ecclesiastical nature. The fiscal and sovereignty prerogatives of the state are temporarily exchanged for services of a specified nature to the ruler.

## THE RATIONALIZATION

The rationalization of bureaucracies by nineteenth-century states was designed to separate bureaucrats from their private interests. This was sought to be done in several ways.

Bureaucratic office was depersonalized through merit-based selection, which precluded private means of entry. The uniformity of rule-bound administration ensured that personal predilection did not affect the fulfillment of official responsibility. Expertise in the application of these rules eliminated private knowledge and interests from administration. It was assumed that a public bureaucracy based on merit and expertise would be insulated from politics. Merit and expertise were to be the linchpins of depoliticized administration. However, the efficacy of merit and expertise required equally the operation of a set of incentives.

## INCENTIVES

The question of incentives is important because the idea of a career civil service was based on the principle of life-time employment. This called for early commitment—possibly by foregoing other career opportunities—and early commitment demanded attractive incentives.

Several incentives were offered. A career in government meant secure employment and old-age security in the form of pension. As Weber said, 'Entrance into an office . . . is considered an acceptance of a specific obligation of faithful management in return for a secure existence.'

There was also the assurance of career advancement in two ways. Entry into higher offices of a public bureaucracy being limited to those who had made the early commitment meant the monopoly of higher offices by such individuals. The other was the assurance of a career path with predictable promotions based on seniority.

Employment in public bureaucracies was based on the guarantee of security of service conditions. A civil servant risked losing position or right to regular promotions, only for reasons duly established as being adequate by impartial bodies. In other words, there could be no arbitrary decision affecting the civil servant's career adversely. As Weber said, what was being offered was 'the opportunity of a career that is not dependent upon mere accident and arbitrariness'.

Since a permanent career in the government meant association with sovereignty functions, important public decisions and vital information, civil servants were granted certain privileges. These privileges consisted of special ranks and protection in the criminal codes against 'insult of officials' and 'contempt of the state'. These privileges along with appointment on the basis of merit brought status in society.

Above all else, serving the state was regarded as a higher duty. As Weber said, 'the position of the official is in the nature of a duty. This determines the internal structure of his relations, in the following manner: Legally and actually, office-holding is not considered a source to be exploited for rents or emoluments, as was normally the case during the Middle Ages and frequently up to the threshold of recent times'.

This paradigm of impersonal administration assumed that with a meritocratic recruitment and promotion system which shielded civil servants from political patronage, an incentive structure which rewarded them for honest effort, mechanisms which punished misuse of public office and the inculcation of organizational loyalty, civil servants would be motivated to put the goals of public administration over their private interest. The four sources of this motivation are: *meritocracy, rewards, control systems,* and *identification with the organization.*

## MERITOCRACY

In a meritocratic system incumbents are chosen on the basis of merit. Meritocracy is important in two ways.

Merit-based recruitment to office invests the office with prestige and makes it attractive to talented individuals.[9] Passing the entrance examination is akin to being inducted into a hall of fame: it is an indication that an individual who has been admitted to the civil service is possessed of extraordinary merit.[10]

A merit-based system tends to attract to its ranks individuals who seek to contribute to public good, or at least, those who have strong preferences for 'having an impact' on the government's task of providing collective goods, i.e. general welfare. This increases the probability of such individuals not seeking to promote their private interests at the cost of the general welfare.[11]

Merit-based recruitment is generally of two types: the mandarin system and open recruitment.[12] A mandarin system is a closed-entry, hierarchical system in which civil servants are selected on the basis of a competitive entrance examination. In this system, selective recruitment takes place on a centralized basis. The entrance examination is rigorous, and candidates with the highest scores are selected. Mandarin systems are found in France, Germany and Japan.

Open recruitment systems have lateral, flexible and market-driven entry mechanisms for civil servants. There is no age limit to entry. The United States and New Zealand are the examples of an open recruitment system.

Different merit-based systems employ different signalling devices to indicate merit.[13] In some countries, for instance, it takes the form of a civil service entrance examination. In others, the primary filter is performance in school or the completion of a graduate degree from a reputable university, and in some others, it is a combination of examination, performance in school, and a graduate degree.

Problems are likely to arise when the merit signalling device is diluted by making recruitment serve other purposes. For example, many governments become employers of the last resort and recruitment to the civil service becomes a solution to the problem of the educated unemployed. Merit in such cases ceases to be the primary criterion.

This also happens when recruitment to the bureaucracy addresses social concerns, such as representation in the civil service on the basis of ethnicity, caste, and social or economic backwardness. This is the case when access to civil service positions is seen as an important privilege to be shared in proportion to caste or communal disadvantages.

## REWARDS

The relationship between an incentive structure which rewards honest effort and an honest bureaucracy has been recognized in the policy debate. It is now accepted that if the incentive structure is poor, civil servants may succumb to temptation. The description of the Ugandan civil servant in the 1980s is telling: 'The civil servant had either to survive by lowering his standard of ethics, performance and dutifulness or remain upright and perish. He chose to survive.'[14] The contentious issue, however, is the level of compensation at which corruption is discouraged, and the cost-effectiveness of such an arrangement.

The problem, essentially, is how to value the output of civil servants, because such output cannot otherwise be marketed. The solution to the problem has been to compare civil service compensation to the compensation of equivalent skills in the private sector to evaluate the adequacy of civil service compensation. This is because civil servants often compare themselves with their peers in the private sector, and they expect to achieve similar income levels. The larger the gap between civil service and private sector compensation, the greater is the tendency of the civil servants to resort to corruption. Hence, the ratio between the government and private sector compensation is called the 'rate of temptation'.[15]

Comparison between civil service and private sector compensation can, however, be tricky. To make such a comparison, the level of compensation has to be adjusted to account for the fact that employment in the civil service offers greater security than employment in the private sector, inducing civil servants to perhaps accept a lower level of compensation. In countries where civil service system is merit-based, civil servants enjoy a degree of prestige which is not associated with employment in the private sector, and therefore, civil servants enjoy a form of psychic income. Empirical evidence[16] suggests that the implicit discount for these two considerations is about 20 to 30 per cent.

Recent studies have tried to establish a numerical correlation between compensation in the civil service and in the private sector. A study by Rijckeghem and Weder,[17] drawing on a multinational corruption index,[18] has attempted to grade civil service compensation levels in twenty-five countries as ratios of compensation in the private sector, and provide rough estimates of pay differentials. Not surprisingly, Rijckeghem-Weder found that corruption is lower in countries where civil servants are paid relatively well. Based on this finding, the study suggested that increasing civil service compensation from 100 to 200 per cent of the compensation in the private sector would reduce corruption by about one unit in the corruption index, by no means an unimpressive reduction.

Such correlations are, however, not without problems. For one, they do not conclusively prove that an increase in compensation in public bureaucracies is sufficient to eliminate corruption. For example, civil servants in El Salvador are paid more than those in the private sector, but El Salvador is at the very bottom of the list of non-corrupt countries in the corruption index. On the other hand, Singapore, which is at the top, is the only country among the twenty-five countries in the list which pays its civil servants more than the average compensation in the private sector.[19]

At what point, therefore, does civil service compensation become attractive enough to discourage corruption? The Rijckeghem-Weder study estimates that government compensation should be between 2.8 and 7.4 times the compensation in the private sector to reduce corruption to a negligible level. This, of course, entails an increase in compensation by a factor of at least three or four, a very expensive proposition, indeed.

Models of efficiency wages in tax collection[22] also yield similar conclusions. Besley and McLaren show that the 'reservation wage' for a tax inspector—a wage equal to the earning in a private sector job— is substantially higher than the 'capitulation wage' that induces corruption by necessity, while the 'efficiency wage', competitive with bribery, is higher still.[21]

According to these models, ensuring honesty in the civil service can be expensive. When incidence of corruption is high and the probability of getting caught is low, the level of compensation at which corruption can be eliminated is high. Governments may, therefore, find it cost-effective to restrict compensation in the government to the capitulation level—the level at which only the dishonest are attracted to the civil service—rather than increase compensation to the prohibitively expensive level at which corruption can be eliminated.[22]

Low level of compensation to civil servants occupying high positions in the government is of serious concern. Wage compression—where salaries of senior civil servants are compressed relative to the minimum pay in the salary structure, and compression is measured as the ratio of the basic salary of the highest category to the starting salary of the lowest category—affects the motivation of senior civil servants. This is significant, because civil servants occupying senior positions control dispensation of benefits whose value far exceeds their compensation. This, clearly, is an incentive to be corrupt.

Compensation to civil servants occupying senior positions has been allowed, for political or ideological reasons, to erode in value more than the compensation paid to civil servants at the lower levels. Wage compression has, in fact, been used as a deliberate mechanism under socialism in order to satisfy considerations of equity.

The adequacy of civil service compensation also needs to be viewed from the perspective of fairness.[23] It is not merely a question of determining the level of compensation at which corruption is eliminated altogether, but equally a question of whether the civil servants are forced to be corrupt, because they cannot meet their reasonable commitments with the compensation they receive from the government. The fairness argument suggests that civil servants may perhaps choose to forego opportunities for corruption, if their level of compensation is such that it can meet their reasonable commitments.

The fairness argument is important, because considerations of fairness influence the behaviour of society, which is often called upon to regulate civil service behaviour. Society may condone acts of corruption if compensation paid to civil servants is seen to be at miserably low levels. If people feel that the compensation paid to civil servants is so low that it is not adequate to meet their reasonable commitments, they may not be willing to cooperate with the government in policing corruption.[24]

The policy debate, therefore, is far from conclusive. If civil servants are driven to be corrupt because their remuneration is not adequate to meet their reasonable commitments, it makes sense to pay them a fair wage. But it is possible that civil servants are driven by greed. In that case the adequacy of civil service compensation is not the issue. In fact, the Rijckeghem-Weder study makes a telling point: from the trends in individual countries over a 12-year period, changes in the level of government compensation did not have any significant impact on the extent of corruption.

## *Promotions and Placements*

Promotions have traditionally been regarded as rewards that motivate civil servants. In order to motivate, the promotion system should be both merit-based and internal to the organization. If promotions are personalized and politicized, civil servants will concentrate on doing personal favours for their superiors.

Campos and Pradhan[25] argue that an internal promotion system based on merit tends to attract such people into the ranks of the civil service who want to make an impact on the government objective of providing general welfare. It can be assumed that such individuals are less likely to be corrupt, an assumption validated by an empirical study.[26] The study found internal promotion and broader career building elements of a bureaucratic structure to be the most important factors in minimizing corruption.

While it is accepted that promotions may establish the needed deterrence to corrupt behaviour, lack of promotion can also lead to personal frustration and, therefore, to selfish behaviour. A sound personnel system should take care of such a situation. It should, at a minimum, assure that even those in the civil service who fall behind their peers in the race for promotions, should not be allowed to get frustrated, drop out of the system, and indulge in corrupt practices.

So, the key feature of a sound promotion policy should be to prevent any civil servant from dropping out of the system after his appointment to the civil service. The objective should be to ensure that amongst civil servants of the same age group, while the most successful individuals maintain a high degree of motivation, the less successful ones are not left feeling frustrated.

In the context of a public bureaucracy, it is not easy to define merit while promoting civil servants and constructing a merit-based promotion system linked to performance and productivity can be problematic. Work in most public agencies is inter-connected, and individual contributions are not easily captured. Most governments get over this problem through promotions on the basis of seniority. In the process, everyone in the organization gets to be promoted without reference to their contribution. This does not help because the value of rewards stems from the fact that they are scarce.

Placements in civil service positions are also seen as rewards which can motivate civil servants. If the system of personnel placements is so designed that the best jobs go to those individuals who are honest and have proved themselves in earlier positions, placements can be a source of motivation and reduce corruption. On the other hand, if the placements are on the basis of personal or political or caste considerations, civil servants are more likely to use their public offices to further personal or political interests.

CONTROL SYSTEMS

Control systems are, in essence, mechanisms designed to detect punish, and curtail use of public office for private gains. Control systems can be of several types: the statutory penalty rate, internal controls, external controls, and social control.

*Statutory Penalty Rate*

The instrument most commonly used is penalty. Penalties—typically of a legal nature—can range from prison sentences to termination of employment to redemption of assets acquired illegitimately. For example, the Prevention of Corruption Act in Singapore stipulates penalty for corruption at imprisonment for five years and a fine of S$ 10,000. The Act further provides that a civil servant against whom charge of corruption is proved, has to pay back the amount of bribe in addition to the judicial penalty. A separate legislation, the Corruption (Confiscation of Benefits) Act, 1989, empowers the Corrupt Practices Investigation Bureau to confiscate gains made by corruption.

Models of efficiency wages in tax collection argue that the penalty rate can directly substitute for wage increases, and sufficiently high penalties can have the effect of eliminating corruption even when detection probabilities are low. If that is the case, optimal penalty has to be very high in a degraded environment of endemic corruption.

Most countries provide high penalties for corruption. Thailand is a case in point. The Thai Penal Code prescribes life imprisonment or death penalty for an offender convicted of corruption. In fact, punishment in the Thai penal system is significantly higher than the punishment provided for similar offences in other countries. Yet, Thailand figures among countries with the highest level of corruption.

Stringency of penalty may not necessarily provide the needed deterrence. There are several reasons for this. First, the penal system does not work in most cases. The fact that the law provides stiff penalties, is no indication that the penalties are actually imposed. Rather, the higher the penalties are, the more likely it is that they will not be awarded to those who get caught.[27] Second, the very stipulation of stiff penalties could easily produce the contrary effect. This, in fact, is the finding of the model on gang activity.[28] The model infers that the society does not indict gangs if it feels that the penalty is unfair. Third, many societies feel uncomfortable about singling out and punishing individuals as if almost by a lottery process, when many other individuals might have committed similar offences.[29]

What is important, therefore, is that penalties should be capable of being implemented. At a minimum, corruption, if proved, should be penalized with termination of government employment. Where civil service employment is highly regarded and brings prestige, dismissal means disgrace for the entire family, and therefore, members of the family have an incentive to discourage corruption. A stipulation prohibiting employment of such civil servants in the private sector makes the cost of indulging in corruption even higher.

Korea has made such stipulations. The General Administrative

Reform Movement (*Suhjongshoeshin*) of 1975 prohibited the private sector from reemploying civil servants who had been dismissed on charges of corruption. The Movement even went a step further. A person who initially recommended the case of the official who was later found to be guilty of corruption, was also dismissed, and prohibition in respect of reemployment was extended to the sons and grandsons of a person found guilty of corruption.[30]

Logically, penalties should be directed at not merely those who receive bribes but also those who pay them. This, unfortunately, is not a common practice, and most countries have been shy of punishing those who pay bribes. It is only in the United States that the Foreign Corrupt Practices Act imposes sanctions against multinational companies offering bribes.

## Internal Control System

Since public bureaucracies are based on the principle of hierarchy, an internal control system, which allows supervision of the lower offices by the higher ones, is built into the hierarchy. The superior in the hierarchy is invested with authority to monitor corruption by his subordinates. The internal control system is often institutionalized by enactment of disciplinary rules and establishment of mechanisms internal to the civil service system.

Independent watchdog institutions can also monitor and punish corruption. For example, independent commissions investigate allegations of corruption and bring offenders to book. A strict independent commission can effectively check corruption, particularly when the internal control system is plagued by collusive behaviour. But there is a danger that independent bodies directly reporting to the top can also be used as personal instruments of those at the top.

Many countries have instituted ombudsmen to look into complaints of citizens on acts of corruption. The ombudsman investigates cases of corruption, and it prepares reports which are made public. However, the ombudsman's efficacy ultimately depends on the integrity of the individual heading it.

There are several factors which can undermine the efficacy of the internal control system. For example, the internal control system can be subverted by collusion. Corrupt civil servants can buy off their official and political superiors by sharing bribes with them. The sharing mechanism produces collusive behaviour, and collusive behaviour, in turn, undermines the internal control system.

Collusive behaviour is often found in hierarchical public bureaucracies, where a sharing mechanism can be conveniently embedded in the line of hierarchy. In such a system, civil servants at the lower level collect bribes and pass a share to the official and political superiors in the hierarchy.

The internal control system is also weakened by excessive administrative rules, regulations, and procedures. Obscure and intransparent procurement regulations are a case in point: Klitgaard demonstrates how even an apparently open rule like the acceptance of the lowest bid leads to corruption.[31] Too many rules and regulations lead to red tape. Red tape confers officials with discretionary powers which are exercised only to collect bribes, and also obfuscates the fixing of responsibility, and in that sense, undermines the detection process.

The internal control system is likely to be ineffective in cases where the government intervenes extensively in the economy, and opportunities are created for discretionary interpretation of regulations and allocation of resources. Government monopolies in the provision of goods and services give civil servants the power and opportunity to appropriate rents that shortages create, with very little chances of being caught.

Klitgaard points out that monopoly power plus discretion minus accountability produces serious corruption. Corruption, in fact, thrives in the context of institutional monopolies, because monopolies, by definition, defy checks and balances. Monopolies preclude economic and political alternatives. Lack of economic alternatives compel citizens to satisfy corrupt civil servants to obtain any service. Lack of political alternatives prevents enforcement of accountability.[32]

When endemic corruption of public institutions is accompanied by reduced economic growth, the internal control system is diluted. Knack and Keefer show how prolonged, slow or negative growth perpetuates the scarcity of economic alternatives, inhibiting the development of new economic activities and political interests, while preserving dependency on corrupt civil servants.[33] Ades and Tella also point to the link between scarcity of economic alternatives and corruption. They show that the degree of competition has a significant effect on corruption. According to them, this occurs through rents which absence of competition creates, and which bureaucrats and politicians then extract.[34]

The control system is also undermined when the bureaucracy is layered in with loyalist civil servants by ruling politicians. Such layering-in helps politicians politicize the administration by making it fully responsive to the demands of politics.[35] This process ends up creating a patronage system.

The process of layering-in erodes the authority of those at the top of the public bureaucracy, and it leads to a disengagement of authority and control. Even when authority is centralized, the power of the top bureaucracy in disciplining subordinates and controlling their activities is weakened. As a result, the balance of authority to control subordinates becomes highly equivocal.[36] This weakens the internal control system.

The internal control system does not work when corruption is sanctioned by politicians in power. The bureaucracy is then made the instrument by which the politicians in power extract rent from the system either to buy political support or to enrich themselves. In such an event, the bureaucracy becomes the lever for surplus extraction from the clients of the bureaucracy.[37]

In countries where corruption is sanctioned by politicians, the mechanism typically involves internal coordination, shared knowledge, and a vertical exchange of benefits.[38] In fact, it creates an internal economy, linking principals and agents. The principals (politicians) provide protection while bureaucratic agents extract bribes and share them with the politicians. Such concerted corruption closes off political and bureaucratic alternatives, giving the entire administration more leverage for corruption. It creates a network of operatives sharing not only the rewards but also the risks, and therefore, the entire administration acquires a stake in protecting corruption and increasing its proceeds.[39]

It is likely that political and official corruption can flourish independently. France, for instance, experiences political corruption, while the bureaucracy is reasonably free from corruption. But more often than not, the two coexist, and they are likely to be interlinked. An interlinked system of political and official corruption is formidable, and can evade the most carefully designed internal control system. This is so, because, in such a scenario, bureaucratic rents are coordinated and shared across both the political and official realms, while monopoly power allows ruling politicians to undermine the system of control and even preempt any opposition.[40] In such cases, the functional distinction between political and official corruption almost disappears.

## External Control System

Typically, the external control system acts as a formal mechanism of restraint, and in an administration in which the principle of separation of powers is applied, checks and balances are exercised by other branches of government. In fact, the broader the separation of powers, the greater the number of veto points which corrupt civil servants have to navigate in order to indulge in corruption.[41]

The two formal mechanisms of restraint which are common to most countries, are a system of external audit and an independent judiciary. An efficient external audit can be an effective restraint. An effective audit should be independent of the executive and external to it. An independent and external audit enforces control over government by exposures and sanctions against corruption. But there should be mechanisms to act on the results of the audit. It is necessary that there should be no significant lag between an act of corruption and its exposure in the audit.

For the judiciary to be an effective instrument of restraint, four core conditions should be met. First, there should be judicial independence. Second, the decisions of the judiciary should be capable of being enforced. Third, citizens should be empowered to approach the courts to make the civil servants comply with the law. Fourth and most important, there should be judicial effectiveness—there should be organizational efficiency in disposing off cases without long delays.[42]

## Social Control

A developed civil society can fight corruption through direct countervailing action.[43] This is important because transparency is meaningful only when people outside the state structure are in a position to monitor government processes and procedures. In fact, as is the common experience, there is no dearth of vigilance organizations, anti-corruption bodies and watchdog agencies in a corrupt state, but these institutions end up protecting corruption rather than exposing and punishing it, only because accountability is not demanded of these institutions. Even the most comprehensive set of formally democratic institutions may not be able to enforce accountability in the absence of a strong civil society to energize them and demand action.

It is important to remember that individual citizens may not have the resources or the will to act alone. That is why collective activity is important. But the depth and intensity of collective activity depend, to a considerable extent, on the 'social capital' of the community[44]—the informal rules, norms and long-term relationships which facilitate coordinated action and enable people to undertake cooperative ventures for mutual advantage. Social capital improves the collective efficiency of the community.[45]

For civil society to be in a position to fight corruption, an important condition has to be met. It has to develop strong and legitimate norms on corruption. Robert Cooter shows that where people freely interact on a repeated basis, they are more likely to form strong and legitimate norms. Surveys and interview research on popular conceptions of right and wrong suggest that most citizens judge civil servants by social norms learned in these everyday interactions. In countries where civil society has been a successful check on corruption, a range of social groups—trade and professional associations, or community groups—have functioned as 'law merchants'. They have succeeded in promulgating codes of good practice and have been able to impose anti-corruption sanctions relatively quickly, on a lower burden of proof than that required for criminal penalties.[46]

For civil society to undertake direct countervailing action against corruption, it should have access to information about the government. Information is a precondition for any meaningful anti-corruption effort. Easy public access to government records is very important to fight corruption.

Freedom of information law is an effective instrument in anti-corruption efforts. Freedom of information laws in the United States of America and a number of European countries have been important in overseeing of government by civil society. The important thing about such freedom of information laws is that they enable citizens to secure information about the government without having to show how their lives are affected by it.

Civil society can fight corruption only when members of the public are able to seek effective redress. If mechanisms addressing citizens' complaints are not in place civil society's capacity to fight corruption is blunted. If anti-corruption institutions such as the ombudsman or the judiciary cannot take note of complaints and act against corruption, civil society cannot provide the countervailing force.

In societies where social capital is weak, it is unlikely that citizens will organize themselves to fight corruption. But the absence of social capital is not necessarily a permanent condition. It can be generated by participation itself, and here, governments and voluntary organizations can play a very positive role.

Hence, the participation of civil society, either formally or informally, in the processes of the government assumes importance. Citizen's participation has been institutionalized in some countries by establishing public-private deliberation mechanisms. Such mechanisms provide the fora for civil servants and key stakeholders from the civil society such as business, labour, consumers, academia, and the press, to evolve public policy. These mechanisms have succeeded in reducing the scope for corruption. The repeated game feature of these mechanisms provides incentives for participants to collaborate with each other, and civil service corruption has been more or less constrained by the repeated nature of the collaboration. In other words, because the rules which govern the behaviour of participants are effectively established within the mechanism, cheating and reneging on them become less likely.[47]

Successful examples are the Deliberation Councils in Japan, the National Wages Council in Singapore, the Budget Dialogue Group in Malaysia, the Consensus Councils in North Dakota in the USA, and the Business–Labour Sector Councils in Canada. In these countries, participatory mechanisms have been involved in crucial areas of decision-making. It has been the experience that transparent, collaborative deliberations in these participatory bodies have reduced the scope for corruption.

Citizens' voice can be useful in expressing social disapproval of civil service behaviour. In Japan, for example, social disapproval has been the principal means of regulating civil service behaviour. Social disapproval in Japan is expressed in several ways. One is social shaming of civil servants of questionable integrity. The other is political embarrassment, and as Japanese civil servants admit, political embarrassment can be a very effective form of expressing social disapproval of official conduct.[48]

Social disapproval can be particularly effective as a mechanism of restraint in hierarchical bureaucratic structures in which the top civil servants are held responsible for the acts of their subordinates. In the Japanese system, in which senior civil servants in the agencies are responsible for the acts of omission and commission of the subordinates whose work they supervise, social disapproval has played a key role in limiting corruption. Social disapproval in Japan is as much directed at the erring civil servant as at the senior civil servants supervising his work. Therefore, in cases where official misconduct is exposed in the courts, the media or the Diet, the impact is felt throughout the agency concerned as senior civil servants along with the minister in charge, suffer the social consequences of the resulting public disapproval.

Klitgaard has shown the effectiveness of shaming those guilty of corruption.[49] But social disapproval can be effective only in those countries in which tradition has placed a high premium on the civil servants, and the civil servants, on their part, value the opinion of society.

It is necessary, therefore, that civil society should come forward to denounce corruption and express its disapproval. Unfortunately, this is not the case in countries where there is a high societal acceptance of corruption. Such acceptance is essentially an expression of social capitulation, and it is detrimental to the detection and punishment of corruption, because citizens do not come forward to cooperate with the government in reporting corruption. In fact, such social capitulation is a familiar sight in developing countries. In such countries economic development is slow, negative and uneven; there are institutional monopolies and a lack of economic and political alternatives; and people see corruption as inevitable and efforts to fight it as futile. In such a setting, there are few alternatives to dealing with corrupt civil servants except on their terms, and it is in the interest of corrupt civil servants to preserve the captive situation for as long as they can.

## IDENTIFICATION WITH THE ORGANIZATION

The function of identification consists of creating conditions which induce the members of an organization to identify their interests with the interests of the organization. Identification with the organization produces a shared commitment to the objectives of the organization. It includes a common understanding among its members about what is desirable and undesirable behaviour, and a devotion to upholding the honour of the organization based on such a common understanding. It also gives members a sense of purpose and belonging, and it imposes a degree of self-discipline which guides them towards achieving the goals of the organization.

When employees identify with the organization, they use the goals of the organization as the basis of their action. Such identification restrains corrupt behaviour, since the use of office for private gains detracts from the goals of the organization.

In the context of public bureaucracies, such identification may be with the civil service as a group rather than with the governmental organization in which the civil servants work. Identification with the civil service presupposes the existence of a certain ethos being shared by the civil service as a group. It is assumed that whether by a process of conscious acceptance or unconscious internalization, the ethos of the service is recognized as binding on the individual civil servant, and in that sense, it becomes an autonomous determinant of civil service action.

The main dimension, of course, is a system of shared belief and orientation, which serves as a definitive standard for official conduct. In the course of official interaction, common notions evolve as to how civil servants should act, and what objectives are worthy of attainment. It happens in several ways. First, common values that are directed towards the goals for which the civil servants as a community work, which are a combination of their ideals as civil servants and their ideas of what is desirable, crystallize over time. These values define the ends of official conduct.

Second, norms of conduct i.e., a set of common expectations concerning how civil servants should behave, develop. If values define the ends of official conduct, norms separate behaviour which is legitimate for achieving these ends from behaviour which is not legitimate.

Third, in addition to the values which define the ends of official conduct and the norms that all the civil servants as a group are expected to adhere to, differential role expectations which become associated with various positions in the bureaucratic hierarchy, also emerge.

These values, norms, and differential role expectations work in tandem to direct the conduct of the individual members of the civil service. The spirit is neatly captured by such expressions as 'conduct unbecoming of a gentleman and an officer' or 'officer-like quality'. As civil servants conform more or less closely to the expectations of their peers in the civil service, and as the degree of their conformity in turn influences their relations with others and their social status, and as their status affects their inclinations to adhere to norms and their chances to achieve valued objectives, the pattern of their behaviour becomes directed along the lines of the values, norms, and the differential role expectations sanctioned by the civil service as a group.

These values, norms, and differential role expectations bind the individual civil servants to forms of behaviour that are acceptable to the entire civil service. They determine whether an individual civil servant is straying from what the civil service as a group is committed to. To the extent that corrupt behaviour of an individual civil servant does not form a part of these shared values, norms, and role expectations, it is discouraged.

Most public bureaucracies today lack the *esprit de corps* which binds their members to acceptable forms of behaviour. Very few public bureaucracies have them, and in the case of these lucky ones, it has taken them many years, even centuries of tradition, to create and nurture the *esprit de corps*.

Whether it is identification with the organization in which civil servants work or with the civil service as a group, there are certain minimum conditions that have to be met to create and nurture *esprit de corps*. First, *esprit de corps* is fostered to the extent to which the recruitment and the reward system is merit-based. The fact that merit and performance are the only requirements for being inducted into the organization or the civil service, and ultimately into its higher echelons, makes it likely that commitment to the goals of the organization rather than pursuit of private interest, becomes a valued attribute. The obverse is also true. If entry and career progression depend on personalism and patronage, *esprit de corps* is not likely to develop.

Second, the organization concerned or the civil service should have a corporate identity. It should have a clear mission and mandate, with a distinct corporate personality, and more importantly, it should give its members the sense of belonging to a corporate organization with an avowed mission.

Third, there should be internal coherence. Its members should be homogeneous with some degree of commonality in educational background. This commonality binds recruits in a common understanding of what is expected of them, and it creates the necessary basis for building trust among them. Internal coherence is impaired when the members owe loyalty to informal alignments based on ethnicity, religion, caste or language, and attach themselves to sub-goals of these alignments. Identification can be a powerful force for combating externalities produced by attachment to sub-goals, by the loyalty it induces to the goals of the organization.

In sum, these four sources of motivation—*meritocracy, rewards, control systems*, and *organizational identification*—help separate the civil servant from the pursuit of his private interest. When nineteenth-century states rationalized their public bureaucracies, they acted on this assumption. Did the rationalization succeed in what it set out to do?

Before studying the Indian experience, we take a look at the evolution and history of public bureaucracy in India, and the conditions that led to its rationalization in the nineteenth century.

## NOTES

1. Max Weber, 'Bureaucracy' in H.H. Gerth and C. Wright Mills (eds.), *From Max Weber: Essays in Sociology* (New York: Oxford University Press, 1946). Also see Guenther Roth and Claus Witich (eds.), *Economy and Society: An Outline of Interpretative Sociology*, Vols 1–3 (Berkeley, 1978).

2. For a very insightful exposition of the Weberian thesis, see Bernard S. Silberman, 'The Structure of Bureaucratic Rationality and Economic Development in Japan', in Hyung-Ki Kim, Michio Muramatsu, T.J. Pempel and Kozo Yamamura (eds.), *The Japanese Civil Service and Economic Development* (Oxford: Clarendon Press, 1995). For a comparative perspective, see Silberman, *Cages of Reason:*

*The Rise of the Rational State in France, Japan, the United States, and Great Britain* (Chicago: University of Chicago Press, 1993).

3. Fulton Committee, *The Civil Service*, Vol. I (London: HMSO, 1975), p. 9.

4. G.E. Aylmer, *The King's Servants: The Civil Service of Charles I, 1625–1642*, (London, 1973), p. 7.

5. See Weber (1978), particularly Vols. 1 and 3. For a cogent analysis, and also about how patrimonialism can be used as framework to study concrete situations, see Stephen P. Blake, 'The Patrimonial-Bureaucratic Empire of the Mughals', in Hermann Kulke (ed.), *The State in India 1000-1700* (Delhi: Oxford University Press, 1997).

6. Hermann Kulke, 'Introduction: The Study of the State in Premodern India', in Kulke (1997), p. 5 and pp. 36–7. The point to be noted is that the patrimonial state is essentially a fragile institution as it depends strongly on the personal abilities of the ruler to contend with the various autonomous and centrifugal forces. The model emphasizes the precarious and often weak position of the patrimonial state which is temporarily overcome through the personal abilities of the ruler.

7. Weber(1978), pp. 1054 ff.

8. Blake(1997), p. 282.

9. Ed Campos and Sanjay Pradhan, 'Building Institutions for a More Effective Public Sector', 1996 (Background Paper for the *World Development Report, 1997*). See Ed Campos and Hilton L. Root, *The Key to the Asian Miracle: Making Shared Growth Credible* (Washington D.C.: Brookings Institution, 1996). Also see T.J. Pempel and Michio Muramatsu, 'The Japanese Bureaucracy and Economic Development: Structuring a Proactive Civil Service', and Hyung-Ki Kim, 'The Japanese Civil Service and Economic Development: Lessons for Policymakers from Other Countries', in Hyung-Ki Kim, Michio Muramatsu, T.J. Pempel, and Kozo Yamamura (eds.), *The Japanese Civil Service and Economic Development* (Oxford: Clarendon Press, 1995).

10. *The East Asian Miracle: Economic Growth and Public Policy* (Oxford University Press, 1993), pp. 174–8.

11. Campos and Pradhan (1996), p. 7.

12. Barbara Nunberg, 'Managing the Civil Service: Reform Lessons From Advanced Industrial Countries' (World Bank Discussion Paper 254, Washington D.C.: The World Bank, 1995).

13. Campos and Pradhan (1996), p. 6.

14. David Lindauer and Barbara Nunberg (eds.), *Rehabilitating Government: Pay and Employment Reform in Africa* (Washington D.C.: The World Bank, 1994), p. 27.

15. Caroline Van Rijckeghem and Beatrice Weder, 'Corruption and the

Rate of Temptation: Do Low Wages in the Civil Service Cause Corruption?', 1996 (Background Paper for the *World Development Report, 1997*).

16. Rino Schiavo-Campo, 'Civil Service and Economic Development— A Selective Synthesis of International Facts and Experience, 1996' (Background Paper for *World Development Report, 1997*). Also see, Campos and Root (1996).

17. Rijckeghem and Weder (1996).

18. Multinational corruption index is prepared by a company called Political Risk Services. The index is based on surveys of business opinion. It is a country-wise assessment of the relative likelihood of top civil servants demanding bribes as well as the extortion of smaller bribes by petty officials.

19. 'Reasons to be Venal: Can Governments Reduce Corruption by Paying More to Public Servants', *The Economist*, August 16, 1997.

20. Timothy Besley and John McLaren, 'Taxes and Bribery: The Role of Wage Incentives', *Economic Journal* V. 103 (1993), pp. 119–41. See Frank Flatters and Bentley McLeod, 'Administrative Corruption and Taxation', *International Tax and Public Finance* V. 2 (1995), pp. 397–417. These models assume that civil servants maximize expected monetary value or indulge in economically rational behaviour. Therefore, these models are known as the rational choice models.

21. Besley and McLaren (1993). An interim step, it is suggested, might be to create a legal schedule of fees for services, payable by citizens directly to civil servants. This would raise pay, reward efficiency, and create a kind of accountability to the client. Such payments may be difficult to supervise and regulate. See Michael Johnston, 'What Can Be Done About Entrenched Corruption?' (Paper for Annual Bank Conference on Development Economics, April 30 and May 1, 1997, Washington D.C.: The World Bank).

22. Rijckeghem and Weder (1996), p. 2.

23. Ibid., p. 3.

24. Ibid., p. 6. In Tanzania, society condoned the practice of government teachers offering private tuition on the ground that teachers were paid poorly and needed to supplement their income, even though the practice of private tuition affected the standard of teaching because it left no time for teachers to prepare for their lessons. In fact, when the government put a ban on private tuition, there were protests from the parents.

25. Campos and Pradhan (1996), p. 7.

26. Peter B. Evans and James Rauch, *Bureaucratic Structure and Economic Growth: Some Preliminary Analysis of Data on 35 Developing Countries* (Berkeley: University of California Press, 1996).

27. Vito Tanzi and Parthasarathi Shome, 'A Primer on Tax Evasion' (IMF Working Paper 93/21, 1993).
28. George A. Akerlof and Janet Yellen, 'Gang Behaviour, Law Enforcement and Community Values', in Henry J. Aaron, Thomas E. Mann and Timothy Taylor (eds.), *Values in Public Policy* (Washington D.C.: Brookings, 1994).
29. Tanzi and Shome (1993).
30. A.T. Rafique Rahman, 'Legal and Administrative Measures Against Bureaucratic Corruption in Asia', in Carino (ed.), *Bureaucratic Corruption in Asia: Causes, Consequences, and Controls* (Quezon City, The Phillipines: NMC Press, 1986), pp. 118-21.
31. R. Klitgaard, *Controlling Corruption* (Berkeley: University of California Press, 1988). Transparency International recommends that the bidders sign an integrity pact, pledging to refrain from corruption. The Transparency International has proposed the idea of 'Islands of Integrity'; these are mutual undertakings among the bidders for government contracts that they will not pay bribes—commitments backed up by posting sizable bonds subject to forfeiture in the event of violations.
32. Johnston (1997).
33. Stephen Knack and Philip Keefer, 'Institutions and Economic Performance: Cross-Country Tests Using Alternative Institutional Measures', *Economics and Politics* 7(3), November 1995, pp. 207–27.
34. Alberto Ades and Rafael di Tella, 'Competition and Corruption' (Working Paper, Institute of Economics and Statistics, Oxford University, United Kingdom, 1994).
35. Joel D. Aberbach and Bert A. Rockman, 'Political and Bureaucratic Roles in Public Service Reorganization', in S.J. Colin Campbell and B. Guy Peters (eds.), *Organizing Governance: Governing Organizations* (Pittsburgh: University of Pittsburgh Press, 1988), p. 83.
36. Mamadou Dia, 'A Governance Approach to Civil Service Reform in Sub-Saharan Africa', (Technical Paper Number 225, Africa Technical Department Series, Washington D.C.: The World Bank, 1993), p. 20.
37. R. Wade, 'The System of Administrative and Political Corruption: Canal Irrigation in South India', *Journal of Development Studies* 18(3), 1982. Also see, Wade, 'Recruitment, Appointment and Promotions to Public Office in India', *World Development* 13(4), 1985.
38. Johnston (1997).
39. Ibid.
40. Ibid.
41. *World Development Report, 1997* (New York: Oxford University Press, 1997), p. 100.
42. Ibid., p. 100.
43. Johnston (1997), p.16.

44. For a very useful discussion on social capital, see Eva Cox, *A Truly Civil Society* (Sydney: ABC Books, 1995), and Hutton, *The State We're In* (U.K.: Vintage Books, 1996). They argue that social capital is critical for the development of civil societies. Cox defines social capital as, 'the process between people which establishes networks, norms and social trust and facilitates co-ordination and co-operation for mutual benefit'. An excellent contribution on the subject is from Robert Putnam, with Robert Leonardi and Rafaella Y. Nanetti, in *Making Democracy Work: Civic Traditions in Modern Italy* (Princeton, N.J.: Princeton University Press, 1993). For a discussion of high-trust and low-trust societies, see Francis Fukuyama, *Trust: The Social Virtues and the Creation of Prosperity* (New York: The Free Press, 1995).

45. *World Development Report, 1997*, p. 114.

46. Robert D. Cooter, *The Rule of State Law Versus the Rule-of-Law State: Economic analysis of the Legal Foundations of Development* (Proceedings of the Annual World Bank Conference on Development Economics, 1996). Also see, Johnston (1997).

47. *The East Asian Miracle: Economic Growth and Public Policy*, A World Bank Policy Research Report (Oxford University Press, 1993), p. 187.

48. John O. Haley, 'Japan's Postwar Civil Service: The Legal Framework', in Kim, Muramatsu, Pempel and Yamamura (1995), p. 99.

49. John Braithwaite argues that social disapproval can be the principal means of societal regulation of civil service behaviour. See John Braithwaite, *Crime, Shame and Reintegration* (Cambridge: Cambridge University Press, 1989). Also see, Haley (1995).

# 3

# Bureaucracy in India:
# Evolution and History

It is difficult to think of an administrative system in India before 600 BC. During that period, the early pastoral nomadism of the Ganges valley was changing itself into a village economy based on agriculture. Inherent in the process of change was a degree of sedentarization. Sedentarization in a configured geographical area both for settling down and carrying on agriculture created the necessary conditions for the emergence of an administrative system. Administrative arrangements evolved, if only to ensure the continued possession of the area of settlement.

The legends of the Aryans speak of this administrative evolution. The gods, at war with demons, were on the verge of defeat. In desperation, they got together and elected a king to lead them. The origins of the early Aryan administrative system may perhaps be traced to these legends.

A rudimentary administrative system evolved with the king as the focal point. A court of elders assisted the king, but his principal advisers were the commander of the troops and the chief priest who also doubled as an astrologer. Spies, messengers and a superintendent of dicing completed the king's establishment. These kingdoms were essentially patrimonial kingdoms. They were small in size, and the administrative organization resembled a family set-up of which the king was the patriarch.

# THE MAURYAS

The early settled period in the Gangetic region saw the emergence of a number of kingdoms, but the three kingdoms of Kashi, Koshala, and Magadha held sway. In the battle for supremacy among the three kingdoms, which lasted for about a hundred years, Magadha emerged victorious and established the Mauryan empire. From a patrimonial kingdom, Magadha under the Mauryas became an empire.

## THE EMPEROR

At the top of the Mauryan administrative structure was the emperor. The *Arthasastra* tells us that the emperor descended from the gods: 'When people were oppressed by the law of the fishes (*matsyanyaya*, according to which the bigger fish swallow the smaller ones) they made Manu, the son of Visvavat, the king.'[1] Visvavat is the sun; so, the first ruler is a divine descendant. As the *Arthasastra* elaborates, 'Kings occupy the position of Indra and Yama on earth; their favours and displeasures are manifest to all. Divine punishment also falls on those who treat kings with disrespect.'[2]

The Mauryan emperor was the state and there was no concept of a state above or beyond the present ruler. The *Arthasastra*, for example, stipulates seven basic elements which constitute a state. These elements are embodied in the doctrine of the *prakrtis*. They are: *svamin* (the ruler), *amatya* (the bureaucracy), *janapada* (territory), *durga* (the fortified capital), *kosa* (the treasury), *danda* (the army), and *mitra* (the ally).[3] The prakrtis are enumerated in order of their relative importance. The *Arthasastra*, in the course of a long discussion, clarifies that each earlier prakrti in the list is more important than the latter one. The ruler is the most important of all the prakrtis, and it is significant that the word used for the ruler is svamin, which means the owner. According to the *Arthasastra* 'The king and (his) rule, this is the sum-total of the constituents.'[4] The ruler constitutes the sum-total of all the prakrtis.

This is evident from the appropriation of revenues in the Mauryan government. All the revenues, whether tax or impost or the profit of state enterprises, were pooled into the *ayasarira* or the 'body of income'. Often, what was realized in the ayasarira, was represented as going to the ruler. There is also mention of the *raja haret* (the king shall take that property to which the claim of both is rejected, also that the owner of which has disappeared),[5] *raj gami nidhih* (a treasure-trove over one hundred thousand shall go to the king)[6] and *dravyam rajadharamyam syat* (in cases of sale without ownership)[7].

It was the same with the composition of the *vyayasarira* or the body of expenditure. In the body of expenditure, the expenses of the royal household were ranked alongside items of expenditure of government. Vyayasarira also included items of personal expenditure of the ruler. Vyayasarira was accounted under fifteen heads. U.N. Ghoshal points out that the first four items of the vyayasarira referred directly to royal household or king's personal expenditure.[8]

The Mauryan ruler was the patriarch. Ashoka's dictum, 'All men are my children' bears testimony to this. When subjects are afflicted by natural calamities, the ruler is enjoined to take care of them like a father. The *Arthasastra* counsels, 'In all cases (in cases of all kinds of danger), he (the king) should favour the stricken (subjects) like a father.'[9] Yet again, while dealing with the settlement of the countryside, the *Arthasastra* enjoins, 'He (the ruler) should grant exemptions at the time of settlement or as people come. He should, like a father, show favours to those whose exemptions have ceased.'[10] Benevolent patriarchy was the basis of the relationship between ruler and subject.

THE BUREAUCRACY

According to the *Arthasastra*, the higher bureaucracy consisted of the *mantrin*s and the amatyas. While the mantrins were the highest advisors to the king, the amatyas were the civil servants. There were three kinds of amatyas: the highest, the intermediate and the lowest, based on the qualifications possessed by the civil servants.[11]

The key civil servant was the *samahartr*. The samahartr prepared the annual budget, kept accounts, and fixed the revenue to be collected. He was responsible for distributing income under the seven heads and expenditure under the fifteen heads. It was his job to ensure that the expenditure did not exceed the revenues.

Another key civil servant was the *samnidhatr* who enjoyed the same rank as the samahartr. The samnidhatr, assisted by a number of civil servants, kept records of the body of taxes that came in from various parts of the empire. He was in charge of the stores, of the actual revenue and other income received by the government. He maintained the stores dealing with precious minerals, grains, timber, armoury, and prison house. Everything that needed to be stored and guarded, was the responsibility of the samnidhatr.

The major departments of government were: Revenue, Exchequer, Stores, Armoury, Prisons, Accounts, Agriculture, Mines, Metals, Mint, Salt, Forest, Cattle, Pastures, Passports, Shipping, Ports, Commerce, Trade Routes, Customs, Frontiers, Excise, Weights and Measures, Spinning and Weaving, Religious Institutions, and Intelligence. Each department had a large complement of staff consisting of superintendents and subordinate civil servants.[12]

The *Arthasastra* recommended that the kingdom should be divided administratively into four divisions. Each division was under a civil servant called the *sthanika*. Under the sthanika, there were junior civil servants called the *gopas*, each in charge of five or ten villages. It was the duty of the gopa to maintain records of all agricultural and other holdings in the villages in his charge and take a census of the households, recording the number of inhabitants, with full details of their profession, property possessed, the income, the expenditure and the revenue received from each village. With such information, the samahartr maintained a record of all towns and villages, classifying them as big, middling, and small, and providing information about their wealth in grains, cattle, and money.

Next in line was the village headman, who the *Arthasastra* designates as *gramika* or *gramakuta*. He was also a functionary of the state and had the power to imprison. The *Arthasastra* also mentions the *gramasvamin*, the owner of the village. He was also an employee, and not the owner of the village, since there was a prohibition against granting a village as a gift or a pension.

The metropolitan area of the capital, Pataliputra, was directly administered. It did not come under the purview of the samnidhatr. The administration of the metropolitan area was the responsibility of the *paur*, or the chief of the town. The paur had his own hierarchy of civil servants. He maintained law and order and the general cleanliness of the city, and was assisted by accountants and tax collectors.

Megasthenes, the Selucid ambassador at the Mauryan Court, describes the administration of Pataliputra in great detail. The city was administered by thirty civil servants, divided into six committees of five each. Each committee supervised one of these functions: industry and arts, welfare of foreigners, registration of birth and death, trade and commerce, public sale of manufactured goods, and collection of tax on articles sold.

*Aksapatala*, the record-cum-audit office, was an important office in charge of the *adhyaksa*. Records maintained in the office related to the activities of state departments, state factories, prices, standard of measures, laws and customs in force, and salaries of all the civil servants working in the state structure.

It is from the records-cum-audit office that civil servants recieved their specific assignments. Once the assignment was completed, civil servants were expected to bring the accounts and balances to the records-cum-audit office for comprehensive audit. The adhyaksa was assisted by clerks, accountants and inspector of coins.

The evidence of the *Arthasastra* would seem to suggest a complex system of hierarchical offices, stretching from villages to central departments manned by civil servants with specific charters of duties and responsibilities. In other words, there was an articulated hierarchy of precisely circumscribed offices.

CONTROL OF CIVIL SERVANTS

All civil servants in the Mauryan empire served at the pleasure of the king. Assurance of tenure did not exist in the Mauryan bureaucracy. There were no definite rules about promotion. The *Arthasastra* suggests that civil servants who increased revenues and served the king loyally, should be made permanent on increased emoluments. The *Arthasastra* also suggested transfers of government servants as an administrative measure, to prevent misappropriation of government funds.[13]

Mauryan rulers seem to have toured extensively to keep a watch on their civil servants. Ashoka, for instance, travelled widely throughout the empire to inspect the work of his civil servants. The *Arthasastra* even detailed how an inspection should be conducted. One entire section of Chapter Nine is devoted to 'inspection of the work of officers'.

Ashoka sent inspectors from the capital once in five years for an audit and check of the provincial administration. There were specially appointed judicial officers both in the urban and rural areas. In the rural areas, these officers were known as *rajukas*.

The Mauryan administration boasted of a well-developed system of secret agents whose services were used for a variety of purposes, primarily for monitoring the administration. There were two types of secret agent organizations: the *samstha* or the establishment, consisting of secret agents who were stationed in a single place, and the *samchara* or peripatetic secret agents who moved from place to place.

Samstha had five categories of secret agents: (1) *kapatika* (apprentice) who observed and reported any conspiracy against the king, (2) *udasthita* (apostate monk) who gathered intelligence disguised as a monk, (3) *grahapatikavyanjana* (farmer) who had a network of intelligence agents working under him, (4) *vaidehakavyan- jana* (merchant) who maintained a number of intelligence agents, and (5) *tapasavyanjana* (bogus ascetic) who posed as a seer and collected intelligence.

Samchara had four categories: (1) *sattrin* (orphan trained for gathering intelligence), (2) *tiksna* (desperado who was used to liquidate the enemies of the king), (3) *rasada* (who administered poison to inflict silent punishment), and (4) *bhiksuki* (Brahmin nun who spied on the houses of the top civil servants).

The *Arthasastra* mentions that secret agents, in the guise of householders, should find out the number of fields, houses and families in those villages in which civil servants were stationed, and their income and expenditure. In effect, agents were to keep a check on and report the work of revenue officers such as the *gopas*.

Secret agents, in the guise of traders, were instructed to find out the quantity and price of the king's goods, obtained from mines, water-works, forests, factories and fields. In respect of goods produced in other countries and imported along a water-route or a land-route, secret agents were asked to find out the amount of duty, road-cess, escort charges, dues at the police station and the ferry. The *Arthasastra* also enjoined that agents, in the guise of ascetics, should make enquiries about the integrity of departmental heads.

## A PATRIMONIAL BUREAUCRACY?

The Mauryan empire exhibits some features of a patrimonial-bureaucratic empire. The ruler was descended from the gods. He was seen as the father of the people who protected them from danger and injustice. Benevolent patriarchy was the basis of the relationship between the ruler and his civil servants.

Civil servants in the Mauryan empire held office on the pleasure of the ruler. Candidates for office had to demonstrate personal loyalty. In fact, the tests mentioned in the *Arthasastra* such as *dharmopadha, arthopadha, bhayopadha,* and *kamopadha* were designed essentially to test the loyalty of the incumbent. There were no rules about progression in one's career except continued loyalty and integrity.

The instruments of control were typical of a patrimonial-bureaucratic empire. Rulers travelled widely and frequently, renewing in face-to-face meetings the personal bond between the master and servant. They rotated civil servants from one assignment to another, and maintained a very elaborate network of intelligence-gatherers outside the regular administrative structure, who reported directly to the top.

There were, however, some features of the Mauryan empire which did not partake of the character of a patrimonial-bureaucratic empire. The most notable is that civil servants' salaries were paid in cash. On the evidence of the *Arthasastra*, it appears that civil servants in the higher echelons were particularly well-paid. The chief minister and the commander of the army received 48,000 *panas*, the treasurer and the chief collector 24,000 panas, the accountants and the clerks 500 panas, whereas the ministers were paid 12,000 panas, and artisans, 120 panas.[14]

A remarkable feature of Mauryan administration was that there was no wage compression. The ratio of the salary of a clerk to that of the seniormost civil servant worked out to 1 : 96, and the ratio of the artisan's wage to the salary of a minister was 1 : 100. The Mauryan economy was put to great financial strain as a result of such huge salaries; in fact, according to the *Arthasastra*, one-quarter of the total revenue of the state was to be earmarked for payment of salaries to civil servants.

Significantly, compensating officials with prebends or benefices was not popular with the Mauryas. Limited land grants, on a strictly temporary basis, was recommended for village-level functionaries. The *Arthasastra* recommended grants of land without the right of sale or mortgage to village-level revenue officials. Thus, such land grants entitled grantees only to usufruct.

It is clear that in the Mauryan administration office-holders were separated from the ownership of the means of administration. This meant that the Mauryan administration was freed from the financial limitations of relying on the private household of civil servants. Mauryan officials maintained themselves on the salaries paid by the rulers.

This separation meant that the officials were obliged to account for the management of property belonging to the state. Rendering accounts was an important part of Mauryan administration. Accounts of administrative departments were properly kept and presented jointly by all the ministers to the king. This was obviously intended to ensure that civil servants did not misappropriate revenues.

Another feature of the Mauryan administration which does not correspond to a patrimonial-bureaucratic empire, is the elaborate system of hierarchical public offices. This contrasts sharply with a patrimonial-bureaucratic structure in which offices are loosely defined and imperfectly ordered.

On the whole, a careful distinction was made between the interests of the state and the private interests of civil servants. The use of the public office to further the purely private interest of the civil servant amounted to an offence inviting severe penalties. According to the *Arthasastra*, embezzlement of government funds was the most reprehensible act a civil servant could ever commit. The *Arthasastra* mentions more than forty ways of *apahara* or embezzlement of government funds.[15]

Large parts of the *Arthasastra* are devoted to detailed discussion of how to prevent and punish misappropriation of the king's revenue by civil servants. The *Arthasastra* provides a comprehensive inventory of penalties to be awarded in such cases. It recommends that errant civil servants be disgraced by smearing them with cowdung and ashes, and proclaiming their offences throughout the town or village, and by shaving their heads and showering them with brickbats. In more serious cases of corruption, the punishment suggested is death, and for effect, death caused by official torture. Clearly, the statutory penalty rate could not have been more stringent.[16]

Interestingly, the *Arthasastra* discusses in detail the relative degree of harm that is likely to be caused to the ruler if the samahartr and samnidhatr indulge in corrupt practices. The *Arthasastra* argues that a corrupt samahartr is likely to cause greater harm than a corrupt samnidhatr. The samnidhatr merely accepts what is guaranteed by others as to the quality, and as such, he has only limited opportunities to be corrupt at a cost to his patron. The samahartr has far greater opportunities. For example, while fixing the quantum of revenue, he may clandestinely receive something for himself first, and, then, fix the dues at a lower rate.

What was really remarkable about the Mauryan administration was that it made a distinction between public interest and private interest. This, however, did not mean that there was no corruption in the Mauryan administration. The elaborate discussion in the *Arthasastra* about corruption and the stringent penalties it suggested would beg the inference that civil servants did, more often than not, succeed in diverting the king's revenues.

## THE ERA OF ADMINISTRATIVE FLUX

After the disintegration of the Mauryan empire and till the Delhi Sultanate was established, politics and administration were in constant flux. During that time, a succession of rulers came, ruled, and sank without leaving behind any memorable administrative system. They gained and lost territories; the more heroic among them succeeded in founding a dynasty here and a dynasty there, writing their names into rock edicts and folklore, but on the whole, they failed to provide abiding administrative and bureaucratic systems.

The Delhi Sultanate (1200–1526) was an exception. It was able to found a recognizable administrative structure, although it failed to establish an all-India empire, leaving the south of India free from the control of the Sultanate. The Bahamanis ruled over the northern Deccan for two centuries, and the Vijayanagara empire emerged to the south of river Krishna.

## A NEW SYSTEM

A new stage of state formation becomes discernible at the time of the Delhi Sultanate. The Sultanate was initially a classical conquest state, and therefore, it became necessary for the rulers to establish and consolidate their authority and control over the newly conquered territories. This was done by a process of sharing the spoils with their followers. But it was important, at the same time, to ensure that the followers were also kept under control. In particular, the tendency of the followers to establish autonomy had to be curbed.

The strategy was to assign land on a temporary basis to the followers, while, at the same time, transfer the holders of these assignments as frequently as possible in order to exercise control over them. Interestingly, it was about fifteen hundred years after the Mauryas that, for the first time, a successful attempt was being made, during the period of the Delhi Sultanate, to establish control over far-flung areas situated away from the core region of the state.

Such a system—the system of simultaneously appropriating a sizeable part of the social surplus and distributing it to the members of the ruling elite—so successfully introduced by the Delhi Sultanate, was adopted by contemporary states outside the Sultanate such as in Orissa and Vijayanagara. In Orissa,[17] 39 governors or *Pariksa* of Kalinga were part of an incipient patrimonial-bureaucracy of the Ganga dynasty between 1271 and 1426. Between 1376 and 1405, there were 16 pariksas who held sway.

In fact, the entire south Indian state system from the fourteenth to the sixteenth centuries was moving towards a patrimonial order.[18] Vijayanagara is an example. As Fernao Nuniz documents about the Vijayanagara kingdom,

This king Chitrao has foot soldiers paid by his nobles, and they are obliged to maintain six lakh of soldiers, that is 600,000 men and 24,000 horses which the same nobles are obliged to have. These nobles are like renters who hold all the land from the king, and besides keeping all the people, they have to pay their cost; they have to pay to him every year 60 lakhs of rents as royal dues. The lands they say yield 120 lakhs of which they must pay 60 to the king, and the rest they retain for the pay of the soldiers and expenses of the elephants which they are obliged to maintain. . . .[19]

The system was responsible for bringing about a new conception of public office which, though radically different from the Mauryan practice defined, in general, the structure and role of public bureaucracies in later years. Rulers now started granting land to their civil servants. The land grants stipulated certain conditions. First, civil servants were required to pay a part of the revenue from the land to the rulers. Second, they were called upon to maintain a specified number of troops for the ruler to be deployed at the time of war. During times of peace, the ruler reviewed, regularly to start with and perfunctorily over time, collection of revenue, the state of the administration, and the mobilization of troops.

Over a period of time, only one aspect of the obligations—supply of troops at the time of wars—came to be emphasized. As wars between kingdoms became frequent, rulers now relied increasingly on their civil servants for regular supply of troops and their replenishment. Often, the troops maintained by civil officials outnumbered the regular army of the ruler.

With the greater frequency of wars and the increasing reliance of the ruler on officials for supply and replenishment of troops, land grants to officials became more frequent. Initially, it was only the revenue from the land which was granted in lieu of salary and not the land itself, with the stipulation that if the grantee defaulted on his obligations, the grant was terminated, and the land and its revenues were resumed by the ruler. In fact, in the initial period at least, the grant was only for the life of the grantee.

As central authority waned over time, it became difficult to enforce the conditions of the original grant. Although it was still open to rulers to terminate a grant, they did not always find it a feasible option because the civil servant, in case of termination of the grant, could well be in political opposition to the ruler. Under the circumstances, it became customary to assume that the grant was in perpetuity, with the grantee assuming the right to dispose of the revenue and the land itself in any manner that he liked. In other words, with efflux of time the grants assumed a hereditary character.

The system of land grants to officials had important administrative and political implications. Revenues were collected by these grantees, and it obviated the need for a centrally administered bureaucracy. Grantees performed administrative functions such as maintaining the peace and imposing order. They, also discharged judicial functions such as settling disputes. The grantees thus came to exercise political, judicial, and administrative functions.

This Sultanate pattern of assigning land to civil servants as compensation for services rendered in lieu of cash salaries was known as the *iqta* system. The Sultan had his own *khalsah* or the crown lands which were reserved for his personal needs and administered directly by his retainers.

Under the iqta system, only revenue from the land was granted, and not the land. The grant was at the pleasure of the Sultan, and the iqta could not be treated as hereditary property. Iqta-holders undertook to pay a fixed annual sum to the Sultanate, irrespective of the revenue collected.

*Iqtadars* were required to maintain a specified number of troops and provide them to the Sultan at times of war. The troops maintained by the iqtadars were supposed to owe allegiance to the Sultan; but in practice, they were loyal only to the iqtadars.

Over time, iqtadars started treating the iqtas as hereditary. Ala-ud-din effected changes in the iqta system to ensure that the grants were not appropriated as hereditary property. He revoked all grants made by previous Sultans. Land was reassessed, and fresh grants were made. But, Firuz Shah, Ala-ud-din's successor, returned all the lands to previous holders or their descendants, and in the process, it came to be recognized that the iqta system had become hereditary over time.

The iqtadars of the Delhi Sultanate had begun their career from being personal retainers of the Sultan. In course of time when the iqtas acquired a hereditary character, the holders invented elaborate and impressive genealogies to establish their aristocratic origins.[20] The ample income from the iqtas enabled civil servants to maintain a life style of great luxury.

The head of the civil administration in the Delhi Sultanate was the *wazir*, who supervised the collection of revenue, the checking of accounts, and the regulation of expenditure. There were three other ministers—one was the head of the military, the second was the head of inter-state relations, and the third, the chancellor, who dealt with state correspondence, and relations between the court and the civil servants in the provinces. The chancellor had agents stationed throughout the Sultanate.[21] The power of the civil servants in the provinces was limited by the presence of these agents who reported directly to the chancellor.

On the whole, there is no mistaking the patrimonial-bureaucratic features of the administration of the Delhi Sultanate. Officials were selected on the basis of their loyalty to the ruler and assigned prebends or benefices as compensation for their services. Officials served at the pleasure of the ruler, and what was demanded of them was personal loyalty and allegiance to the ruler. There was no articulated hierarchy of precisely circumscribed offices. Rather, officials held positions that were loosely defined and imperfectly ordered.

More importantly, there was no distinction between the public and the private, or the official and the personal. Officials could use their office in furtherance of their private interests so long as they rendered to the ruler services of a personal or military nature.

## THE MUGHALS

The Mughal state was, like the Delhi Sultanate, a classical conquest state to start with. Mughal rulers, like the rulers of the Sultanate, were called upon to establish and sustain their authority through sharing of spoils with their followers, and, at the same time, keeping their followers under control. Assignment of land on a temporary basis and frequent transfers of holders of assignments was the strategy adopted by the Mughals, but where the Mughals scored over the Sultanate was in sustaining the temporariness of the land assignments, and in the process, exercising total control over the holders of these assignments.

### THE EMPEROR

Abu al-Fazl's *Ain-i Akbari* portrays the Mughal ruler as a divinely inspired patriarch.[22] Abu al-Fazl says, 'Sovereignty is a ray of light from the Divine Sun.'[23] So, when the ruler receives this ray of light, he acquires the qualities and virtues needed to govern successfully. This meant that the Mughal ruler enjoyed the position of a spiritual guide to his people, and this position derived directly from God. That the rulers were touched by God, singled out, and called to the throne is a major theme of Abu al-Fazl's book. Combined with the fact that the ruler was also the patriarch, this meant that the moment the ruler ascended the throne, he was inspired by God to govern his state with the strength, wisdom and compassion of a father looking after his household.

The second theme of Abu al-Fazl's discussion is the overlap of the imperial household and the state. In the imperial household, departments dealing with purely domestic matters coexisted with departments of wider reach and significance such as those dealing with the administration of the entire state.

The third theme is the importance of the imperial household. The finances of the imperial household indicate its importance. For example, in 1594 the income of Akbar's household was about 25 per cent of total state revenues, and salaries for clerks, servants, and labourers amounted to nearly 9 per cent of the revenues.

These are also the typical features of a patrimonial-bureaucratic empire. The Mughal ruler was regarded as a divinely-aided father to his people, and therefore, was in a position to establish the traditional, family-rooted authority of the patrimonial-bureaucratic emperor. The centrality and importance of the imperial household in the organization of the empire corresponded to the patrimonial-bureaucratic type. The inclusion of state offices in the imperial household, and the combination of the personal and the official was a successful attempt to absorb the state into the imperial household, and to rule the realm as one great extended family.

THE BUREAUCRACY

The Mughal bureaucracy was based on the *mansabdari* system. Every *mansabdar* was invested with a *mansab* (a rank or a command) which determined his position in the Mughal bureaucracy. The mansabdari system was graded across thirty-three categories of command, ranging from a commander of ten to a commander of five thousand. A *panch-hazari* or the commander of five thousand, was a top civil servant. The ministerial staff of the higher grades also formed part of the mansabdari establishment, and therefore, the intermediate class of mansabdars consisted of all those whose commands ranged between contingents of ten to below 200 in Akbar's time, and 500 in Shah Jahan' time.

The title to a mansab was not hereditary. The appointment to grades and promotion across them, depended on the pleasure of the ruler. In other words, the mansab, in itself, did not confer office. The mansabdari system was essentially a pool of civil servants available for civil or military deployment. The concept of a mansab, to start with at least, had military connotation because it meant holder of a command, but it was not always that a mansabdar had military obligations. Over a period of time, the military designations became merely symbolic. The mansabdari system, as it finally evolved, became a combination of the higher civil service, the peerage, and the army, all rolled into an omnibus service organization.

There was also a system of assignment of land revenue to civil servants in lieu of payment of salary. This was the *jagirdari* system. Under this system, an incumbent, after presenting his troops for inspection, was given a *jagir*. By the seventeenth century, the jagir system had become the norm, and it was the accepted way for the ruler to reward the loyalty of a civil servant.[24] It is noteworthy, however, that under the Mughals the mansab and the jagir accompanying it, were not hereditary.

Abu al-Fazl describes the categories of civil servants. The *sipah salar* (or commander of the army) was a mansabdar who controlled the largest body of troops in the area. He was in charge of provincial affairs and was primarily responsible for keeping the peace. The *faujdar*, a subordinate of the sipah salar, commanded the largest body of cavalry, and was in charge of tackling recalcitrant cultivators and monitoring local revenue collectors and jagirdars. The *qazis* were responsible for the administration of justice. The *kotwal*, the chief officer in urban areas, maintained order in the cities. The *amal-guzar* was the chief financial officer at the sub-provincial level, in charge of collecting revenue.

The seven civil servants who made up the administrative structure, are not presented in the *Ain-i Akbari*, as progressive links in an administrative chain joining individual villages to central departments in the Mughal capital through sub-districts, districts, and provincial offices. The responsibility of these civil servants cut across several of these divisions which were essentially fiscal in nature. Individual civil servants were not posted at each separate level. Most civil servants were expected to report directly to the ruler. In any case, civil servants from the imperial establishment were assigned, in a supplemental capacity, to district and sub-district levels to help regular civil servants with the collection of taxes, particularly for the lands of the imperial domain. In the process, they were expected to oversee the functioning of the civil servants working in the field.

Civil servants of the Mughal administration, for the most part, did not specialize in either the civil or military branches of the government. All civil servants were from one class, and were considered capable of handling both civil and military assignments. There was no correspondence between the mansabdari rank and the position in the government actually held. High-ranking civil servants sometimes held provincial or sub-provincial posts, and civil servants from intermediate ranks were often assigned to central level offices in the imperial household.

On the whole, in Mughal governance, there are no clear-cut lines of authority, no separate departments at successive levels of administration, and no clean lines of hierarchy in administrative organization. Groups of men in the imperial household oversaw, on behalf of the emperor, the working of civil servants at the provincial and sub-provincial levels who exercised military, financial or legal powers with jurisdictions which varied across geographical areas.

## CONTROL OF CIVIL SERVANTS

Mughal rulers established and consolidated control over their civil servants in several ways. Rulers travelled widely and frequently so that they could keep a watch over their civil servants.[25] Of their two hundred years of rule the Mughal rulers spent almost 40 per cent of their time on tour.[26]

Mughal civil servants were expected to attend the imperial court regularly. Mansabdars were required to visit the imperial court on a number of occasions—after each change in assignment, after a change of jagir posting, on being promoted, and on most days of special celebration. It was said that, for mansabdars, progression in their career depended as much on putting in regular, obsequious appearances at the imperial court as on the quality and value of the gifts they presented to the Mughal rulers.

Another successful technique of control was the introduction of a rigorous system of checks and balances. This was done by appointing civil servants with competing, overlapping areas of responsibility. In the provinces, the functioning of the provincial governor was subject to checks and balances by two other civil servants—the finance officer and the military officer. For example, no major amount of money could be drawn from the treasury without finance officer's authorization. The military officer encroached on the provincial governor's jurisdiction in matters concerning the army. At the sub-provincial level, a similar system of checks and balances prevailed between the collector, the local assignees, the treasurer, the finance officer, and the army captain.

Frequent transfer of civil servants was another technique of control. No civil servant was allowed to keep his jagir or stay at his post for more than three or four consecutive years. This ensured that the mansabdars who were posted in places away from the royal seat of power did not form subversive alliances with local elements and build independent bases of authority.

Abu al-Fazl also speaks of news-gatherers stationed in cities and towns throughout the realm. These news-gatherers were responsible for keeping the emperor informed of the doings of the mansabdars in their areas of assignment.

But the most important technique of control was the strictly enforced temporariness of the jagir assignments. This created the necessary feeling of insecurity and helplessness. A mansab under the Mughals and the jagir accompanying it, were ex officio and governed by the doctrine of escheat. The jagir was given to the mansabdar only so long as he held office, and was resumed by the emperor upon the death of the mansabdar or his removal from the mansab. The jagir could not be passed on to the progeny of the mansabdar.

It was the common Mughal practice, for the next generation of the mansabdars to start once again from the bottom of the heap with a fresh official appointment. A letter written by the young Aurangzeb to his father depicts a graphic yet poignant picture of how an estate and its belongings actually escheated to the Mughal ruler. Even as the mansabdar was on his deathbed, it was the usual practice to put royal seals on his coffers and to beat the servants in order to get the details of the property of the departing mansabdar.[27] Pelsaert's chronicles of the Mughal times

are also replete with accounts of how on the death of a mansabdar, his estate and savings escheated to the Mughal Emperor.[28]

Since the jagir was only for the life time of the mansabdar and
could not be bequeathed, the result was a prodigal bureaucracy
which indulged in wild extravagances while the mansab lasted.
In fact, the chronicles of the time depict an unending saga of os-
tentation and high living. Surrounded by huge hordes of
retainers who pandered to the indulgences of their masters, the
Mughal bureaucrats, at least those in the higher echelons,
celebrated life by acquiring elaborate harems, building exquisite
summer houses, and laying intricate gardens, and death, by constructing domed tombs.[29]

The prodigal nature of the Mughal bureaucracy made it
almost imperative that its members maximized income using
every possible opportunity. The civil servant was required to give
expensive presents to the emperor, and his career progression
depended largely upon it. They had also to support their own
establishments—the wives and retinues. They had to sustain the
pomp and splendour of their offices and the courts. It was almost
a compulsion for the Mughal civil servants to use their public offices to make as much money as possible.

Mughal civil servants, driven by an unrelenting urge to accumulate wealth, appropriated to themselves whatever they could
lay their hands on. Bernier describes the sense of general insecurity which prevailed among the citizenry as a result of the
unremitting predation by the Mughal civil servants: the wealthier
ones buried their gold and silver at great depth and went about
with the lugubrious manner of the very penurious, and the ordinary folks made themselves scarce.[30] Bernier graphically depicts
the conduct of the wealthy merchants—how they made an art
form of hiding their wealth lest they arouse the curiosity of
Mughal civil servants, who combined the authority and the in-
clination to part any person from his belongings.[31]

To augment their income, governors and their civil servants
engaged in trade themselves. They used their public office to
declare government monopoly of any trading activity which
would yield them optimal returns, and more generally, to control
prices to enrich themselves.[32] They even went to the extent of
monopolising food grains, particularly when it carried a scarcity
premium. For example, the Governor of Surat monopolized the

entire available supply of food grains in 1632, and he did so at a time when Gujarat was in the grip of a terrible famine.[33] Evidently, the ingenuity of Mughal bureaucrats in cashing on scarcity premia to enrich themselves, provided the inspiration to the later-day Indian bureaucrats.

The general feeling of insecurity caused by the predation of the Mughal bureaucracy was responsible for inhibiting the flow of capital into commerce or industry. In the Mughal regime, there was a clear pecking order—the ordinary merchants were subordinate to business magnates, and the magnates, in turn, to local governors and their civil servants who had the option of entering the market and preventing competition whenever it was beneficial to them. Under the circumstances, investment plans by private merchants had to take into account the fact of the local governors and his civil servants entering the market capriciously, and this, more than anything else, inhibited the smooth flow of capital into commerce and industry during the Mughal times.[34]

The strategy of the Mughals to control their civil servants by strictly enforcing the temporariness of the jagir assignment was successful. But it had very serious social and economic consequences. It led to unlimited exploitation of the people,[35] and, in turn, to agrarian unrest and social crisis. Irfan Habib has argued that this was the cause of the decline of the Mughal empire, a thesis whose validity is now generally accepted.[36]

A PATRIMONIAL BUREAUCRACY?

There is no mistaking the features of a patrimonial-bureaucratic empire in the Mughal period. The Mughal ruler was seen as a divinely inspired patriarch. There was the overlapping of the imperial household and the state, and the combination of the personal and the official. The Mughal administration was an extended patriarchal system.

The Mughal bureaucracy partook of the patrimonial nature of the political organization, and exhibited all the characteristics of a patrimonial bureaucracy. The candidates for posts in the Mughal administration had to demonstrate personal qualifications—loyalty, family, and position—to be awarded a mansab. Loyalty to the ruler was considered the most important qualification. Civil servants in the Mughal bureaucracy were assigned land in lieu of salaries and held office only at the pleasure of the Mughal ruler.

## THE EAST INDIA COMPANY

The British founded a state in India to promote and protect their trade interests. The British government had conducted several wars in India to support the trade of the East India Company, and then found, to its pleasant surprise, that the Company had acquired, through the actions of Robert Clive, a dominion in India on its own. The founding of the British Indian state by Clive was in the style of a robber baron;[37] it is not altogether surprising that the administration which followed, only matched that style.

### THE COMPANY

By 1765, the word 'civil servant' had started being mentioned in the records of the East India Company to describe its functionaries. The usage, interestingly, was to distinguish those who did work of a mercantile nature from others engaged in military activities. Before 1765, the lowest functionary of the East India Company was called a 'factor', meaning a commercial agent. The trading station where factors worked was called a 'factory', and the place where a number of factories were grouped together under the administration of a president and his council, was called a 'settlement'.

By 1674, the East India Company had already introduced salary scales and conditions of tenure for its employees. At the bottom of the structure was the factor. A young man inducted into the services of the Company was recruited as an apprentice, and he had to serve in that capacity for seven years. The qualifications required were good penmanship and an elementary knowledge of accounts. He earned an annual salary of 5 pounds for the first five years and 10 pounds for the remaining two. On the expiry of the contracted seven years, he could be considered for a further tenure of three years at 20 pounds a year after which he was eligible for promotion to superior grades. A junior merchant was paid an annual salary of 30 pounds, and the senior merchant, 40 pounds. On promotion to the council, the senior merchant got an enhanced salary of 150 pounds, while a president's salary could go up to 500 pounds.

Seniority in service determined all promotions. In each presidency, the president and his council were required to submit annually to the Court of Directors, a complete list of all the functionaries of the Company, arranged strictly in order of seniority in their respective grades, along with a report assessing their performance and conduct. A final seniority and gradation list was prepared by the Court of Directors on the basis of the list provided by the president and the council.

Appointment to the service of the East India Company was only by nomination. To be appointed as a recruit, it was necessary to get a nomination from a director of the East India Company. In 1765, the Company decreed that henceforth, only writers were to be recruited, and therefore, the point of entry to the service of the East India Company became that of the writer.[38]

Nominations were made by the directors either for financial considerations or in exchange for political support, and in many cases, to provide for family and friends. The directors, in fact, made a lot of money out of nominations. Writership commanded high prices. A newspaper article in 1772 reported that writerships had been sold for 2000 to 3000 pounds each, and in 1783, there was an advertisement in a newspaper offering 1000 guineas for a writer's place in Bengal.[39]

A statistical analysis of the nominations on the basis of different considerations makes interesting reading. Of those nominated to the service of the East India Company between 1809 and 1850, 23 per cent were relatives of the members of the Court of Directors, and 55 per cent were nominated on the basis of friendship. The shares of other nominations were Company's service (4.69 per cent), the recommendations of the Board of Control (6.57 per cent), business relationships(1.64 per cent) and political recommendations (0.70 per cent).[40]

THE FUNCTIONING OF THE COMPANY'S BUREAUCRACY

The rule of the East India Company was one of sheer plunder by its civil servants. Almost all the young people who joined the services of the Company, came to India with the avowed mission of amassing a fortune as quickly as possible, and colonial India did not let them down. India was considered a gold mine, and sizable fortunes were made.[41] Corruption had become a way of life, and it was customary in colonial India to give money or expensive presents to civil servants of the Company to get favourable orders.

In addition, civil servants of the East India Company indulged in private trade to make money for themselves, although it was clearly against the interest of the Company. Initially, the Company opposed the practice on the ground that those of its civil servants who indulged in private trade sacrificed the interest of the Company to their own. The Company even directed that stringent bonds should be taken from the civil servants not to indulge in private trade. But the Company had to finally give in. Private trade by its employees in India became so pervasive that the Company was forced to recognize the right of its employees to indulge in private trade.

By the time the administration of the Diwani provinces was taken over by the Company, corruption among its civil servants had reached an all-time high. Clive was entrusted with the specific mission of cleaning up the administration. He started out with a number of stringent measures. Notable among them was his attempt to make the civil servants of the Company sign an undertaking not to accept bribes or presents. Clive did not exactly succeed in his mission, because he had himself earlier received 234,000 pounds and a land grant worth about 30,000 pounds a year as his own personal share in exchange for support to Mir Jafar against Siraj-ud-daula.

A frustrated Clive returned to England in 1760, and the civil servants of the Company started making money once again. As Sir Alfred Lyall said, 'finding themselves entirely without restraint or responsibility, uncontrolled either by public opinion or legal liabilities (for there was no law in the land), they naturally behaved in such circumstances, with such temptations, men would behave in any age or country'.[42]

The Company had been forced to recognize the right of its civil servants to indulge in private trade,[43] but they found more innovative ways of augmenting their income. For example, they started making money by trading privately even without the payment of internal customs duties. Such a move put the Indian merchants at a clear disadvantage. They had to pay duties, and the added burden made them uncompetitive. Indian merchants bribed civil servants for the privilege of trading in their name and buying immunity from payment of internal customs duties. As Clive said, 'the evil was contagious and spread among the civil and military down to the Writer, the ensign, and free merchant'.[44]

The practice of civil servants of the Company passing favourable orders in exchange for expensive presents had become so widespread that the directors of the East India Company had to step in and take corrective measures. Instructions were issued that the civil servants should pay to the treasury of the Company, all presents that exceeded Rs 4000 in value, unless the receipt was sanctioned by the directors, and they should not accept any present above Rs 1000 in value without sanction from the president or the council. As expected, these instructions were openly flouted.

When the East India Company took over the administration of the diwani provinces, opportunities for making money became even more plentiful, particularly for those working in the Revenue Department.[45] When the system of auctioning revenue collection to the highest bidders was introduced in the diwani provinces, civil servants working in the Revenue Department used the new system to make money in two ways. First, they held land in *benami* transactions and granted themselves hefty remissions of revenue.[46] Second, the amount of rentals due to the Company was deliberately depressed in exchange for bribes from the landlords.[47]

However, parking the ill-gotten wealth remained a problem. The fortunes made were so sizable that they soon overflowed the normal channels of remittance through the bills of the Company. Many of these fortunes found their way to Europe through foreign channels, but these foreign channels were not particularly dependable, and therefore, considered risky.

That is why when English agency houses such as Alexander & Company, Palmer & Company, Colvin & Company, Fairlie-Fergusson & Company, and Cruttenden-Mackillop & Company were established at Calcutta, a felt need was fulfilled. These agency houses became the depository of the illicit earnings. The earnings now came to stay in India itself. Taking all the three presidencies together, these savings were estimated at nearly four million pounds per annum.[48]

These earnings, now parked in India, were invested mostly in commerce.[49] Some of them were also invested in industrial enterprises, and it is because of such investment that the civil servants of the East India Company have often been described as the first industrial capitalists of India. While deposing before the Select Committee on Colonization and Settlement, one of the settlers clearly acknowledged the capital contribution of the civil servants of the East India Company, and applauded that 'the root of independent British enterprise in Bengal is to be found in the civil service'.[50] When the Europeans were permitted to own agricultural property of their own, the illicit earnings found yet another outlet. The Company's civil servants advanced them capital and guaranteed them, by using their official positions, all manner of facilitation and security of enterprise.

Not all the illicit earnings were invested in industry or lent out for acquisition of agricultural farms. A large part was used to lead a life of great luxury. As Clive said,

The sudden and, among many, the unwarrantable Acquisition of Riches had introduced Luxury in every shape, and in its most pernicious Excess .... Every Inferior seemed to have grasped at Wealth, that he might be enabled to assume that Spirit of Profusion, which was now the only distinction between him and his Superior .... In a country where Money is plenty, where Fear is the Principle of Government, and where your Arms are ever victorious, ... it is no Wonder that the Lust of Riches should readily embrace the proffered Means of its Gratification, or that the Instruments of your Power should avail themselves of their Authority, and proceed even to Extortion, in those Cases where simple Corruption could not keep Pace with their Rapacity.[51]

Civil servants made no secret of their getting rich at the expense of the Company or the government. The large sums of money and the lavish presents, as Clive, no puritan himself, had occasion to observe,

were so publically known and vindicated that every one thought he had a Right to enrich himself at all Events, with as much Expedition as possible; the Monopoly of Salt, Beetle, Tobacco was another Fund of immense Profits to the Company's Servants, and likewise to such others as they permitted to enjoy a Share, while not a Rupee of Advantage accrued to the Government, and very little to the Company, from that trade.[52]

A PATRIMONIAL BUREAUCRACY?

Conceptually, it is difficult to situate the rule of the East India Company in the framework of patrimonialism because of the problem of colonial politics. But the basic premises of patrimonialism—a system in which those occupying public offices fail to distinguish between public and personal patrimony, and the power and authority of office being used as a form of currency—were more than fulfilled during the rule of the East India Company.

There is no mistaking the patronage character of the bureaucracy of the East India Company. The candidates for posts in the Company had to demonstrate personal qualities—family or position or payment of money—to get recruited. The civil servants were selected as nominees of their patrons—the Directors of the Company. Consequently, the loyalty of the civil servant was to his patron rather than to the Company. It was to the patron that the civil servants looked for their protection as well as progression in their career.

Clearly, the bureaucracy of the East India Company was impervious to the distinction between the public and the private. For that matter, there was no distinction between the personal and the professional. All the public offices were seen as opportunities for private gains and were exploited as such.

NOTES

1. R.P. Kangle, *The Kautiliya Arthasastra, Part III* (Delhi: Motilal Banarsidass Publishers, 1992), p. 116.
2. Ibid., p. 117.
3. Ibid., p. 127.
4. Ibid., pp. 127–8.
5. Ibid., p. 128.
6. Ibid., p. 128.
7. Ibid., p. 128.
8. U.N. Ghosal, *Contributions to the History of Hindu Revenue System* (Calcutta, 1929), p. 154.
9. Kangle (1992), Part III, p. 119.
10. Kangle (1992), Part II, p. 56.
11. Kangle (1992), Part III, p. 204. The *Arthasastra* prescribes qualifications for different civil service categories. It recommends that persons possessing qualities of *sattva* or energy, *prajna* or intelligence

and *vakyasakti* or articulation should be considered suitable for appointment to government jobs. It even suggests tests to judge these qualities: dharmopadha, arthopadha, bhayopadha, and kamopadha. Dharmopadha was a test designed to test whether the person was likely to join in a conspiracy against the king. Those who passed the test of dharmopadha were to be appointed as judges and magistrates. Arthopadha was to ascertain whether the person was susceptible to the same suggestion if a large bribe was promised to him; those who passed the test of arthopadha were to be appointed as revenue officers. Bhayopadha was designed to test whether a person would join a conspiracy if he is demoted along with other officers. Those who passed the bhayopadha test were to be appointed to jobs that required close proximity to the king. Kamopadha was to find out the attachment of the person to worldly pleasures. Those who passed the kamopadha test were to be posted to jobs dealing with entertainment.

12. The *Arthasastra* categorizes all the *amatyas, mantrins* and high-ranking functionaries into several *tirtha*s:
    1. *Mantrin* (minister)
    2. *Purohita* (priest)
    3. *Senapati* (commander of the army)
    4. *Yuvaraja* (prince)
    5. *Dauvarika* (chief of the palace attendants)
    6. *Antarvamsika* (chief of the king's guards)
    7. *Prasastr* (magistrate)
    8. *Samahartr* (chief collector)
    9. *Samnidhatr* (chief treasurer)
    10. *Pradestr* (commissioner)
    11. *Nayak* (town guard)
    12. *Paur* (chief of the metropolitan area)
    13. *Karmanta* (superintendent of mines)
    14. *Mantrin-parishad adhyaksa* (president of the council of ministers)

13. The much-used quote from the *Arthasastra*, 'But those who do not consume (the king's) goods and increase them in just ways, should be made permanent in their offices, being devoted to what is agreeable and permanent to the king'. See Kangle (1992), Part II, p. 86.

14. The pana was a silver coin, with a silver content equivalent to three-quarters of a tola. The salaries mentioned could not have been on a monthly basis and were clearly annual salaries. See Kangle (1992), Part III, p. 208.

15. Notable among the ways of apahara were: civil servants could prevent revenues from being raised or realized, they could lend out state goods at interest accruing personally to them, they could

appropriate state goods for personal use; and they could substitute inferior goods for high quality goods.

16. The punishment recommended was proportionate to the value of the money or property misappropriated. Death was decreed only in cases where the value of the property stolen was more than fifty panas.

17. See Kulke (1997), p. 32n.

18. There seems to be some degree of agreement on this point. See Kulke (1997), pp. 38–9. Also see Burton Stein, 'Reapproaching Vijayanagara' in R. Frykenberg and P. Kolenda (eds.), *Studies in South India: An Anthology of Recent Research and Scholarship* (Madras/New Delhi, 1985).

19. R. Sewell, *A Forgotten Empire* (London, 1900), pp. 373–4.

20. The bureaucracy of the Sultanate consisted of diverse strands: Turks, Afghans, Persians, and Arabs, with the first two being predominant. At the beginning, clan affiliations kept them divided, but once they were forced to accept India as their home, they coalesced into a homogeneous group. See Thapar (1990), p. 298.

21. Thapar (1990), p. 292–3.

22. The discussion on the Mughal era draws heavily on Blake (1997).

23. Quoted in M. Athar Ali, 'Towards an Interpretation of the Mughal Empire', in Kulke (1997), pp. 268–9.

24. It was only during Akbar's time that a change was sought to be made. Akbar started paying officers salaries in cash. The remuneration package to the holders of the higher commands in the mansabdari system during Akbar's time was particularly handsome: making allowances for the discounted value of money, the salaries paid to the mansabdars during the Mughal times was somewhere between five to ten times of what it is today in India. For example, a commander of five thousand (the highest rank) had a salary equivalent of 24,000 pounds of Elizabethan or Stuart purchasing power at a time when the total revenue of England was something less than a million pounds. Even two hundred years later, the salary of the Governor General, the highest functionary in colonial India, was only 25,000 pounds a year. See Percival Spear, *A History of India, Vol. Two, From the Sixteenth Century to Twentieth Century* (New Delhi: Penguin Books, 1990), p. 46.

25. An administrative manual, purported to be current during the reigns of Shah Jahan and Aurangzeb divided the reign of each emperor into two parts: the settled (*istiqamat*) and peripatetic (*safar*). Under 'settled', the manual listed the period during which the emperor resided in the major cities of the empire, and under 'peripatetic', it listed the longer journeys of the ruler. See Blake (1997), p. 299.

26. The Mughal rulers were so peripatetic and such was the extensive-ness of their tours, that they had also to carry their imperial harems with them when they toured. Consequently, a curious practice developed among the women of the imperial harem: they got used to giving birth while lying on a saddle cloth. See Blake (1997), p. 299.

27. W.H. Moreland, *From Akbar to Aurangzeb* (London, 1923), pp. 277–8.

28. F. Pelsaert, W.H. Moreland and P. Geyl (tr), *Jahangir's India* (Cambridge, 1925), pp. 54–5. 'Immediately on the death of a lord who has enjoyed the King's *jagir*, be he great or small, without any exception— sometimes even before the breath is out of his body— the King's officers are ready on the spot, and make an inventory of the entire estate, recording everything down to the value of a single pice, even to the dresses and jewels of the ladies, provided they have not concealed them. The King takes back the whole estate ab-solutely for himself, except in a case where the deceased has done good service in his lifetime, when the women and children are given enough to live on, but no more. . . .'

29. B.B. Misra, *The Indian Middle Classes: Their Growth in Modern Times* (Delhi: Oxford University Press, 1978), p. 46. Also see, Spear (1990), pp. 41–7.

30. Misra (1978), pp. 40–2.

31. A. Constable (ed.), *Francois Bernier: Travels in the Mogul Empire, 1656–68* (London: Constable, 1891).

32. Mir Jumla was the typical example of the Mughal Governor who used all means to advance his trade interests. See Misra (1978), p. 34.

33. Misra(1978), p. 34. Tavernier's accounts of Agra and Golconda are telling. While describing the houses, Tavernier classifies them into two groups: those of the nobles being fair and well-built while those of the private persons had nothing fine about them. As for Golcon-da, he says that merchants, brokers and artisans lived side by side with all the common people outside the city and the city was in-habited only by persons of quality, the officers of the king, the min-isters of justice and the military men. See V. Ball (tr and ed.), *Jean Baptiste Tavernier : Travels in India* (London, 1889).

34. Misra (1978), pp. 32–3.

35. Although some historians have admired the efforts of the Mughal government in construction of roads and bridges (see P. Saran, *The Provincial Government of the Mughals, 1526–1658*, Allahabad, 1941), a few bridges, a few roads, and the repair of Feroze Shah's canal per-haps leaves little else to be added. The Mughal administration preferred a garden to a canal and their officers, a tomb to a well. (Spear 1990).

36. See Irfan Habib, *The Agrarian System of Mughal India, 1556—1707* (Bombay, 1963), and 'The Mansab System, 1595–1637', *PIHC* (Patiala, 1967).
37. Spear (1990), p. 93.
38. Clive started his career as a writer with the East India Company, and was called by Lord Brougham as the merchant's clerk who raised himself to celebrity. See L.S.S. O'Malley, *The Indian Civil Service 1601–1930* (London: John Murray, 1931), p. 5.
39. Das (1998), pp. 117–8.
40. B.B. Misra, *The Bureaucracy in India, an Historical Analysis of Development up to 1947* (Delhi: Oxford University Press, 1977), p. 71. Sometimes, the nominations were based on India connections: from families who had worked in India and boasted of a tradition of service which was handed down from generation to generation. Nineteen of the Thackeray family, beginning with the grandfather of the novelist and his father, were members of the service in India. See O'Malley (1931), p. 239. Most of the nominations under friendship were based on family connections with India. Out of 110 directors of the Company who served between 1784 and 1834, almost fifty per cent had resided in India. The result was that almost 35 per cent of those who entered the Company's civil service during 1809–1850 had fathers who had served the Company in India. See Misra (1977), p. 72.
41. John T. Noonan, *Bribes: The Intellectual History of a Moral Idea* (Berkeley: University of California Press, 1987), p. 394. Young men who went out in Company's service 'aspired to the rapid acquisition of lacs', a lac being 100,000 current rupees or 10,000 British pounds, and from 25,000 to 100,000 pounds being regarded as a respectable fortune for an Englishman to acquire in India. According to the dairy of Mackrabie, George Vansittart took home 150,000 pounds with him in 1776, and Barwell who retired in 1781, was credited with a fortune of 40,000 pounds. See O'Malley (1931), p. 31n.
42. O'Malley (1931), p. 11.
43. Ibid., p. 20. The directors of the East India Company had not authorized regular payment of salaries to the collectors, so they were allowed the right of private trade. In any case, this seems to have been the common practice in most of the colonies at the time. The French did the same in Canada and the Dutch in South Africa, with the same result—the underpaid civil servants indulged in private trade.
44. Ibid., p. 12.
45. The instructions issued to the supervisors were inspired by high ideals; the instructions read, 'Aim at no undue influence yourself, and check it in all others. Great share of integrity, disinterestedness, assiduity and watchfulness is necessary not only for your own

guidance but as an example to all others; for your activity and advice will be in vain unless confirmed by example. Carefully avoid all interested views by commerce or otherwise in the province whilst in service. . . .' See O'Malley (1931), p. 19.

46. The Parliamentary Committee of Secrecy of 1773 found no direct evidence to show that the civil and military servants held land. It suggested that 'the Company's servants sometimes share with the Buniayans in the profits of the lands rented by them', and that in one specific instance, this practice 'was directly asserted by the Buniayan who held the land'. See Misra (1978), p. 124. It was common knowledge, however, that almost every officer of the Company, held *benami* lands in the names of their money-lenders. Cauntoo Baboo, the money-lender of Warren Hastings, had considerable land in Baharband Pargana, and it was widely believed that the land held was for the Governor General himself.

47. O'Malley (1931), p. 32. John Shore who was afterwards Lord Teginmouth, wrote an excellent account of the period in his book *Memoirs of Lord Teignmouth* and was tempted to say that as President of the Committee of Revenue, he could easily have made 100,000 pounds on a single mission and that some of Company's servants realized vast sums from the landlords for understating the amount of their rentals.

48. Misra (1978), p. 90.

49. Cornwallis had this to say, 'I have every reason to believe that at present almost all the Collectors are under the name of some relative or friend deeply engaged in commerce, and by their influence as Collectors and Judges of Adaulet they become the most dangerous enemies of the Company's interest and the greatest oppressors of the manufactures.' See O'Malley (1931), p. 34.

50. Misra (1978), p. 78.

51. Quoted in Misra (1978), pp. 80–1.

52. Quoted in ibid., p. 81.

# 4

# Rationalizing the Bureaucracy

The famine which visited Bengal and Bihar in 1770 and killed about one-third of the population of the province, was the turning point. Two civil servants of the East India Company—Sir Francis Sykes and Richard Becher—were believed to have been responsible for the famine. They purchased large stocks of grain for the army at hefty profits to themselves, at a time when the province was already facing the problem of scarcity of foodgrains, and they moved the stocks out. Benjamin Disraeli wrote about it in *Sybil*. Warren, one of Disraeli's more famous characters in the book, makes a huge fortune in rice during a famine in India.

## LEGISLATIVE ENACTMENTS

Lord North's Regulating Act of 1773 was intended to curb the corruption among the civil servants of the East India Company. The Act made a distinction between the civil and commercial functions of the Company, a distinction which called for separate personnel for these functions. The Act expressly forbadé collectors and other functionaries in the Revenue Department and Judicial Department from participating in the commercial transactions of the Company. The Act contained a specific injunction against functionaries of the Company accepting gifts from any of the 'natives of Asia'.[1]

The India Act of 1784 supplemented the provisions of the Regulating Act of 1773. The Act of 1784 made acceptance of presents as well as indulgence in corrupt and sordid bargains as punishable misdemeanour.

The Amending Act of 1786 provided the necessary teeth to the disciplinary provisions of the India Act 1784. The Act of 1786 prescribed specific rules and procedures to punish civil servants of the Company who were guilty of misdemeanour. In addition, the head of the executive government in India was invested with powers to supersede the decisions of the council and punish such misdemeanour. In this respect, the Amending Act of 1786 marked a significant improvement on the provisions of the Regulating Act of 1773 and the India Act of 1784. It invested the executive with disciplinary authority over the civil servants of the East India Company. In the process, it sent down the important message that hereafter, civil servants had to transfer their loyalty from individual patrons in the Board of Directors in the East India Company to the governmental organization in India.

The Charter Act of 1793 went even further. It was a comprehensive enactment which provided for a career structure for civil servants of the East India Company. It also initiated steps for moderating the excesses of the patronage bureaucracy of the Company. The Act of 1793 did this in several ways.

First, it provided that all vacancies in the civil service in India below that of the Member of Council could only be filled from among the civil servants of the Company. This provision was intended to exclude all outsiders from being appointed to public offices under the Company. It also aimed at preventing directors of the Company from pushing the claims of their nominees over those of others who were more suitable.[2]

Second, it prescribed an age limit for entry into the civil service of the Company. The Regulating Act of 1773 had earlier provided that no writer should be sent out to India under 15 or above 18 years of age. The maximum was now raised; the Charter Act of 1793 provided that no person above 22 should be appointed or sent out to India.

Third, it provided for a salary structure, and it linked the level of salaries to the number of years of service in the Company. For a post carrying 500 pounds a year, the minimum period of service was three years. For a job with a salary of 1500 pounds, it was six years. The minimum period of service required for a post carrying a salary of 3000 pounds a year was nine years, while for a post with 4000 pounds, the minimum length of service was twelve years.

Fourth, it linked promotions to seniority. The responsibilities of different departments were defined, and salaries were fixed proportionate to responsibility. Perquisites and allowances were abolished.

Fifth and most important, it required the directors of the Company to take an oath that they would not accept money for making nominations. It seems to have worked because the Parliamentary Committee appointed in 1808–9 to look into rumours of corruption among the directors of the Company found no evidence of any director being involved in corrupt practices while making nominations.

## ADMINISTRATIVE MEASURES

In addition to legislation, administrative steps were taken by Hastings and Cornwallis to curb corruption in the East India Company. Hastings set out to reorganize the administration of the Company and free its trade interests from being opportunities for corrupt practices.[3]

Hastings started with abolishing the plethora of private agencies which had been associated with discharge of public functions, such as maintenance of law and order as well as dispensing of civil and criminal justice. He was of the view that duties in the public realm should be performed by civil servants who are appointed and paid by the government.[4]

Hastings initiated measures to curb corruption in the commercial functions of the Company. He made customs duty equal for all categories involved in commerce and transferred control of customs from the collectors in the Revenue Department to commissioners, who were paid a commission on their collections.[5] He also took measures to stop unauthorized exactions by the civil servants of the Company.

In his drive against corruption, Hastings provided for people to have easy access to the civil servants. He issued instructions that each civil servant should set apart a fixed time for hearing complaints of people. He directed that a box should be installed for petitions at the door of each government office or court house, and that all the petitions found in the box were to be read out to the civil servant on each court day. The idea was that the people who had a grievance, should get it redressed at a higher level of the public bureaucracy without being subjected to extortionate corruption by subordinates.

The measures introduced by Hastings brought about a change in the way public offices were viewed. The power, prestige, and dignity of public office were now seen as flowing out of personal integrity, and not out of affluence and conspicuous consumption. The commercial residents of the East India Company earned much more from their salary and indulgences in private trade than the collectors did, but the collector, because of his integrity and official position, enjoyed a far greater status in the society. There was a fundamental shift of emphasis from affluence to integrity.

As a result of the changes brought about by Hastings, there was a discernible reduction in corruption, but not to the extent as was made out at the time. Major Scott, speaking in the House of Commons' debate on Pitt's India Bill, pointed out that the time when large fortunes were made in India was over. According to him, out of the 504 civil servants appointed between 1762 to 1784, only 37 had returned to England, 150 were dead, and 325 were still in Bengal. Out of the 37 civil servants who had returned, only two were members of parliament, none had immense fortunes, many had less than 20,000 pounds, and some not even a shilling.[6]

Major Scott was exaggerating. When Lord Cornwallis took over, many civil servants were still making money on the side. As Cornwallis pointed out at the time of taking over, his primary concern was to clean the administration—in his own words, to clean the 'system of dirty jobbings' which the East India Company was.

It has been said that Cornwallis was fond of making sweeping statements about corruption, but his statement, at least about the dirty 'jobbings' of the civil servants of the East India Company, was based on facts. In 1787, Cornwallis found plenty of evidence of fraud, speculation, and corruption. A typical case was that of the Resident at Benares, who, in addition to his salary of Rs. 1000 a month, obtained, by illegitimate means, almost Rs 400,000 a year, and this was apart from the monopoly of the trade of the surrounding country.[7]

Cornwallis started out by suspending the entire Board of Revenue for irregularities and sending most of the corrupt civil servants back to England. He was in a position to do this because he was close to Prime Minister Pitt, and as such, he was beyond the control of the East India Company. Such was his clout that he was in a position to refuse even the request of the Prince of Wales for patronage.

He believed that corruption was best curbed by paying civil servants a decent and regular salary. At his instance, a system of paying regular salary to civil servants was introduced, and this was supplemented by the payment of a commission of one per cent of the total revenue collected by civil servant. The salary structure introduced by Cornwallis was attractive by itself, but civil servants earned more from the commission than from their salaries. The actual amount of commission varied from district to district, depending on the quantum of revenues collected, but it was not allowed to exceed the annual ceiling of Rs. 27,000 set by Cornwallis.

The more abiding contribution of Cornwallis was in making the rule of law, the basis of all executive action. He formulated a code—the Cornwallis Code as it came to be known. The code placed legal restraints on the exercise of authority by stipulating procedures to be followed. By defining procedural limits to the exercise of power at different levels, the area of discretion was reduced in order to curb corruption.

The code was a serious attempt to subjugate the arbitrary will of the executive to the rule of law. It was for the first time that the supremacy of a law binding not only on the people, but also on the civil servants who enforced it was recognized. More importantly, the code represented the first ever attempt to introduce a system in which the relationships founded on personal loyalty began to give way to those permitted by law.

## TRAINING

The East India Company did not have a system of imparting training to its civil servants. When writers arrived in India for the first time, they were required to spend some time in the principal town of the presidency to which they were allotted, and pass some tests in law and the local languages. After that, they were given a regular assignment in the field.

It was Lord Wellesley who introduced a system of imparting training to writers on their arrival in India. Wellesley's system consisted of training all writers in one place through a common curriculum irrespective of the presidency to which the writer was allotted by the Company. In fact, Wellesley spoke of a civil service capable of 'an inexhaustible supply of useful knowledge, cultivated talents, and disciplined morals'.[8]

The Fort William College was established at Calcutta in 1800 to provide such training.[9] Every candidate nominated to the service of the East India Company was now required to undergo a full-time probationary training for three years during which he was expected to take two examinations a year. Even those allotted to the Bombay and Madras presidencies were now required to undergo training at Fort William. During the three years of training at Fort William, probationers were not assigned any regular public duties.

The curriculum at Fort William consisted of general principles of ethics, civil jurisprudence, international law and general history, and specialized education consisting of languages and history of India, the customs and manners of its people, the Hindu and Muhammadan codes of law and religion. Several professors were appointed at Fort William to lecture on oriental languages, oriental law and ethics, government regulations, and European studies, which included mathematics, natural philosophy, history, political economy, English literature and the Constitution.

Lord Wellesley, while establishing Fort William College, had not reckoned with the Court of Directors of the East India Company, which did not take kindly to this initiative. The Court of Directors ordered the abolition of the Fort William Training College in 1802 on the ground that it was too grandiose and costly, and that such training could be provided in England itself. The directors however agreed to the existence of Fort William College for the study of Oriental languages. Fort William College was closed down in 1854.[10]

Wellesley's initiative had, however, brought home the importance of providing training to all recruits to the civil service at one place through a common curriculum which was comprehensive enough to equip the future administrators of colonial India with the necessary knowledge to undertake their responsibilities with a modicum of competence. In 1804, the Board of Directors asked the Committee of Correspondence to report on a system of education and training which could be adopted for recruits to the civil service.

The Committee of Correspondence recommended that a college be established in England in which all recruits to the civil service should receive a general education in the classics, mathematics and arithmetic, the elements of general law and Oriental learning. The committee also recommended that it was not advisable to send out writers to India before they were eighteen years of age.

The directors approved the committee's proposal and the estate of Haileybury at Hertfordshire was acquired as the site for the college in 1805. As a temporary measure, Hertford castle was taken, pending construction of the college building at Haileybury, and the East India College was started in 1806. A number of eminent academics from Oxford and Cambridge were appointed professors in the East India College. The East India College was moved to the new building at Haileybury in 1809.

The prospectus issued by the Haileybury College in 1806 summed up the purpose of the college—'to provide a supply of persons duly qualified to discharge the various and important duties required from the Civil Servants of the Company in administering the government in India'.[11] Students were to be admitted at the age of 15, and to remain till they were 18. The curriculum included Oriental literature with practical instruction in the rudiments of Oriental languages, especially Arabic and Persian, mathematics and natural philosophy, classical and general literature, and law, history, and political economy.

In spite of the comprehensiveness of the curriculum at Haileybury, the level of education was never very high. But what Haileybury did was to inculcate a strong *esprit de corps* in its trainees. Haileybury men took pride in the service, and this feeling was shared by the directors who took personal interest in them and treated them more as members of a big official family rather than as mere employees of the East India Company.

# PATRONAGE

In spite of the considerable headway made in the matter of training, the method of selecting candidates was still by patronage. It was by nomination only. A system had developed to apportion nominations among the directors of the Company. The annual quota of patronage of the Company was divided into twenty-eight shares. The Chairman and the Deputy Chairman of the Court of Directors of the Company received two shares each, the President of the Board was allotted two, and each of the twenty-two directors, one each. Such a principle of apportionment of nominations among the directors had been accepted by the Court of Directors in 1806.[12]

The exercise of patronage by the directors was untrammelled except for the provision in the Charter Act of 1793 which enjoined directors to take an oath undertaking not to make nominations in exchange for gifts or money. The system of unlimited patronage continued till the India Act of 1833 introduced the idea of limited competition.

The Act of 1833 sought to limit the discretion of the directors in the exercise of their patronage. The Act stipulated that for every vacancy at the Haileybury College, at least four candidates should be nominated, and the best one among them should be selected through an examination. During the course of the debate on the Bill in 1833, Lord Macaulay had lent full support to the proposal of Charles Watkin Wynn, a former President of the Board of Control of East India Company, who advocated recruitment by competition. The principle of four-fold nomination was proposed as a compromise by Macaulay, who piloted the measure through the House of Commons. In his speech on the bill, Macaulay had emphasized the importance of a literary competition as the most effective means of selecting gentlemen of breeding and culture to the Company's civil service.[13]

The board now decided to hold a preliminary qualifying written examination for selection of candidates to the Haileybury College. The subjects prescribed for the examination were Latin and Greek, history, geography, philosophy, elements of mathematics, arithmetic and geometry. In addition to the written test, a system of interviewing the candidates was also introduced. The Court of Directors was now forced to admit those of the nominated candidates to the Haileybury College who were declared eligible by the board, and to appoint as writers only those whom the board considered qualified after the examination.

Because of the age requirement—the India Act of 1833 had provided that no candidate at the entrance examination should be under the age of 17 or above the age of 20—only a few of those who joined the Haileybury College had the benefit of a university education. In fact, almost all of them came to Haileybury after finishing school. As the Macaulay Committee later observed,

Hitherto, the admissions (to the Haileybury College) have been given by favour. They are henceforward to be gained by superiority in an intellectual competition. While they were given by favour, they were frequently, indeed generally, given to persons whose age was not much above the minimum. A director would naturally wish that his son or his nephew to be handsomely provided for at 19 rather than at 23, and be able to return to England with a competence at 44 rather than at 48. A majority of students have, therefore, been admitted before they were 19, and have gone out before they were 21. But it is plain that, in any intellectual competition, boys of 18 must be borne down by men of 21 or 22.[14]

The result was that almost all writers who went to India were very young and merely equipped with a school education. In fact, the Red Pamphlet (1857) urged that the indigo planters should be made magistrates instead of 'unfledged boys ignorant of the people and imperfectly acquainted with the language of the country'.[15]

The idea of limited competition as introduced by the Act of 1833 evoked opposition from the directors of the East India Company who did not want their power of patronage to be limited in any manner. Eventually, parliament revoked the scheme of limited competition by an Act in 1837. As a result the directors were allowed to nominate candidates.

The Act of 1833 might not have succeeded in moderating the exercise of patronage but it did achieve an important breakthrough. It introduced the agenda of replacing patronage by merit. During the parliamentary debate leading to the enactment of the Act of 1833 and its subsequent amendment in 1837, and the public controversy and debate about restraining the power of patronage of the directors of the East India Company, the need for replacing patronage by merit had been adequately emphasized. This was instrumental in paving the way for introduction of a merit-based civil service.

Patronage was replaced by merit as the basis for selection when appointment to the civil service of the East India Company was thrown open to competition by an act of parliament in 1853. This was also the time when the Charter of the East India Company was being renewed for the last time. As the act stipulated, 'all powers, rights, or the privileges of the Court of Directors—to nominate or appoint persons to be admitted as students' should cease, and that 'subject to such Regulations as may be made by the Board of Commissioners for the affairs of India, any person being a natural-born citizen of Her Majesty, who may be desirous of being admitted to the said College at Haileybury . . . shall be admitted to be examined as a candidate for such admission'. In essence, patronage was replaced by merit.

The Act of 1853, however, allowed the directors of the Company to make nominations till the end of April, 1854. After the act was passed by parliament, Sir Charles Wood, the President of the Board of Control, appointed a committee with Lord Macaulay as the chairman,[16] to advise on the subjects for the examination of candidates for the civil service. The committee submitted its report in November 1854.[17]

The committee's recommendations covered two important aspects. The first concerned the age of the candidates. The committee recommended a minimum age of 18 and a maximum of 23 on the ground that candidates for the examination should have had a college education, preferably with a good degree from some of the best universities in England. In the words of the committee,

We think it desirable that a considerable number of the civil servants of the Company should be men who have taken their first degree in arts at Oxford and Cambridge. At present the line is drawn as if it had been expressly meant to exclude the bachelors of these universities.[18]

The second recommendation of the committee related to the subjects for the examination. The subjects recommended were English language and literature, history, mathematics, natural sciences, moral and political philosophy, Sanskrit, and Arabic. As can be seen, the subjects recommended did not have much to do with the problems which the civil servant was called upon to address in colonial India, but the committee had a reason for recommending such subjects. According to the committee, in case the related branches of knowledge, namely the Oriental, were prescribed, 'The great majority, and among them many young men of excellent abilities and laudable industry, must be unsuccessful'.[19]

The committee also recommended that successful candidates—probationers, as the committee called them—should be on probation for a specified number of years before they were called upon to hold public office. The committee recommended a comprehensive training programme during which probationers were required to undertake special studies in four branches—Indian history and geography, the principles of jurisprudence and law, commerce and finance including banking, and one Indian language. At the end of the probationary period, probationers had to take a second examination. While the position secured in the first examination entitled them to the choice of their provinces, the position in the second examination determined their rank in the service.

The Board of Control accepted these recommendations and framed regulations. The board also appointed examiners, who conducted the first set of examinations in July 1855. In 1858, the powers and functions of the Board and the Court of Directors were transferred to the Secretary of State for India in Council. Consequently, the duties of the examiners were handed over to Civil Service Commissioners who were appointed in May 1855 to hold competitive examinations to the civil service. The Government of India Act, 1858 vested the Secretary of State in Council with the executive power to make regulations for the conduct of examinations and admissions to the civil service in India. The Civil Service Commissioners were required to advise and assist the Secretary of State in Council in framing these regulations, to control and superintend these examinations, and to grant certificates of fitness for appointment. The independence of the Civil Service Commissioners was assured by the fact that they were directly appointed by the Crown, and that too, by Orders in Council. This independence was necessary to ensure that appointments to the civil service were made strictly on the basis of merit, and the process of selection was adequately insulated from political considerations and other forms of patronage.

The merit-based system put in place in the 1850s, has remained unchanged in its basic structure, and continues to the present. The only changes made to the system consist of providing representation on communal and caste lines. The Muddiman pledge started the provision of communal representation in the civil service. Although the Muddiman pledge came in 1925, the agitation for communal representation in the civil service had started much earlier. At the time of Dyarchy, groups had started organizing themselves along caste and community lines, and were pressing for representation. These groups drew up a detailed list of what came to be broadly classified as Scheduled Castes and Scheduled Tribes. The classification was for the purposes of securing representation in the civil service, duly endorsed by statutory provisions.

The questions and points raised by legislators in the Central Assembly in 1921 on the subject of employment in the public services related primarily to this aspect—the need for providing representation in the civil service. The emphasis was generally on caste and religious affiliations. As a result, the British government agreed to extend official sanction to the principle of representation on communal and religious lines. This was done by means of a 'pledge'— an undertaking to reserve employment opportunities to members of minority and scheduled communities. In 1925, Sir Alexander Muddiman, the Home Member, extended to the minority communities, his pledge to have thirty-three and one-third per cent of all direct appointments in the civil service reserved for them.

The Muslims were the first community to seek representation, and as a result, they got the largest share in the beginning. When rules on representation in the civil service on communal lines were defined in the Home Resolution of 4th July 1934, there was clarity in the matter. The resolution laid down that twenty-five per cent reservation would be given to Muslims, eight and one-third per cent to the Anglo-Indians, and an additional six per cent reservation to minorities other than the Muslims and the Anglo-Indians.

The Scheduled Castes had no specific percentage assigned to them before 1943. A Government of India Resolution that year reserved eight and one-third per cent of the vacancies in their favour. This did not initially apply to the posts in the Indian Civil

Service (ICS), but Sir Francis Mudie, the Home Member, assured B.R. Ambedkar in 1945 that representation would be given to candidates belonging to the Scheduled Castes in the ICS, to the extent of eight and one-third per cent. The percentage was increased to twelve in May 1946.

The principle of communal and caste representation was further elaborated in independent India. Reservation in favour of Scheduled Caste and Scheduled Tribes was increased to 18 per cent, while much later, reservation was provided for members of the Backward Classes. In all, a reservation of fifty per cent now exists for different categories in matters of appointment to the civil service.

During the colonial period, the principle of reservation did not apply to promotions. A system was developed over time in which the principle of reservation was made applicable to promotions up to a certain level. In cases of the civil servants belonging to Scheduled Castes and Scheduled Tribes, certain exemptions were also provided in matters of promotion such as relaxation in periods of residency in the lower post.

While the Civil Service Commissioners, and later, the Public Service Commission which was established in 1926, selected candidates for the civil services in colonial India, after independence, the Union Public Service Commission, an independent body, was charged with the responsibility for recruiting candidates to the all-India services and to posts under the central government. As for the state governments, the same functions were given to the state public service commissions.

Article 315 of the Indian Constitution provides for the establishment of the Union Public Service Commission, and Article 320 enumerates the functions of the commission. Several provisions in Articles 316 to 319 create the necessary conditions for the Union Public Service Commission to function as an independent body. Similar provisions exist in the Constitution in respect of state public service commissions.

Candidates successful in the civil service examination set out on a career with well-articulated conditions of service and an assurance of predictable career progression. The conditions of service include salary or wages including subsistence allowance during suspension and periodic increments, leave, provident fund and gratuity, and regular promotions based on seniority.

The course of career progression is well defined and, what is remarkable, without negative overtones. The Constitution itself provides for necessary safeguards against arbitrary dismissal or punishment. Article 311(2) lays down that no civil servant shall be dismissed or removed or reduced in rank except after an enquiry in which the civil servant is informed of the charges against him and given reasonable opportunity to defend himself. It further provides that where it is proposed after such enquiry, to impose any penalty on a civil servant, it can be done only on the basis of the evidence adduced during such enquiry. The predictability of the career cycle is strengthened by uniform retirement and pension rules.

The bureaucratic structure in India is largely an insulated internal labour market. The system is designed to ensure that, by and large, only those who enter the civil service through the examination system, and thus make the early commitment, gain access to senior positions in the public bureaucracy. This is done by declaring senior positions in the public bureaucracy cadre posts and formulating cadre rules for the various services in such a way that these cadre posts can be occupied only by members of the concerned service. The idea is to prevent horizontal entry into the top and middle ranks.

The basic features of the civil service in India are:

1. Higher education with at least a degree, as the basis for eligibility for appointment to the civil service.
2. Entry into service on the basis of examinations.
3. Entrance into a distinct civil service career beginning at the lowest level of the upper civil service and moving through a series of hierarchically linked offices at a predictable rate.
4. Career progression only on the basis of seniority.
5. A higher civil service career involving mobility from one control post to another across almost all departments of government.
6. A uniform career period, (20 years of service and 50 years of age) the completion of which provides the civil servant with a vested interest in a retirement income or a pension.
7. A career structure in which officials are protected from arbitrary imposition of penalty and dismissal. The grounds

for imposition of penalty and dismissal are well-defined in laws and regulations.

On the whole, the move which started initially with restraining corrupt practices, and later, replacing patronage with merit, ended with a structure that looks remarkably like the Weberian definitional model of bureaucracy, at least in its distinguishing aspects.

## NOTES

1. O'Malley (1931), p. 25. The Regulating Act of 1773, however, permitted usury by the civil servants of the East India Company and stipulated that not more than 12 per cent can be charged on such loans. Hastings, by a regulation issued in 1774, prohibited all such advances.
2. Misra (1977), p. 47. Such cases were very common. For example, in 1789 Cornwallis was pressurized by no less a person than the Prince Regent to allow his protege with hardly two years' service to supersede an officer of talent and character. Cornwallis refused.
3. Ironically, Edmund Burke had sought the conviction of Hastings primarily on charges of corruption. According to Burke, Hastings 'did not only give and receive bribes accidentally', he 'formed plans and systems of government for the very purpose of accumulating bribes and presents to himself'; he descended into the 'muck and filth of peculation and corruption' and he was 'not only a public robber himself, but the head of a system of robbery, the captain-general of the gang'. See Noonan (1987), p. 392.
4. In respect of revenue administration, Hastings reorganized the districts and placed each one under a covenanted servant called the collector who was vested with executive authority in the settlement and collection of land revenue. The collectors and their officers were prohibited from giving loans to middlemen, and an interdict was laid on the receipt of presents from the zamindars. The collector was made directly accountable to the government. This model of district administration was adopted by Madras and Bombay with slight local modifications. Misra (1977), p. 49.
5. In the judicial system, Hastings initiated measures to make the process free of corruption. In the Muhammadan courts, almost every decision was a corrupt bargain with the highest bidder. One quarter of the property in dispute was retained by the judge as a reward for his trouble. In the interior places, justice was dispensed by unauthorized courts with the result that in Warren Hastings' words, 'the regular course of justice was suspended everywhere'. See O'Malley (1931), p. 25.

6. O'Malley (1931), p. 31.
7. Ibid., p. 34.
8. B.B. Misra, *The Central Administration of the East India Company, 1773–1834* (Manchester, 1959), p. 386.
9. O'Malley (1931), p. 232. The establishment of Fort William College was made to coincide with the date of the first anniversary of the date of the fall of Tippu Sultan.
10. The building in which the Fort William College was housed, is now the Writers Building which is the seat of West Bengal's government. The name, Writers Building, was given to it because the young writers lived in it while studying languages.
11. O'Malley (1931), p. 236.
12. Das (1998), p. 117.
13. Misra (1977), p. 79.
14. 'Report On The Indian Civil Service' in *The Civil Service, Vol. I* (London: HMSO, 1975), Appendix B, p. 120.
15. Quoted in O'Malley (1931), p. 81.
16. O'Malley (1931), p. 241. Lord Macaulay was the logical choice to head the committee because he was the advocate of the competitive system on the ground that it raised the standard and quality of the entrants to the civil service. The other members of the committee were Lord Ashburton, Henry Melvill (Principal of Haileybury College), Benjamin Jowett (Master of Balliol College, Oxford), and John Lefevre.
17. The philosophy that informed the recommendations of the committee was that of the generalist administrator. The ideal administrator, according to the committee, was the gifted layman who can take a practical view of any matter, irrespective of the subject matter. The gifted layman should have received 'the best, the most liberal, the most finished education that his native country affords', and as the committee further explained, 'Such an education has been proved by experience to be the best preparation for every calling which requires the exercise of the higher powers of the mind.' See *The Civil Service, Vol I.* (1975), Appendix B, p. 119.
18. *The Civil Service, Vol. I* (1975), Appendix B, p. 119.
19. Ibid., p. 120.

# 5

# Meritocracy

The Union Public Service Commission administers a competitive examination annually to select candidates for the higher civil service. The higher civil service in India consists of the Indian Administrative Service (IAS), the Indian Foreign Service (IFS), the Indian Police Service (IPS), and the Central Services, Class I and II. Similarly, public service commissions at the state level conduct competitive examinations either annually or as a bunch of vacancies arises, to recruit candidates to the state civil service.

Recruitment to the IAS, IFS, IPS, and the Central Services, Class I and II is on the basis of the civil service examination which was administered annually by the Union Public Service Commission prior to 1979. The age limit for recruitment to the IAS, IFS, and other Central Services was 21–26 years, and for the IPS, 20–26 years. Relaxation in the upper age limit was permissible only in the case of candidates belonging to the Scheduled Castes and Scheduled Tribes. Candidates were permitted two chances to take the examination within the age limit. The examination consisted of a written examination in three compulsory subjects and several electives depending on the service the candidate appeared for, and an interview.

## KOTHARI COMMITTEE

The Union Public Service Commission appointed a committee under the chairmanship of D.S. Kothari in 1974 to review recruitment methods. The committee reported in 1976, and the Government of India accepted most of its recommendations. The implementation started in 1979.

As a result of the recommendations of the Kothari Committee, there was a change in the pattern of examinations in 1979. The committee had recommended that there should be two written examinations for the higher civil service: the preliminary and the main. Only those who passed the preliminary examination, could sit for the main examination. According to the committee, the preliminary test was to be in the nature of a screening test to weed out less meritorious candidates, and thereby, reduce the number of applicants to manageable proportions. Candidates successful in the main examination were to appear for an interview. The Kothari Committee had specifically recommended the retention of the age limit of 21–26 years. The government, however, decided in favour of an extended age limit of 21–28 years, with the stipulation that the upper age limit was to be further relaxed by another five years in case of candidates belonging to the reserved category of Scheduled Castes and Scheduled Tribes.[1]

There was yet another area in which the Government of India went beyond the Kothari Committee's recommendations. The committee had specifically recommended that aspirants to the civil service should be permitted only two attempts, irrespective of whether they belonged to the general or reserved categories. The Government of India, however, permitted three attempts to the general category and unlimited attempts to the reserved categories. In 1990, the government increased the number of attempts for the general category from three to four.

## SATISH CHANDRA COMMITTEE

The Union Public Service Commission set up another committee under the chairmanship of Satish Chandra, to review and evaluate the system of selection introduced in 1979. The Satish Chandra Committee was asked, in particular, to examine whether the pattern of a common civil service examination in operation during the previous decade had succeeded in identifying candidates who combined intellectual capacity with the requisite traits of personality. The committee reported in 1989, but the Government of India decided to implement only a few of the recommendations of the committee with effect from the civil service examination of 1993.

Some of the recommendations of the Satish Chandra Committee are important. The committee recommended the age limit of 21–26 years for the general category, while suggesting that the usual relaxation of five years should be given to the reserved categories. In other words, the Satish Chandra Committee was making the very same recommendation which the Kothari Committee had made earlier in respect of the age limit. But the Government of India did not accept this recommendation, and it chose to continue with the age limit of 21–28 years.

The Satish Chandra Committee observed that the candidates from the reserved categories got the benefit of as many as eleven attempts because of the relaxation of five years given to them. The committee recommended that while the general category should continue to get three attempts, the reserved categories should be given a maximum of six attempts. The Government of India did not accept this recommendation.

On whether the common civil service examination in operation during the previous decade had succeeded in identifying candidates who combined intellectual capacity with requisite traits of personality, the committee concluded in the affirmative. The committee was of the view that the existing scheme of examination had been able to identify candidates who had the intellectual capacity and traits of personality needed for the civil service.

Under the civil service examination scheme as it exists now after the modifications consequent on the Kothari and Satish Chandra Committees, the age limit is 21–28 years, with the upper age limit being relaxable for candidates from the reserved categories by five years. Candidates with a general degree from any of the universities specified or a technical or professional degree recognized by the government are eligible to be admitted to the civil service examination.

Starting with the civil service examination of 1994, Government of India decided to implement the recommendations of the Mandal Commission providing for reservation for the Backward Classes and as a result, a total of 50 per cent reservation has now been made for candidates belonging to the Scheduled Castes, Scheduled Tribes, and Other Backward Classes.

# EFFECTIVE MERITOCRACY

There has been considerable discussion on whether the candidates selected for the civil service represent the best and brightest of the educational system in India. Research on the subject[2] does not lend credence to the commonly held view that those who join the civil service are the best products of the Indian universities. Raj Singh emphatically states that 'the civil service examination can hardly be called to be a measure of intelligence and creativity of the administrative abilities of the entrants'.[3] In fact, in terms of these studies, approximately half of those selected for the civil service had mediocre academic records in their respective disciplines and obtained their college degrees in the second or even third divisions.[4]

There are essentially two aspects that need to be considered. First is the quality of the degree obtained by the candidate. In India, it is generally the case that the more brilliant students go in for higher degrees while the less meritorious ones are from the pass degrees. Table 5.1 provides data about the degrees obtained by the candidates who appeared for the civil services main examination, while Table 5.2 looks at the distribution of selected candidates according to the degrees obtained by them. On the basis of such data, the success ratios for candidates from both the categories—with higher degrees and pass degrees—have been worked out.

TABLE 5.1
*Educational Degrees of Candidates for the
Civil Services (Main) Examination*

|  | 1983 | 1985 | 1989 | 1993 | 1994 | 1995 |
|---|---|---|---|---|---|---|
| Higher degrees | 6803 | 6756 | 6077 | 6143 | 6529 | 5357 |
|  | (72.73%) | (71.25%) | (64.59%) | (63.21%) | (61.90%) | (61.62%) |
| Pass degrees | 2551 | 2726 | 3331 | 3575 | 4019 | 3337 |
|  | (27.27%) | (28.75%) | (35.41%) | (36.79%) | (38.10%) | (38.38%) |

*Note:*   A. The total number of candidates denotes those who took civil services (main) examination.
B. Percentages shown relate to the totals for that column.

*Source:   The Annual Reports*, UPSC.

There has clearly been a gradual increase in the number of candidates with pass degrees, while the number of candidates with higher degrees is declining. The pool of applicants is getting increasingly filled with candidates whose educational background is qualitatively lower than those in the previous years.

TABLE 5.2

*Educational Degrees of Candidates Selected for the Civil Services*

|  | 1983 | 1985 | 1989 | 1993 | 1994 | 1995 |
|---|---|---|---|---|---|---|
| Higher degrees | 671 | 607 | 588 | 526 | 474 | 417 |
|  | (79.41%) | (76.84%) | (69.18%) | (66.58%) | (67.23%) | (65.05%) |
| Pass degrees | 174 | 183 | 262 | 264 | 231 | 224 |
|  | (20.59%) | (23.16%) | (30.82%) | (33.42%) | (32.77%) | (34.95%) |

*Note:* Percentages shown relate to the totals for that column.

*Source: Annual Reports,* UPSC.

A similar trend is also visible in respect of the selected candidates (Table 5.2). The number of successful candidates with pass degrees has gone up while the number of those with higher degrees has come down. The data in Table 5.2 also shows that the number of those with pass degrees in the list of successful candidates is a significant number. While the number was only 20 per cent of successful candidates in 1983, it is as high as 35 per cent in 1995.

The other aspect to be examined is the grades of the selected candidates in the university degree (Table 5.3).

TABLE 5.3

*Distribution of Selected Candidates by Division*

|  | 1983 | 1985 | 1989 | 1993 | 1994 | 1995 |
|---|---|---|---|---|---|---|
| First division | 542 | 536 | 573 | 526 | 480 | 429 |
|  | (64.14%) | (67.84%) | (67.41%) | (66.58%) | (68.08%) | (66.90%) |
| Other divisions | 303 | 254 | 277 | 264 | 225 | 212 |
|  | (35.86%) | (32.16%) | (32.59%) | (33.42%) | (31.92%) | (33.10%) |

*Note:* Percentages shown relate to the totals for that column.

*Source: Annual Reports,* UPSC

The data in Table 5.3 make it clear that more than 30 per cent of the selected candidates did not have a first division. While the percentage of successful candidates with less than first division was as high as 36 in 1983, this percentage is still high at the prevailing 33 per cent.

## Rate of Success

The rate of success is also an important indicator of effective meritocracy. The rate of success in the civil service examination in India is given in Table 5.4.

TABLE 5.4
*Success Rates for the Indian Higher Civil Service*

| Year | Number of applicants | Total number successful | Ratio |
|------|------|------|------|
| 1960 | 10,376 | 333 | 31.2 |
| 1961 | 9182 | 372 | 24.7 |
| 1962 | 8432 | 374 | 22.5 |
| 1963 | 7113 | 417 | 17.1 |
| 1964 | 6414 | 568 | 11.3 |
| 1965 | 7152 | 426 | 16.8 |
| 1966 | 8305 | 426 | 19.5 |
| 1967 | 8312 | 346 | 24.0 |
| 1968 | 9726 | 354 | 27.5 |
| 1969 | 11,302 | 378 | 29.9 |
| 1970 | 11,710 | 428 | 27.4 |
| 1971 | 15,538 | 542 | 28.7 |
| 1972 | 17,684 | 549 | 32.2 |
| 1973 | 21,032 | 591 | 35.6 |
| 1974 | 24,423 | 611 | 40.0 |
| 1979 | 100,742 | 702 | 143.5 |
| 1980 | 89,277 | 747 | 119.5 |
| 1981 | 94,419 | 873 | 108.2 |
| 1982 | 85,462 | 963 | 88.7 |
| 1983 | 89,312 | 845 | 105.7 |
| 1984 | 130,942 | 814 | 160.9 |
| 1985 | 152,598 | 790 | 193.2 |
| 1986 | 163,530 | 855 | 191.3 |
| 1987 | 149,631 | 817 | 183.1 |
| 1988 | 145,012 | 897 | 161.7 |

*contd.*

| Year | Number of applicants | Total number successful | Ratio |
|------|------|------|------|
| 1989 | 156,414 | 850 | 184.0 |
| 1990 | 309,300 | 940 | 329.0 |
| 1991 | 209,849 | 871 | 240.9 |
| 1992 | 332,343 | 763 | 435.6 |

*Source:* Compiled from the *Annual Reports* of the UPSC for the various years.

How good is this success rate? To evaluate this it is necessary to compare these figures with those of other countries which have similar systems of recruitment. Japan is one such country. An open, competitive civil service examination is administered every year in Japan by the National Personnel Authority to recruit staff for three levels in the civil service: Class I, II, and III. Table 5.5 provides the success rate for Japan.

TABLE 5.5
*Success Rates for the Japanese Higher Civil Service*

| Year | Number of applicants | Total number successful | Ratio |
|------|------|------|------|
| 1960 | 16,364 | 981 | 16.7 |
| 1961 | 11,743 | 1133 | 10.4 |
| 1962 | 14,059 | 1218 | 11.5 |
| 1963 | 16,329 | 1366 | 12.0 |
| 1964 | 15,904 | 1434 | 11.1 |
| | | | |
| 1965 | 21,125 | 1624 | 13.0 |
| 1966 | 24,799 | 1507 | 16.5 |
| 1967 | 21,567 | 1364 | 15.8 |
| 1968 | 20,483 | 1313 | 15.6 |
| 1969 | 17,973 | 1306 | 13.8 |
| | | | |
| 1970 | 17,637 | 1353 | 13.0 |
| 1971 | 23,532 | 1401 | 16.8 |
| 1972 | 27,429 | 1349 | 20.3 |
| 1973 | 30,129 | 1410 | 21.4 |
| 1974 | 30,688 | 1375 | 22.3 |

*contd.*

| 1975 | 37,825 | 1206 | 31.4 |
|------|--------|------|------|
| 1976 | 44,518 | 1136 | 39.2 |
| 1977 | 48,514 | 1,06 | 40.2 |
| 1978 | 55,972 | 1311 | 42.7 |
| 1979 | 51,896 | 1265 | 41.0 |
| 1980 | 45,131 | 1254 | 36.0 |
| 1981 | 40,770 | 1361 | 30.0 |
| 1982 | 36,856 | 1383 | 26.6 |
| 1983 | 34,854 | 1478 | 23.6 |
| 1984 | 34,089 | 1562 | 21.8 |
| 1985 | 36,072 | 1655 | 21.8 |
| 1986 | 32,675 | 1718 | 19.0 |
| 1987 | 32,308 | 1696 | 19.0 |
| 1988 | 28,833 | 1814 | 15.9 |
| 1989 | 27,243 | 1983 | 13.7 |
| 1990 | 31,422 | 2047 | 15.4 |
| 1991 | 30,102 | 2200 | 13.7 |
| 1992 | 30,789 | 2075 | 14.8 |

*Source:* Pempel and Muramatsu (1995)

At first sight, the success rate in India appears to be much lower than in Japan, and this would beg the inference that the method of selection of candidates to the Indian civil service is more meritocratic than in Japan. But a comparative evaluation of the success rate of both these countries should also involve an examination of the relative quality of the applicants for the civil service examination, and also to what extent the civil service examination is competitive and open.

## Quality of the Pool of Applicants

One way of assessing the quality of the applicants would be to look at the background of the successful candidates. Ralph Braibanti, a noted researcher on the Indian bureaucracy, has argued that the better students in India opt for medical, engineering and pure sciences, economics being an exception. He has, in fact, pointed out that sixty-seven per cent of those who join the civil services belong to the arts and the social sciences group.[5] Table 5.6 points to the validity to Braibanti's observation.

TABLE 5.6
*Subject-Wise Distribution of Selected Candidates (Percentage)*

| Subjects | 1983 | 1985 | 1989 | 1993 | 1994 | 1995 |
|---|---|---|---|---|---|---|
| Humanities-A | 50 | 49 | 54 | 54 | 48 | 46 |
| Humanities-B | 19 | 18 | 16 | 13 | 13 | 14 |
| Languages | 7 | 9 | 7 | 7 | 10 | 11 |
| Science | 18 | 18 | 17 | 22 | 25 | 24 |
| Engineering | 6 | 6 | 6 | 4 | 4 | 5 |

*Note:*   Humanities-A: Anthropology, History, Law, Management and Public Administration, Philosophy, Political Science and International Relations, and Sociology
Humanities-B: Commerce and Accountancy, Economics, Geography and Psychology
Languages: Assamese, Bengali, Gujarati, Hindi, Kannada, Kashmiri, Marathi, Malayalam, Oriya, Punjabi, Pali, Sanskrit, Sindhi, Tamil, Telugu, Chinese, Persian, Arabic, English, French, German, Russian, and Urdu
Science: Agriculture, Animal Husbandry and Veterinary Science, Botany, Zoology, Chemistry, Physics, Geology, Mathematics, Statistics and Medical Science
Engineering: Civil, Electrical and Mechanical Engineering.

*Source:*   *Annual Reports*, UPSC.

Candidates with academic background in Humanities-A, Humanities-B and Languages accounted for more than 70 per cent of the candidates selected. It would seem that Macaulay's conception of the generalist administrator with a classical education in the liberal arts continues to prevail.[6]

How does this compare with the academic background of candidates for the civil service in Japan? Table 5.7 indicates the subject-wise distribution of candidates appearing for the higher civil services in Japan.

TABLE 5.7
*Subject-Wise Distribution of Candidates
for the Japanese Civil Service*

| Year | Law | Engineering | Agriculture | Others | Total |
|------|------|------|------|------|------|
| 1978 | 10,630 | 25,567 | 7079 | 12,696 | 55,972 |
| 1979 | 10,034 | 22,532 | 7033 | 12,297 | 51,896 |
| 1980 | 9694 | 18,272 | 6419 | 10,746 | 45,131 |
| 1981 | 9644 | 14,991 | 6253 | 9822 | 40,770 |
| 1982 | 8834 | 12,609 | 5892 | 9521 | 36,856 |
| 1983 | 8421 | 11,719 | 6063 | 8651 | 34,854 |
| 1984 | 8321 | 11,491 | 5714 | 8563 | 34,089 |
| 1985 | 8915 | 11,838 | 5679 | 9640 | 36,072 |
| 1986 | 8043 | 10,776 | 5195 | 8661 | 32,675 |
| 1987 | 7666 | 11,088 | 5055 | 8439 | 32,308 |
| 1988 | 6728 | 9969 | 4788 | 7348 | 28,833 |
| 1989 | 6443 | 9600 | 4433 | 6767 | 27,243 |
| 1990 | 7341 | 9937 | 4597 | 9547 | 31,422 |

*Source:* Pempel and Muramatsu (1995).

The number of applicants with background in engineering and agriculture has been sizable (Table 5.7). The surprising presence is that of law graduates in such large numbers. In Japan, it is accepted that the brightest students go to law, and in particular, the Law School of the Tokyo University attracts the best products of the Japanese educational system. There is a clear preference for law graduates in the Japanese civil service, particularly for graduates from the Tokyo Law School.[7] For example, of the twenty or thirty annual recruits to the ministry of finance, the most prestigious ministry in the Japanese government, 80 to 90 per cent are from the Tokyo Law School (Wolferen 1990: 111). Table 5.8 gives the break-up of law graduates who appeared for the civil service examination in Japan for the different years.

If one goes by the ratio of the total number of successful candidates to the number of applicants, the ratio in respect of law graduates has been better than the general ratio for most of the years.

Although there are a large number of law graduates in Japan's civil service, the fact remains that an overwhelmingly large per-

TABLE 5.8
Number of Law Graduates in the Japanese Civil Service

| Year | Number of applicants | Total number successful | Ratio | Law Graduates | | |
| --- | --- | --- | --- | --- | --- | --- |
| | | | | Number of applicants | Number successful | Ratio |
| 1960 | 16,364 | 981 | 16.70 | 4403 | 262 | 16.80 |
| 1961 | 11,743 | 1133 | 10.40 | 3284 | 308 | 10.70 |
| 1962 | 14,059 | 1218 | 11.50 | 3947 | 316 | 12.50 |
| 1963 | 16,329 | 1366 | 12.00 | 4077 | 298 | 13.70 |
| 1964 | 15,904 | 1434 | 11.10 | 3807 | 298 | 12.80 |
| 1965 | 21,215 | 1624 | 13.00 | 4411 | 299 | 14.80 |
| 1966 | 24,799 | 1507 | 16.50 | 4843 | 290 | 16.70 |
| 1967 | 21,567 | 1364 | 15.80 | 4293 | 269 | 16.00 |
| 1968 | 20,483 | 1313 | 15.60 | 4332 | 266 | 16.30 |
| 1969 | 17,973 | 1306 | 13.80 | 4032 | 251 | 16.10 |
| 1970 | 17,637 | 1353 | 13.00 | 3998 | 252 | 15.90 |
| 1971 | 23,532 | 1401 | 16.80 | 5093 | 261 | 19.50 |
| 1972 | 27,429 | 1349 | 20.30 | 5238 | 242 | 21.60 |
| 1973 | 30,129 | 1410 | 21.40 | 5866 | 262 | 22.40 |
| 1974 | 30,688 | 1375 | 22.30 | 6227 | 249 | 25.00 |

| 1975 | 37,825 | 1206 | 31.40 | 7556 | 237 | 31.90 |
| 1976 | 44,518 | 1136 | 39.20 | 8238 | 235 | 35.10 |
| 1977 | 48,514 | 1206 | 40.20 | 8729 | 240 | 36.40 |
| 1978 | 55,972 | 1311 | 42.70 | 10,630 | 245 | 43.40 |
| 1979 | 51,896 | 1265 | 41.00 | 10,034 | 229 | 43.80 |
| 1980 | 45,131 | 1254 | 36.00 | 9694 | 229 | 42.30 |
| 1981 | 40,770 | 1361 | 30.00 | 9644 | 226 | 42.70 |
| 1982 | 36,856 | 1383 | 26.60 | 8834 | 237 | 37.30 |
| 1983 | 34,854 | 1478 | 23.60 | 8421 | 221 | 38.10 |
| 1984 | 34,089 | 1562 | 21.80 | 8321 | 220 | 37.80 |
| 1985 | 36,072 | 1655 | 21.80 | 8915 | 242 | 36.80 |
| 1986 | 32,675 | 1718 | 19.00 | 8043 | 251 | 32.00 |
| 1987 | 32,308 | 1696 | 19.00 | 7666 | 250 | 30.70 |
| 1988 | 28,833 | 1814 | 15.90 | 6728 | 266 | 25.33 |
| 1989 | 27,243 | 1983 | 13.70 | 6443 | 270 | 23.90 |
| 1990 | 31,422 | 2047 | 15.40 | 7341 | 271 | 27.10 |
| 1991 | 30,102 | 2200 | 13.70 | 6955 | 287 | 24.20 |
| 1992 | 30,789 | 2075 | 14.80 | 7008 | 286 | 24.50 |

*Source:* Pempel and Maramatsu (1995)

centage of recruits to the civil service come from Tokyo University. Roughly 35 to 40 per cent of successful candidates are graduates of Tokyo University. In the 1991 civil service examination, over 50 per cent of the successful candidates for Class I Civil Service came from the University of Tokyo.[8]

Of late, the dominance of the civil service by the graduates of Tokyo University is not quite what it was. Even so, recruits to the higher civil services come from a small number of the more reputable universities in Japan. Waseda University accounts for 11.8 per cent, and Kyoto University graduates made up 7 per cent of the successful candidates in the 1991 civil service examination. Usually only 15 or so of Japan's 460-odd universities see 10 or more of their graduates succeed in the civil service examinations.[9] There has been some broadening of the recruitment process, but the field is still very limited. Waseda University, Kyoto University and the other state universities remain, even now, minority contributors to the list of successful candidates in the civil service examination in Japan.

On the whole, the number of universities producing 10 or more successful candidates in the civil service examination has remained limited in Japan. Since the prestige of civil servants in Japanese society continues to remain very high, the aspiration to enter the civil service is high. Aspirants to the civil service try hard to join Tokyo University, and failing that, the universities of Waseda and Kyoto, because, it is perceived, and rightly too, that admission to these universities is a stepping stone to the civil service.

These universities—Tokyo, Waseda, and Kyoto—require applicants to pass an entrance test before they are considered for admission. Applicants from certain high schools find it easier to pass the entrance examinations to these universities. These high schools are state-run schools which were established between 1877 and 1908. Therefore, those who want a civil service career, try to enter these schools so as to get admission to the Tokyo, Waseda or Kyoto universities, and ultimately enter the civil service. In other words, the decision to make the civil service career is taken very early in life, at the time of getting admission to these state-run high schools.

In India, the position in the first two decades after independence was similar to that of Japan. Recruits to the civil service came largely from three or four of the more reputable universities. In particular, the universities of Delhi and Allahabad contributed more than 50 per cent of the recruits to the civil service. The share of these two universities has declined in recent years. For example in 1994, the universities of Delhi and Allahabad provided only 1976 candidates, accounting for 18.73 per cent of the candidates who appeared; and 122 of them qualified for appointment, accounting for 17.31 per cent of the successful candidates. In 1995, the universities of Delhi and Allahabad between them, provided 1787 candidates, accounting for 20.55 per cent of the total number of candidates who appeared; and 129 of them qualified for appointment, accounting for 20.13 per cent of the successful candidates.

The position has broadened in recent years. For example, 707 candidates who qualified for the higher civil services in 1994 came from 109 universities spread all over India. Unlike in Japan, no single university has an overwhelming presence in the list of successful candidates for the civil service, as is clear from Table 5.9.

TABLE 5.9

*Success Ratio of the First Ten Universities in Relation
to the Number of Successful Candidates in the
Civil Services (Main) Examination, 1995.*

| S. no. | University | Candidates appeared | Candidates qualified | Success ratio |
|---|---|---|---|---|
| 1. | University of Delhi | 977 | 112 | 1 : 8.72 |
| 2. | Indian Institute of Technology, New Delhi | 204 | 45 | 1 : 4.53 |
| 3. | Indian Institute of Technology, Kanpur | 153 | 36 | 1 : 4.25 |
| 4. | Jawaharlal Nehru University, New Delhi | 259 | 31 | 1 : 8.35 |
| 5. | University of Rajasthan, Jaipur | 377 | 23 | 1 : 16.39 |
| 6. | Patna University, Patna | 333 | 20 | 1 : 16.65 |
| 7. | Punjab University, Chandigarh | 155 | 19 | 1 : 8.1 |

*contd.*

| S. no. | University | Candidates appeared | Candidates qualified | Success ratio |
|---|---|---|---|---|
| 8. | University of Allahabad | 810 | 17 | 1 : 47.65 |
| 9. | Osmania University, Hyderabad | 231 | 16 | 1 : 14.44 |
| 10. | University of Lucknow | 252 | 13 | 1 : 19.38 |

Source: 47th Report 1996–97, UPSC.

The top 10 universities provided 3751 candidates, i.e. 43.14 per cent of the total number of candidates for the examination. They provided 332 successful candidates, accounting for 51.79 per cent of the total number that qualified for appointment in the civil service. But the performance of these top ten universities varied considerably. The success ratio of four institutions, namely the University of Delhi, Indian Institute of Technology, New Delhi, Indian Institute of Technology, Kanpur, and Jawaharlal Nehru University, New Delhi was higher than the overall success ratio of 1 : 13.56, while the success ratio of the remaining six was considerably lower.

## COMPETITIVENESS IN CIVIL SERVICE EXAMINATION

The degree of competitiveness of a civil service examination depends on two factors: (a) whether there is a system of reservation of jobs, and (b) how many attempts a candidate is permitted to appear for the civil service examination.

There is reservation to the extent of 50 per cent of total recruitment in favour of particular communities in India. This means that candidates from a reserved category compete among themselves within the category, and not with the candidates from the general category or other reserved categories. For example, a candidate from the Scheduled Tribes category competes only with other candidates from the Scheduled Tribes, and not with candidates from the general category or the candidates belonging to the Scheduled Castes or the Other Backward Classes. In Japan, there is no reservation of any sort. All the applicants compete with each other, and the best ones are chosen on the basis of merit.

It is by now established that the number of attempts which a candidate is allowed for appearing in the examination detracts from the competitiveness of the civil service examination. In Japan, a candidate is allowed only one attempt. In India, on the other hand, an applicant from the general category is allowed four attempts, and a candidate from the reserved categories, as many as twelve attempts. The large number of attempts that the candidates are allowed in India, inflates the number in the pool of applicants for the civil service.

A recent study by the Lal Bahadur Shastri National Academy of Administration has the following comment to make,

Under the present system, many candidates waste valuable years of their lives taking the examination year after year. The psychological toil on the unsuccessful candidates is enormous. At the end of the process, whether due to crossing the age limit or due to exhausting all permissible attempts, such young men and women cannot but feel a sense of rejection and suffer a loss of confidence.[10]

Because of multiple attempts and relaxation in maximum age, the number in the pool of applicants has been inflated artificially. More fundamentally, this has also had the effect of subtracting from the effective meritocracy of the civil service. As the study by the Lal Bahadur Shastri National Academy of Administration points out, 'It is statistically self-evident that the average quality of entrants to the service is inversely proportional to the number of attempts that a candidate should be allowed to each candidate.'[11]

The same study recommended that the age of recruitment should be between 20–25 years. According to the study,

This is being suggested keeping in view the need to mould fresh entrants into the ethos of the service. It is imperative that we start the process with young minds. A fresh entrant to the service is less likely to imbibe new qualities and values, the greater is the age at entry to the service.[12]

In addition to the UPSC, Government of India has set up staff selection commissions, Railway Recruitment Board and other agencies, and entrusted them with the responsibility of recruitment at the lower levels of the civil service. Vacancies occurring in the lower echelons of the civil service in central government establishments other than those filled through the UPSC or agencies like the staff selection commissions are filled by the respective departments from among the candidates listed in the employment exchanges. The recruitment by all these bodies is not any more meritocratic than that of the UPSC. At the level of the state governments, recruitment to the state civil services is done by the public service commissions of the states in a manner very similar to that of the UPSC. Of late, there have been reports that the recruitment done by the state public service commissions is based on considerations other than merit.

## ATTRACTING TALENTED INDIVIDUALS

Where does it leave us in the matter of attracting talent to the civil service?

A recent survey conducted by the Lal Bahadur Shastri National Academy of Administration, Mussoorie, indicated that one of the prime motives for joining the civil service was to make money.[13] Commenting on the findings of the survey, Sen has this to say,

A recent survey has elicited startling response from a substantial section of the intending aspirants to the civil service. According to the respondents, one of the prime motivating forces for joining the civil service is the scope and opportunity for making money! Such reactions would not have been forthcoming if it is not ingrained in the psyche of the people at large, that civil service is a mechanism to make money. Even if the perception is incorrect or exaggerated, the very fact that it exists should be cause for worry and concern. . . . Civil servants should not only be honest and upright, but they should also appear to be so.[14]

A survey of civil servants in the Delhi Administration reported the following response from a civil servant, 'I see that my juniors, fresh from the Cadre, come with a single motto *Jaldi paisa banao aur jao* (make money quickly and leave).' He added, 'They ask for a particular post, they lobby for it and are happy even if they get a short tenure in the seat.' The survey also found that the most-sought-after posts involved public dealing, the departments which have a high budget outlay, and those which included issuing of numerous work contracts.[15]

There is an added dimension to it in recent years. With the

liberalization of the Indian economy and the entry of multinationals, there has been a sharp rise in the salaries and perks of those in the private sector. Consequently, two interrelated trends are visible. First, serving civil servants feel less privileged than their counterparts in the private sector. Second, to a large number of bright men and women, a career in the civil service is becoming increasingly less attractive. In other words, the civil service in India is not in a position to attract talented and bright individuals.[16]

According to journalist Praful Bidwai, who has extensively analysed the change in character of the civil service in India, it is inconsequential whether the 'brightest elements' are joining the civil service. Says Bidwai, 'What is important is that people with the right aptitude for good governance and with progressive and liberal ideas join the ranks. This regrettably is not happening'.[17]

The contrast with Japan could not have been starker. In Japan, when asked to choose from ten possible reasons for choosing the civil service as their career, the most cited reasons were 'suitability to one's own character' (21 per cent), 'breadth of vision' (18 per cent), to serve the state (16 per cent), and to serve the public (12 per cent). Only 10 per cent cited 'security of position' as the reason for their joining the civil service.[18]

Clearly, the civil service in India is not in a position to attract the kind of talented individuals who are less likely to be corrupt. On the other hand, it seems to attract mostly individuals who are likely to be corrupt. As a 1995 report on India's bureaucracy describes the process,

the culture of corruption and opportunism has become so dominant that the youngsters now joining the civil services draw up their preferences on the basis of opportunity to make money through corruption. Consequently neither the Indian Foreign Service nor even the Indian Police Service seem to attract examining candidates as much as the Indian Administrative Service, the Indian Revenue Service, and the Indian Customs and Central Excise Service. Presumably, the opportunity for corruption in IAS/IRS/IC & CES is more than even in the IPS.[19]

## NOTES

1. The age limit of 21–28 years was in operation from 1979 to 1987 when the Government of India reconsidered the matter and reduced the upper age limit to 26 years. However, due to pressure

from the affected parties, the government under V.P. Singh reconsidered the matter and the upper age limit was restored to 28 years
in 1980.

2. See L.P. Srivastva, *Public Personnel System in India* (Patna: Janaki
Prakashan, 1987), Pradeep Saxena, *Public Policy and Administration
and Development* (Jaipur: Print Well, 1988), K.K. Katyal, 'How
Autonomous are the Public Service Commissions?' *The Hindu*,
December 1, 1990, Niru Hazarkla, *Public Service Commissions* (New
Delhi: Leela Devi Publications, 1979), J.B. D'sousa, 'Selection for
Civil Services, Change in the System Vital', *The Economic Times*, May
9, 1981.

3. Raj Singh, 'Indian Bureaucracy and Development', *Indian Journal of
Public Administration*, Vol. xxxiv, No. 2, 1985, p. 269.

4. See T.C.A. Srinivasavardan, 'Some Aspects of Indian Administrative
Service', *Indian Journal of Public Administration*, Vol. vii, No. 1, 1961.
Also see, V. Subramaniam, *Social Background to India's Administra-
tion: A Social Economic Study of the Higher Civil Services in India* (New
Delhi: Publications Division, Government of India, 1961), p. 149.

5. Ralph Braibanti, 'Reflections on Bureaucratic Reforms in India', in
R. Braibanti and J. Spengler (eds.), *Administration and Economic
Development in India* (Durham: Duke University Press, 1963).

6. S.K. Das, *Civil Service Reform and Structural Adjustment* (Delhi: Oxford University Press, 1998), p. 154.

7. The preference for law graduates in Japan's civil service has a historical basis. The Regulation of 1887 prescribed the subjects for the
civil service examination under two categories: the mandatory and
the elective. The mandatory subjects were six in number and consisted of constitutional law, criminal law, civil law, administrative
law, economic law, and international public law. The elective subjects consisted of public finance, commercial law, criminal procedure law, and civil procedure law. While the candidates were
required to take all of the six mandatory subjects prescribed, they
had to opt for one of the elective subjects. Background in law was
thus made a major requirement to succeed in the civil service examination.

8. Pempel and Muramatsu (1995), p. 45n. In fact, Tokyo University
graduates constitute 88.6 per cent of all the section chiefs and civil
servants of the higher rank in the Ministry of Finance. It is 76 per
cent in the Foreign Ministry, 73.5 per cent for the National Land
Agency, and 68.5 per cent for the Ministry of Transportation. See K.
Wolferen, *The Enigma of Japanese Power* (New York: Vintage Books,
1990), p. 111.

9. Pempel and Muramatsu (1995), p. 45.

10. Atindra Sen (ed.), *Civil Service Reforms* (Mussoorie: Lal Bahadur Shastri National Academy of Administration, 1995), p. 34.
11. Sen (1995), p. 33.
12. Ibid., p. 34.
13. Sumita Paul, 'A Bureaucracy in Need of Servicing', *Sunday Times*, July 23, 1995.
14. Sen (1995), p. 5.
15. Kota Neelima, 'Bureaucrats' Choices—Plum Inducements or Transfers', *Indian Express*, September 15, 1998.
16. Ramesh K. Arora and Rajni Goyal, *Indian Public Administration: Institutions and Issues* (New Delhi: Wishwa Prakashan, 1995), p. 632.
17. Praful Bidwai quoted in Sakina Yusuf Khan, 'Fatal Attraction', *Sunday Times*, July 23, 1995. See Praful Bidwai, 'Reforming the Bureaucracy: Recruitment, Training must Change', *The Times of India*, September 8, 1994. Also see Bidwai, 'Are We Killing the IAS?' *The Tribune*, August 2, 1995.
18. Pempel and Muramatsu (1995), p. 47.
19. *Governance and Government: Emerging Scenarios in the 21st Century— From Administrative Bureaucracy to Service-Driven Result-Oriented Management by Government in India*, The Report of the Strategic Management Group's Working Party on Modernising and Downsizing India's Bureaucracy, September 1995, pp. 234–5.

# 6

# Rewards

The reward system, as discussed in Chapter 1, is an important source of motivation. The relationship between an incentive structure which rewards honest effort and an honest civil service has been recognized in the policy debate. The reward system in a public bureaucracy can take the form of compensation, promotions, and placements in civil service assignments.

## COMPENSATION

It is the government which determines the level of civil service compensation in India. This is done generally on the basis of the recommendations of pay commissions which are set up from time to time. While the central government sets up its own pay commissions for its employees as well as members of the all-India services working both with the state governments and the central government, the state governments also set up their pay commissions periodically to determine the level of compensation to their employees.

### PAY COMMISSIONS

There have been, so far, five pay commissions set up by the central government: the First Pay Commission (1946–50), the Second Pay Commission (1957–9), the Third Pay Commission

(1970–3), the Fourth Pay Commission (1983–6), and the Fifth Pay Commission (1995–7). Although these pay commissions have enunciated independent principles of pay determination, there has been a remarkable degree of uniformity of approach. The variations were minimal, and were determined by the socio-economic environment prevailing at the time.

In general, there have been three characteristics which have guided the deliberations of the pay commissions—inclusiveness, comprehensibility, and adequacy. Inclusiveness means that the broad patterns of the remuneration structure should apply to all cases without exception. Comprehensibility means that a recommended pay scale should reflect a total picture of the emoluments of a post rather than being fragmented into a number of allowances. Although the characteristics of inclusiveness and comprehensibility are important determinants of the body of civil service compensation, we are concerned with the third characteristic—adequacy of compensation.

*Adequacy*

There were two important considerations which the First Pay Commission addressed while deliberating upon adequacy of civil service compensation: (a) moral principles have a role in determining the compensation structure in the government, and (b) fairness and adequacy of civil service compensation cannot be judged only from the perspective of the civil servants; it should be from the perspective of the employer and the community as a whole. The first consideration guided the commission to declare that civil service compensation cannot be less than a living wage. The second consideration prompted the commission to state that the perception of the employer namely the state and the community regarding the adequacy and fairness of civil service compensation, has to be the guiding factor. In other words, civil service compensation should not be disproportionate to the general level of income of the society. What it means is that the civil service should not be treated as an elite group in the matter of being compensated for its services.

The First Pay Commission made a number of weighty pronouncements. It declared, 'there should be no great disparity between a commercial and official career', and 'adequacy of remuneration certainly bears on the efficiency of the employee because it affects his freedom from care and anxiety and promotes his willingness to work'.[1] But the commission did nothing to end or lower the disparity. On the contrary, the commission, reduced the salaries of the higher categories in the civil service. It recommended the lowering of the salary of a secretary to the Government of India from Rs 4000 to Rs 3000 a month.

The Second Pay Commission agreed with the views of the First Pay Commission, and declared that a combination of social and economic considerations should be taken into account while determining civil service compensation. The commission suggested that the compensation of senior civil servants should be 'sufficient to enable them to maintain a standard of living not conspicuously below that of other groups in the community with which they are socially linked'.[2]

The Third Pay Commission, while calling for a reappraisal of the principles enunciated by the earlier two commissions, examined in some detail the effect of salaries in the private sector on those in the government. The commission stated that while disproportionate importance should not be attached to the compensation prevailing in the private sector, it was necessary to take note of the level of compensation and other conditions of service in the private sector, so that necessary corrections could be made in government pay structure. But the commission also sounded a note of caution. It warned against an uncritical use of comparison between salaries in the government and private sector without considering the work content and the totality of the prevailing circumstances.

In spite of its rhetoric, the Third Pay Commission did not go into the details of the differential between private sector and civil service compensation to determine the desirable levels of compensation. Instead, it relied on the inability of the government to pay salaries comparable to those in the private sector. It pointed out that the wide gap between the emoluments of civil servants and employees in the private sector need not be closed because of the resource constraints of the government.

The Third Pay Commission, however, recognized the need for paying a living wage to civil servants—a wage which will meet their reasonable commitments. It said:

While government employees naturally both need and value security, they also need and value a reasonable standard of living. Besides bare physical needs, every family also has its conventional or social needs. A family should not be obliged to live in a manner that sets it apart from other families in the social group to which it belongs and that makes it unable to live according to the established customs of the community.[3]

The Third Pay Commission also recognized the link between low salaries and corruption. It said,

While it is not argued that the payment of high salaries by itself is a guarantee for the honesty and integrity of the public service, it can be confidently stated that the payment of a salary which does not satisfy the minimum reasonable needs of a government servant is a direct invitation to corruption.[4]

Interestingly, the Third Pay Commission did not recommend any change in the salary structure at the level of joint secretary to the Government of India and above. This was in spite of the fact that by the time the commission submitted its recommendation in 1973, persistent rise in prices had eroded much of the real worth of government salaries, and any cushion which the salary structure might have contained, had disappeared. The Third Pay Commission went on to explain,

so far as the upper range of the salaries are concerned, we have stated that a limit is set by considerations of social acceptability, even though it may be militating against demand and supply principles in the market sense. We have also observed that increasing salaries at the upper level would lead to inevitable demands from the lower income groups and these demands would have large financial implications. At this end of the spectrum, therefore, social considerations, including reduction of disparities in income acquire importance.[5]

The Fourth Pay Commission merely reiterated the points made by the earlier commissions, notably the Third Pay Commission with some minor change in emphasis. It concluded that the pay structure could not be determined by a rule of the thumb or by a formula of universal allocation, but it had to be correlated to the nature and culture of the employment, the degree of satisfaction it generated both to the employees and others, the totality of what it took and gave to the employees, the resources of the employer, and the public assessment of the satisfaction rendered. The decision about pay, in the views of the commission, had to be judgemental, and not merely arithmetical or mechanical.

The Fourth Pay Commission did not favour parity with the private sector, but it recognized the necessity of paying the civil servant a living wage. It pointed out that the requirement of a satisfactory pay structure was to enable the employees to lead a simple life at a level considered satisfactory by him and the society, and in addition, the pay scale should be such that it did not give rise to a sense of deprivation or frustration on comparing his lot with his social peers. In the words of the commission,

Another requirement of a satisfactory structure of emoluments is that it should enable the employee to lead simple life at a level or standard considered satisfactory by him and his likes and the society where he belongs. It should not be derogatory to his work and responsibilities.[6]

The Fourth Pay Commission raised the salary of secretary of the Government of India from Rs 3500 to Rs 8000 per month, of the additional secretary from Rs 2750 to Rs 7300, and that of the joint secretary from Rs 2500 to Rs 5900 per month. In all other categories of the civil service, the commission recommended increases in salaries.

The Fourth Pay Commission also held that the real income of the civil servants should not be allowed to erode with increases in the cost of living. The commission recommended full neutralization of price rise to employees drawing pay up to Rs 3500, 75 per cent to those getting basic pay between Rs 3501 and Rs 6000, and 65 per cent to those getting basic pay above Rs 6000 subject to marginal adjustments.

The Fifth Pay Commission studied the question of the pay differential between the government and the private sector in some detail, and came to the conclusion that 'it is indisputable that there has come to be a yawning gap between the salaries and benefits available in the private sector and the government at all levels'.[7] The commission even sounded a word of caution about what was going to happen if things were allowed to remain that way. It warned, 'we believe that this problem if not addressed at this juncture is likely to gradually spell a rot in the system. Not only is a flight of talent an immediate possibility, a tendency towards corruption is equally likely'.[8] The commission also took note of the fact that in Singapore, salaries in the government had been benchmarked to the salaries of the private sector, and in the United Kingdom, the salaries of the permanent secretaries were close to the salaries of the chief executives in the private sector.

Although the Fifth Pay Commission noted the huge differential between civil service and private sector compensation, and it even hinted that this might constitute the rate of temptation, nothing positive came out of it. According to the commission, 'We also observe that it may not be possible to lift the remuneration system prevailing in the private sector and transplant it in its entirety on to the Government as there are vital differences between the two sectors'.[9] True to the traditions of the pay commissions before it, the Fifth Pay Commission cited the resource constraints as the reason. It said, 'We are, however, constrained by the availability of funds within the Government in making recommendations of this sort'.[10]

The Fifth Pay Commission also endorsed the view that civil service compensation should be a living wage. It took note of the fact that 'a rational salary structure for senior functionaries should allow a salary level which is adequate to meet the current levels of consumption and reasonable additional requirements'.[11] It also pointed to the adverse consequences which would follow if this was not done, but, as it transpired, the recommendations of the commission fell far short of what it professed.

The different pay commissions have been reluctant to establish any parity between civil service and private sector remuneration, and this has been so, in spite of the fact that the remuneration of the top management in the private sector in India has been subject to regulation by the Government of India itself. The Companies Act, in Sections 198 and 309 as well as in the Schedule XII to the act, contain enabling provisions for the government to regulate private sector remuneration.

Before 15th June 1988, the upward restrictions on the salaries and perks of the managerial personnel of the private sector were specified in guidelines issued by the central government from time to time. After 1988, the restrictions came to be incorporated in the Companies Act itself. Table 6.1 summarizes the restrictions placed by the central government on salaries, specified perks and commission on net profit including bonus.

TABLE 6.1

*Ceiling on Remuneration of Managerial Personnel in Private Sector in India*

(Monthly Equivalent)                                                  (In Rupees)

| Period | Salary | Perks | Commission |
|---|---|---|---|
| 1969 to March 1983 | 7500 | 2500 | 3750 |
| April 1983 to June 1988 | 7500 | 3750 | 3750 |
| June 1988 to July 1993 | Between 6,000 to 15,000* | Monthly salary subject to a ceiling of 11,250 | 50% of the salary |
| July 1993 to Jan 1994 | Between 20,000 to 50,000* | Monthly salary subject to a ceiling of 37,500 | No ceiling† |
| Feb 1994 onwards | No ceiling for companies making adequate net profit, subject to the condition that the remuneration consisting of salary, perks and commission, does not exceed 5% or 10% of the net profits of the company in any year depending on whether the company has one or more MD/WTD. For companies making losses, all inclusive remuneration varying from Rs 40,000 to Rs 87,500 per month, but higher payment can be made with approval of the government. | | |

*Note:* *depending on the effective capital of the company.
†subject to the condition that the total of salaries, perks and commission does not exceed 5% of the net profits of the company in any year depending on whether the company has only one or more MD/WTD.

*Source:* Prasad (1996)

In spite of the periodic restrictions put by the Government of India on the maximum compensation of the managerial personnel, the compensation in the private sector has always been higher than the maximum salary payable to the civil servants. For example, the compensation of managerial personnel in the private sector was more than three times the salary of a secretary to the Government of India up to 1978, about 1.5 times between January 1986 and May 1988, and about two times till July 1993. After 1993, private sector compensation has registered a quantum leap (Table 6.2).

TABLE 6.2

*Comparative Compensation across Sectors*

(As on 1st July 1997)                                                    (In Rupees)

| Positions | Basic salary | Dearness allowance | City compensatory allowance | Cost to company |
|---|---|---|---|---|
| CEO private sector* | 23,303 | — | — | 102,255 |
| Secretary to GOI | 26,000 | 4160 | 240 | 58,590 |
| HOD private sector† | 15,155 | — | — | 65,283 |
| Jt. secy‡ to GOI | 18,400 | 2944 | 240 | 45,250 |
| Entry level private sector | 3772 | 2058 | — | 10,837 |
| Entry level GOI | 8000 | 1284 | 240 | 16,783 |

*Note:*    Cost to the Company represents all direct and indirect cost to the company for hiring an employee. This includes all monthly payments, statutory obligations (Provident Fund, ESI dues, Pension, etc.) and subsidies (Canteen, Conveyance, Uniform, etc.).
*taken for an average company
†taken for an average company
‡taken at lowest of the scale of pay for Jt Secretaries.

*Source:*   Sethi, Balaji and Shrimali (1996) as modified by the government pay increases in 1997.

It can be seen that a secretary to the Government of India clearly lags behind his counterpart in the private sector—the chief executive officer (CEO) of a private company. The same is true at the level of the head of the department (HOD), but to a much smaller extent. At the entry level, the government does better than the private sector.

We can see from Table 6.2 that a CEO in the private sector costs much more to his company than a secretary to the Government of India costs the government, although the basic pay of a secretary to the Government of India is higher than that of the CEO. There are several reasons for this. First, a CEO in the private sector draws an incentive pay of Rs 14,752 which works out to 65 per cent of his basic salary. A secretary to the Government of India, or for that matter any top functionary in the government, does not get anything on this account.

Second, a CEO in the private sector draws sundry allowances such as for books and periodicals, club membership, credit cards, leave travel concession, medical care, entertainment, services and amenities, which are estimated on an average at Rs 12,645 per month—almost 55 per cent of the basic salary. A secretary to the Government of India is entitled to leave travel concession and unlimited medical benefits at government hospitals. The value of these facilities to a secretary to the Government of India is estimated at about Rs 2700 per month which works out to 10.38 per cent of the basic salary.

Therefore, the cost of a CEO in an average private sector company is Rs 102,255 per month while in the case of a secretary to the Government of India, the cost per month is Rs 58,590. In other words, the cost of employing a secretary to the Government of India is about 57 per cent of what it costs to employ a CEO in an average private sector company.

However, when it comes to a comparison between the HOD in the private sector and a joint secretary to the Government of India, the picture is not so stark. The cost of employing a joint secretary at Rs 45,250 per month is 69 per cent of the cost of employing an HOD in the private sector at Rs 65,283 per month. There is an explanation for this.

The differential of remuneration between the CEOs and the HODs is very wide. An HOD gets about 40 per cent less than the CEO. On the other hand, differential of remuneration between a joint secretary and a secretary is only marginal. It was as low as Rs 2000, but with the recent pay revision, the differential is about Rs 4000. At the HOD level, the private sector organizations are very liberal with designations, but parsimonious with compensation. It should also be noted that while an HOD has approximately 8 to 10 years of experience, a joint secretary has already completed at least 18 years of service.

At the entry level, government remuneration appears to be better than in the private sector. Although the compensation package at the entry level is lower in the private sector, entry-level executives in the private sector reach a much higher compensation level within a short span of time because of performance-related rewards. In the government hierarchy, the climb is long and slow.

There is also a great deal of difference in the superannuation benefits in the government and the private sector. In the private sector, the CEOs are given superannuation benefits which are significantly better than the pensionary benefits to a secretary to the Government of India.[12]

On the whole, there is a significant gap between civil service compensation and the compensation in the private sector. The matter is compounded by the fact that the gap is widening every year. The annual increase in compensation in the case of a secretary to the Government of India is in the range of 8 to 9 per cent, while the annual increase in the compensation for a CEO in the private sector is 30 to 35 per cent. If this trend continues, and the only offset which is likely, is with a pay commission which awards on an average, an increase of about 40 per cent once in ten years or so, the gap will increase dramatically.[13]

Such a gap, is certainly greater than the notional income which civil servants enjoy because of their status in society and security of tenure. Chapter 1 estimated that the implicit discount for this notional income could be around 20 to 30 per cent. Even if we discount for this, the gap is still significant. In other words, the rate of temptation exists in India. The incentive for civil servants to succumb to the temptation of corruption is, indeed, undeniably large.

*Erosion in Compensation*

But this is only half the story. A truer picture of civil service compensation emerges when one looks at the serious erosion in compensation on account of inflation, especially at the higher levels. The percentage increase in salaries at the various levels in the government between 1st January 1986 and 1st January 1996 is decidedly lower than the percentage increase in per capita income during the same period (Table 6.3).

TABLE 6.3

*Increase in Per Capita Net National Product and Compensation of Civil Servants during 1986 and 1996*

| Items | 1.1.86 | 1.1.96 | Percentage increase |
|---|---|---|---|
| Per capita net national product Rs at current prices | 2962* | 8237† | 178.1 |
| Civil service compensation of | | | |
| (a) Peons | 750 | 2060 | 174.7 |
| (b) LD Clerk | 950 | 2556 | 169.1 |
| (c) UD clerk | 1200 | 3196 | 166.3 |
| (d) Assistant | 1640 | 4331 | 164.1 |
| (e) Group A | 2200 | 5776 | 162.5 |
| (f) Secretary | 8000 | 16,580 | 107.3 |

*Note:* *relates to 1986–7
†relates to 1994–5

*Source:* *Report of the Fifth Central Pay Commission, Vol. I (1997).*

Table 6.3 reveals some disturbing facts. While the increase in per capita net national product at current prices between 1986 and 1996 has been 178 per cent, the increase in civil service compensation has ranged only between 107 and 174 per cent. The percentage increase in per capita income is a measure of the average increase of income in the country. It is unfortunate that the increase in the income of a secretary to the Government of India should be less than the average increase of income in the country at large. This seems like an open invitation to corruption.

In fact, it becomes even clearer when one looks at the real income of a secretary to the Government of India. The erosion in real income can be seen from Table 6.4.

During the period between 1949 and 1996, the pre-tax emoluments of a secretary to Government of India increased 5.53 times. During the same period, however, the All India Consumer Price Index increased 18.74 times. Thus, there was an erosion of 71 per cent in the real earnings of secretary to the Government of India during the period 1949-1996.

TABLE 6.4

*Trends in the Emoluments of Secretaries to the Government of India, 1949–1996*

(Emolument in Rs)

|  | 1949 | 1959 | 1965 | 1970 | 1973 | 1986 | 1996 |
|---|---|---|---|---|---|---|---|
| Emoluments (pre-tax) | 3000 | 3000 | 3500 | 3500 | 3500 | 8000 | 16,580 |
| Emoluments (post-tax) | 2263 | 2281 | 2422 | 2399 | 2331 | 5896 | 12,615 |
| Index of emoluments (pre-tax) | 100 | 100 | 117 | 117 | 117 | 267 | 553 |
| Index of emoluments (post-tax) | 100 | 101 | 107 | 106 | 103 | 261 | 557 |
| All India Consumer Price Index* | 100 | 124 | 163 | 211 | 252 | 754 | 1874 |
| Real earnings index (pre-tax) | 100 | 81 | 72 | 55 | 46 | 35 | 29 |
| Real earnings index (post-tax) | 100 | 81 | 66 | 50 | 41 | 35 | 30 |

*Note:* *Base 1949 = 0

*Source: Report of the Fifth Central Pay Commission, Vol. I (1997).*

## Pay Compression

Successive pay commissions have tried to compress the salaries of the senior civil servants with a determination that can only be described as obsessive. The First Pay Commission which had been constituted even before the country became independent, deliberated on the question of salaries paid to senior civil servants in some detail. At the time the First Pay Commission was finalizing its recommendations, there was an impression that the salaries of the top civil servants were too high and needed to be pruned. It was believed that such high salaries in the government were responsible for attracting the best and brightest of the educational system and concentrating them in the civil service to the exclusion of the other sectors of the society. The First Pay Commission even quoted the statements of Prof. D.R. Gadgil and K. Santhanam, who were firmly of the view that the salaries of the top civil service needed to be pruned.

The First Pay Commission was also conscious of the fact that any reduction in the existing level of salaries for the higher civil servants was likely to raise temptation for corruption. The commission observed, 'any drastic reduction in the existing scale of salaries for the higher posts would result in serious loss of efficiency and integrity'.[14] The commission, however, proceeded to recommend lowering of the salary of the secretary to the Government of India from the existing level of Rs 4000 to Rs 3000 per month.

The Second Pay Commission devoted one entire chapter to a discussion on wage compression. The commission appeared to be greatly disturbed by what it considered to be high salaries paid to senior civil servants, and it dwelt rather expansively on the issue whether maximum salaries in the civil service should be reduced still further; that is, below the levels which were in force as a result of the recommendations of the First Pay Commission. The commission, in fact, showed a good deal of concern for reducing the ratio between the maximum and the minimum salary.

The approach of the Second Pay Commission seems to have been influenced by the view points of the service associations of the lower level employees in the government. The commission achieved its objective of compressing wages by recommending that the compensation of the senior civil servants should be frozen at the same level, while the salary of all other civil servants should be increased. In its obsession to compress wages, the Second Pay Commission seems to have ignored all other legitimate factors of pay determination. The approach of the Second Pay Commission in compressing the compensation paid to senior civil servants set the tone for the succeeding pay commissions, and it became, over time, the single most important factor governing the fixation of salaries for the senior civil servants.

Both the Third and Fourth Pay Commissions followed the approach of the Second Pay Commission in compressing wages in order to satisfy the criteria of equity. The obsession of the pay commissions with wage compression overshadowed all other considerations including that of a comparison with the compensation structure prevailing in the private sector, and of the need to provide a decent standard of living to senior civil servants.

Such an approach was the result of the general upsurge of socialist ideas, and a Fabian crawl toward some nebulous goal of egalitarianism which favoured a general compression in wages of senior civil servants. This is confirmed by the attitude of the pay commissions in the matter of recommending the payment of dearness allowance to senior civil servants. The first three pay commissions were not in favour of giving any dearness allowance to the top civil servants. It was only the government which, in its executive capacity, decided in 1978 to give some partial neutralization for the increased cost of living to senior civil servants. The Fourth Pay Commission recommended only limited neutralization for senior civil servants. The result of such a half-hearted recommendation was a partial neutralization of the increased cost of living for senior civil servants while there was complete neutralization for civil servants at the lower levels.

The Fifth Pay Commission looked at the question slightly differently. It conceded that inadequate salaries for civil servants were an expense and not an economy. In its own words, 'Although it can be argued that corruption is a state of mind, it cannot be denied that beyond a certain point the penury of a powerful civil servant can have disastrous consequences for his integrity'.[15] But in its ultimate recommendations, the Fifth Pay Commission did not live up to what it preached.

Did successive pay commissions succeed in their single-minded aim of compressing wages? Table 6.5 provides the compression ratio as it has emerged as a result of the recommendations of the various pay commissions.

Table 6.5 provides some interesting insights. During the period 1948–96, the minimum salary of the lowest civil servant in the government increased from Rs 55 to Rs 2060. During the same period, the pre-tax maximum salary in the government increased from Rs 3000 to Rs 16,518 while the post-tax salary increased from Rs 2263 to Rs 12,615. The compression ratio went down progressively from 54.5 in 1948 to 8.0 in 1996. The post-tax compression ratio went down even more drastically from 41.0 in 1948 to 6.1 in 1996.

TABLE 6.5
*Compression Ratio: 1948–1996*

(Emolument in Rs)

| | 1948 | 1949 | 1960 | 1965 | 1970 | 1973 | 1986 | 1996 |
|---|---|---|---|---|---|---|---|---|
| Maximum Salary (pre-tax) | 3000 | 3000 | 3000 | 3500 | 3500 | 3500 | 8000 | 16,580 |
| Maximum salary (post-tax) | 2263 | 2263 | 2281 | 2422 | 2399 | 2331 | 5896 | 12,615 |
| Minimum salary | 55 | 65 | 80 | 103 | 141 | 196 | 750 | 2060 |
| Pre-tax compression ratio | 54.5 | 46.2 | 37.5 | 34.0 | 24.8 | 17.9 | 10.7 | 8.0 |
| Post-tax compression ratio | 41.0 | 34.8 | 28.5 | 23.5 | 17.0 | 11.9 | 7.9 | 6.1 |

*Source: Report of the Fifth Central Pay Commission, Vol. I (1997).*

Evidently, the pay commissions have succeeded in ensuring wage compression. In the forty years between the First and the Fourth Pay Commission, the compression ratio was brought down sharply as is obvious from Table 6.5; but, in their preoccupation with compressing wages, pay commissions were only adopting an ad hoc approach. They did not make any systematic study of the extent to which the ratio between the maximum and minimum compensation in the civil service should be reduced, and the impact it would have on the integrity of the senior civil servants, although these are aspects which the pay commissions dwelt on rather expansively in their general discussion on the principles of pay determination.

*A Fair Compensation?*

As discussed in Chapter 1, the question of adequacy of civil service compensation needs to be looked at from the perspective of fairness. Viewed from this perspective, it is not merely a question of compensating the civil servants at a level that makes them incorruptible (eliminating the rate of temptation), but one of paying a salary on which the civil servants are forced to be corrupt to meet their current level of consumption and reasonable commitments. In other words, the question is: is the civil service compensation in India a living wage?

A study by Professor Kamta Prasad conducted in 1996 looked precisely at this aspect.[16] The study, taking a sample of 100 civil servants in the rank of joint secretary to the Government of India and above, worked out a compensation package which, it suggested, should be adequate to provide for a consumption pattern which is more or less similar to that of the social class to which the civil servants belonged, and also meet their reasonable additional requirements.

The study computed Rs 6490 as average current expenditure per month, and Rs 8349 as reasonable additional requirement for the civil servants of the rank of joint secretary. In order to ascertain the income which is necessary to enable these civil servants to spare Rs 14,839 (Rs 6490 of current expenditure + Rs 8349 of reasonable additional requirement) per month, the study used the ratio between the current average emoluments (Rs 13,245) and current average consumption (Rs 6490). Using this ratio (2.04 : 1), an average emolument of Rs 30,284 per month was estimated to enable the officers of the rank of joint secretaries to meet their current consumption expenditure and reasonable additional requirements. The study estimated an average emolument of Rs 33,500 for additional secretaries, and Rs 36,000 for secretaries to Government of India on the basis of a similar logic.

At the time the study reported in February 1996, the actual compensation paid to these categories of civil servants, fell far short of the levels estimated by the study to be the living wage. The recommendations of the Fifth Pay Commission were accepted in 1997, and as a result, an increase of about 40 per cent was given to these categories. Interestingly, in spite of the increases, the compensation given to these civil servants is still lower than the living wage as estimated by the study.

EXPERIENCE OF OTHER COUNTRIES

How have other countries dealt with this problem? Singapore, for example, has been very sensitive to this problem. When the People's Action Party (PAP) came to power in 1959, the civil service in Singapore was very corrupt. The PAP government adopted a number of measures to minimize corruption in the civil service. One measure was to improve the level of civil service compensation. Lee Kuan Yew, the Prime Minister of Singapore, while speaking before parliament on 22nd March 1985, justified the increase in civil service compensation on the ground that civil servants should be paid top salaries to ensure a clean and honest government. In his speech, he reasoned that the best way of dealing with corruption was 'moving with the market', which is 'an honest, open, defensible and workable system', instead of hypocrisy, which results in duplicity and corruption.[17]

The Singapore government has periodically increased civil service compensation to bring it on par with or to make it even higher than the compensation in the private sector. The civil service compensation package now averages 114 per cent of the compensation in the private sector. The first salary revision took place in 1973, when the salaries of civil servants were raised substantially to reduce the gap between the civil service and private sector compensation. A second salary revision was effected in 1979 to put civil service compensation on par with that in the private sector. The third salary revision occurred in April 1982, and once again, civil service salaries were made comparable to those in the private sector.

The most recent and the most substantial salary revision for the civil service was effected in 1989. As a result of the 1989 salary revision, civil servants in Singapore are ahead of their counterparts in the private sector, and interestingly, they are also the highest-paid civil servants in the world. While introducing the proposal for the salary hike in the Singapore parliament, Lee Hsien Loong, the Minister for Trade and Industry, stated that the fundamental philosophy of the PAP government was to 'pay civil servants market rates for their abilities and responsibilities'. Singapore has certainly succeeded in keeping the rate of temptation at bay as a matter of deliberate policy. As Rafique Rahman says, 'The (Singapore) government believed that an efficient bureaucratic system is one in which the officers are well-paid so the temptation to resort to bribes would be reduced'.[18]

In Japan, the position is only slightly different. The salaries which a civil service position commands is still high, but not higher than that in the private sector. Salaries for the civil service are marginally below those for comparable private sector positions. In 1990, a new recruit to the civil service received 168,000 yens per month while the private sector equivalent was 10 per cent higher.[19]

It is the Diet that determines the civil service pay, but as recommended by the National Personnel Authority. The Authority annually surveys thousands of private companies,[20] and it has evolved a complex formula linked to private sector compensation to make its recommendations to the Diet. The Diet has generally accepted the compensation schedules and the annual adjustments as recommended by the National Personnel Authority.

## Why Capitulation Wages?

As the successive pay commissions in India have never tired of pointing out, they would have been inclined to recommend a more attractive compensation package for the civil service, but for the resource constraints of the government. In other words, what has mattered is the capacity of the employer to pay. The Fifth Central Pay Commission had the following to say on the subject, 'We should have fewer but better-paid employees. . . . In case the numbers can be brought down, Government can very well afford to pay its employees a decent salary.'[21]

As correctly pointed out by the Fifth Pay Commission, it is the massive bureaucratic sprawl which has affected the capacity of the government to pay its civil servants a decent wage. The sprawl has been formidable by any standard. The central government is a case in point. The number of posts in the central government increased from 17.37 lakhs in 1957 to 29.82 lakhs in 1971, to 37.87 lakhs in 1984 and to 41.76 lakhs in 1994. During the period between 1957 and 1971, the number of posts increased by 71.7 per cent, between 1971 and 1984 by 27 per cent, and between 1984 and 1994 by 10.3 per cent.[22] Viewed on an annual basis, while there was an annual growth rate of 3.9 per cent for the period 1957 to 1971, an annual increase of 1.9 per cent was observed for the period 1971 to 1984 and an annual increase of 1 per cent, for the period 1984 to 1994. The bureaucratic sprawl for the state governments and the union territories has been no less formidable.

India, like most other developing countries, has, as a matter of deliberate policy, tended to protect government employment and neglect wages. In fact, the preferred policy in India has been to overstaff and underpay. The result, regrettably, has been capitulation wages—wages below reservation wages which attract only the dishonest to government employment. And it has proved to be costly for the citizens in the longer run, because it has increased the incentive of civil servants to succumb to the temptation of corruption, and the entire citizenry has been subjected to extortionary corruption for access to goods and services provided by the government.

The experience of Japan, as we have seen, has been refreshingly different. Japan has been able to pay its civil servants well. This has been because of the fact that Japan has maintained a very small government with relatively fixed number of agencies and personnel since the early 1960s. Japan has enforced manpower ceilings mandated by law and adjusted recruitment to such ceilings. Since 1968, the manpower ceilings have been lowered year after year with the result that the Japanese civil service has now progressed to net reductions in its numbers. For example, in 1965, Japan had a total of 834,391 general account national public employee positions. By 1989, the number had decreased to 824,769. The number of all budgeted national employee positions in 1970 was 1,992,793. By 1991, the number had decreased to 1,180,700.[23]

In the matter of its civil service compensation policy, Japan has a lesson to offer. Japan has followed a deliberate policy that has reduced public employment and increased wages to be almost on par with the private sector. The happy result is that it has been less costly in the longer run. The adequacy of civil service remuneration has reduced the incentive of the civil servant to succumb to the temptation of corruption, and Japan's civil service has been in a position to attract individuals who are committed to general welfare rather than pursuit of their private interest.

## PROMOTION

Promotion is an important incentive. India follows what is known as a closed multi-track model of promotion. Since the entry track is what governs how far a civil servant can rise in the system, the level of entry of the civil servants has determined the opportunities for promotion in the civil service.

In India, there is a bewildering array of promotion schemes.

The schemes vary not only between departments of the same government, but across them, in the civil service organizations of the different state governments. All promotion schemes, however, profess to follow two common norms namely, (a) reasonable promotional opportunities ranging from two to four promotions in a civil servant's career and (b) the more competent among the civil servants should get faster promotion.

## ARE THE PROMOTIONAL OPPORTUNITIES REASONABLE?

Assurance of reasonable promotional opportunities ranging from two to four promotions in the career of a civil servant, which spans upwards of thirty years, has generally been the accepted norm. The practice, however, has sharply departed from the accepted norm. Promotional opportunities in actual practice have depended on vacancies in the higher grades, and not enough vacancies have been forthcoming to provide more than two promotions to all civil servants. The result has been unrelieved stagnation and lack of adequate career progression for an overwhelming majority of civil servants in India.

The general demoralization in almost all the departments of government as a result of large-scale stagnation, had been brought to the notice of the successive pay commissions. For example, this was brought to the notice of the Second Pay Commission by government employees who had demanded better promotional opportunities. The commission attributed such stagnation to the principle that the grade structure of a service and the number of civil servants to be positioned in the different grades were determined on the basis of the functional requirements of the organization. Promotional opportunities were further limited because quotas were prescribed for direct recruitment and promotional vacancies in the interest of efficiency of the organization. On a balance of considerations, the Second Pay Commission decided to give precedence to the functional requirements and efficiency of the organization over the promotional opportunities for civil servants.

A similar demand was made before the Third Pay Commission with a request that the commission should explore ways and means of relieving the stagnation in the civil service. The specific demand was to consider restructuring of service cadres so that at least two promotions were assured in the entire career of a civil servant. The commission recommended some marginal improvements in the career prospects of civil servants belonging to Groups C and D. But, on the whole, it was of the view that creation of additional posts in the higher grades only for promoting civil servants, can be justified on the basis of functional requirements of the organization and should not be resorted to as an easier option for improving promotional opportunities and relieving stagnation. The commission specifically recommended that the standard of recruitment should not be diluted only to open up promotional avenues.

In order to avoid stagnation and to provide adequate promotional opportunities, the Fourth Pay Commission suggested provision of a rational cadre structure and elongated pay scales, but with a word of caution. It warned that any system of career progression of civil servants should be consistent with the functional requirements of the organization. The commission refrained from laying down any rigid formulation about the number of promotions which a civil servant should get in his entire career and the length of service that should qualify for time-bound promotions. The commission recommended cadre reviews to be conducted at regular intervals to identify grades and posts which could be upgraded.

While implementing the recommendation of the Fourth Pay Commission, detailed guidelines were issued by the government for conducting cadre reviews. The guidelines provided for cadre reviews to be conducted by all the ministries, but the general experience with cadre reviews, on the whole, has been disappointing. Wherever cadre reviews have been conducted, it has taken a long time, and the process has generally remained inconclusive. As if to compound matters, no cadre review has been conducted in many departments.

As a result, promotional opportunities for a large number of civil servants have not improved in spite of the scheme of cadre reviews. In fact, perfunctory implementation of the scheme has resulted in a situation in which stagnation continues unrelieved in different cadres in a large number of organizations, and the situation is particularly bad in respect of small cadres and isolated posts.

The position in the state governments is only marginally better. In a number of states such as Arunachal Pradesh, Kerala, Rajasthan, Karnataka, Punjab, Haryana and Himachal Pradesh, schemes providing for time-bound promotions have been introduced. In Arunachal Pradesh, all civil servants are placed in the next higher grade after completion of 13 years of service in the lower grade. After another 7 years of service or on the completion of 20 years of service, they are entitled to the next higher grade. In Karnataka, three time-bound promotions are available after 10, 20 and 25 years of service in the lower grades. In Punjab, Haryana and Himachal Pradesh, two time-bound promotions are assured after completion of 8 and 15 years of service in the lower grades.[24]

The idea in general is to provide an assured progression or *in-situ* promotion on a personal basis to all civil servants who have completed a specific period of service. Regrettably, this has not happened uniformly across the government, and there is a lot of stagnation. In fact, the Fifth Pay Commission was so disillusioned with the persisting stagnation in large areas of the civil service that it recommended an Assured Career Progression Scheme for all the civil servants in the central government.

While calling for the introduction of an Assured Career Progression Scheme, the Fifth Pay Commission suggested that a comprehensive and coherent promotion scheme should be evolved which should ensure adequate career progression in a reasonable time frame to all categories of employees. The scheme recommended by the commission aims at providing a minimum of two promotions to each Group B, C, and D employee and three promotions to each Group A employee, in their entire career span. The promotion contemplated under the scheme is limited to financial upgradation in the pay scale and not linked to the availability of posts in the higher grade. Government of India finally accepted the recommendation of the commission for the introduction of the Assured Career Progression Scheme in August 1999.

## DO THE MORE COMPETENT GET FASTER PROMOTIONS?

It is an accepted principle that the more competent among the civil servants should get faster promotion. This is reflected in the adoption of the Limited Departmental Competitive Examination as a method of promotion. In order to ensure that merit is given due consideration in such promotions, a concept of benchmarking has been introduced in grading of the annual confidential reports. But, in spite of the formulation of detailed principles to sift the brighter amongst the civil servants for accelerated promotions, promotions have finally been made on the basis of seniority, because even in the case of accelerated promotions, most civil servants are able to obtain the required benchmark in their confidential reports.

## PROMOTIONS IN THE ALL-INDIA SERVICES

The all-India services, however, present a different picture altogether. Promotions, and at least four of them in the career of any civil servant belonging to the all-India services, are guaranteed. This has been possible because of regular cadre reviews, and the creation of a large number of posts to take care of the promotional requirements of the civil servants belonging to the all-India services.[25]

What is disturbing, however, is the almost guaranteed nature of the promotions without any attempt at sifting the brighter and the more competent among the officers of the all-India services or relating the process of promotion to any system of performance-indication. The Indian Administrative Service is a typical example. Although there is a procedure for empanelling officers from the Indian Administrative Service for appointment as joint secretaries, additional secretaries and secretaries to the Government of India, and on occasions, there are a number of IAS officers who do not get empanelled for a variety of reasons, the same officers return to their parent cadres in the state governments and get appointed to posts which are equivalent in respect of responsibility and remuneration, to those of joint secretaries, additional secretaries and even secretaries to the Government of India.

There is a certain contradiction involved in the practice, and the Fifth Pay Commission took serious note of this. In the words of the commission,

The logic for this is the supposed difference between the qualities required of an officer for a Central Government posting, and those needed for a State Government posting. That the argument was specious is proved by the fact that officers who were overlooked in the Central Government because of the CBI cases pending against them have been appointed by the State Governments to high positions![26]

The commission called for a change in the present system of almost guaranteed promotions in the all-India services, especially in the state governments. The commission proposed a system of joint empanelment in which the central government and the state governments could jointly decide as to who is or is not fit to be empanelled. In other words, fitness or unfitness of a civil servant belonging to the all-India services should be the same for both central and state-level assignments. The idea is nothing new; it had been proposed in the 1980s, but it fell through because most of the state governments refused to be a party to such a process of joint empanelment.

EXPERIENCE OF OTHER COUNTRIES

In Singapore, promotions are entirely merit-based. The promotions are effected by the Public Service Commission on the basis of official qualifications, experience, and merit. Eligible candidates for promotion are interviewed by the members of the Pubic Service Commission and Selection Boards. The merit of the civil servant is determined by his performance in grade, and by an assessment of the civil servant's ability to carry out the responsibilities and duties of the next grade. More specifically, three factors are taken into account by the Public Service Commission when considering civil servants for promotion—the reports of the supervisors on performance of the civil servant, the recommendations of ministerial or departmental committees, and an assessment of the ultimate potential of the civil servant.

The speed of promotions of the civil servants in Singapore depends on two factors—the civil servant's Currently Estimated Potential (CEP), and the time norms for promoting civil servants with that potential. Therefore, the higher a civil servant's CEP and the shorter the time norm, the faster is his speed of promotion. In 1989, the government introduced a scheme for accelerated promotion for high-fliers because 'promotions are a much more selective and discriminating method to reward good officers than pay raises alone'.[27] To hasten promotions, the government shortened the time norms so that the civil servants could be promoted to their final ranks by the age of forty-five instead of fifty. For example, all civil servants of proven ability reach the rank of principal assistant secretary two years earlier than was the norm; that is, by the age of thirty and within eight years of joining the civil service.

This system links promotion mainly to performance. The government has moved from a confidential evaluation system to a participatory performance appraisal system developed by the Shell Oil Company. Performance appraisal has two parts. One reviews and assesses past job performance, and the other assesses the management and leadership potential (the so-called 'helicopter capacity' of the civil servant) in an effort to identify and groom talent within the civil service.[28]

In Japan, promotions are fully merit-based. Promotion within the civil service takes place on the basis of a combination of seniority and a number of performance indicators which differ across agencies, but the internal merit system is designed to ensure that the promotions go to those civil servants who, in the eyes of their superiors in the civil service, have proven themselves in earlier positions. The internal merit system in Japan makes sure that individual efforts congruent with agency or national goals are rewarded. Successful civil servants can hope to attain the position of section chief after approximately 15 years of service, assistant bureau chief after 22–25 years, and bureau chief after 25–28 years. The position of administrative vice-minister is achieved after 28–30 years.[29]

Since the number of promotional vacancies are limited by law, competition for promotion is intense. Competition begins with the entrance examination to the civil service, and in most cases, with the long educational competition that precedes it. By the time they enter the civil service, recruits have internalized values and norms of hard work, high competition, and dedication to the goals of the agency.

Japan follows a closed, multi-track model of promotion. The closed nature of the model intensifies the process of competition. One knows precisely who one's competitors are, and the absence of horizontal entry sets limits to the competing group. In effect, competition is a life-long proposition in Japan. The result is a high level of initiative, aggressiveness, and dedication to the goals of the agency in which the civil servant works. But the point to note is that positive performance, however nuanced, is seen and rewarded.[30]

Politicians in power have no inputs in the matter. The total absence of political involvement in the process of promotion merely reinforces the merit-based nature of the civil service system.[31] Only positive performance and total dedication to the goals of the agency matter for promotion, and corruption is held against the individual civil servant. The way the system of promotion is structured in Japan has tended to incline the civil servant against corruption, either for personal gain or in the service of partisan politics.[32]

Significantly, the personnel practices in the agencies are designed to ensure that no civil servant is left with a feeling of such frustration that his private interests get the better of him in the discharge of his public duties. This is because of the fact that even the less successful civil servants achieve social as well as financial position much better than individuals of their age group who went directly from college to a private corporation, and who have successfully climbed the corporate ladder. In other words, elegant and stable second jobs await even those who are less successful in the race for promotions. The difference between success and failure in the promotion competition is thus small, but the competition among the civil servants for promotion and career advancement is so intense that even such small differences are perceived as significant.[33]

In India, in perfect contrast, the promotion system is only remotely linked to internal merit, and therefore, it has not succeeded in raising the stakes for corruption. The promotion system in the state governments is not related to merit and performance-indication at all, and in the central government where the situation is marginally better in terms of linking the system of promotion to performance-indication, civil servants think nothing of bringing political pressure to get themselves empanelled for senior posts. There have been cases when civil servants who were not found fit to be empanelled as a joint secretary, have been posted as secretary to Government of India or even as the Cabinet Secretary! Civil servants with established lack of integrity have been empanelled for higher posts while several others of impeccable honesty have been disregarded. The process of promotion in India is not one of healthy competition, but only an abominable rat race, and in this rat race, consummate operators in the civil service have routinely made use of the services of power brokers, fixers, godmen, astrologers, politicians, and even top industrialists to get themselves empanelled.[34] One shudders to think what happens in the state governments!

The Central Administrative Tribunal had laid down in Jetli's case that clear criteria, procedures, and guidelines should be prescribed for promotion of civil servants.[35] The Government of India took the matter to the Supreme Court to get the judgement of the Central Administrative Tribunal overruled, and in its enthusiasm to see that the promotion system is not shackled by any clear criteria, argued that the promotions were only a subjective exercise of governmental discretion.

The Supreme Court judgement upheld the argument of the Government of India. While striking down the judgement of the Central Administrative Tribunal, the Court said:

> The appointment of the Secretary to Government of India is not on the basis of a competitive examination where a candidate who secures 99 per cent of marks has to be appointed. Even when a person appoints a cook or a watchman, he looks for a person in whom he has faith. How can Government of India appoint any person as Secretary in whom it has no faith?[36]

The judgement of the Supreme Court does sound a trifle jarring in the modern times. In fact, a secretary to the Government of India being compared to a personal cook or watchman only evokes memories of patronage bureaucracies in which, as we have seen, a civil servant was given an assignment and continued there, only because the ruler had faith in him.

## PLACEMENTS

Placements in civil service positions are rewards that could motivate civil servants. If the system of placements is so designed that the best jobs were given to those with merit and integrity, placements could be a source of motivation. On the other hand, if placements are done on the basis of personal or political considerations, civil servants are more likely to use their public offices for personal or political considerations.

In India, the Department of Personnel and Training which is the nodal agency of the Government of India for the personnel function of the government, issues guidelines from time to time on various issues relating to transfers of civil servants. These guidelines are not mandatory in nature, but they provide policy options within the overall constraints of administrative convenience. Similarly, the various ministries and departments of the central government and state governments also formulate detailed policy guidelines about how transfers are to be effected, on the general lines of the instructions issued by the Department of Personnel.

All these guidelines take pains to stress the norms that the right job should go to the right person, that there should be an unbroken tenure of at least three to five years in a post, and that the consideration for transfer should be non-ascriptive and free from political pressure. But the guidelines remain on paper as pious exhortations, and the transfers of civil servants are done only at the behest of politicians. More often than not, transfers are not linked to considerations of competence, suitability of the incumbent for the job, or the need of the organization.

Transfers of civil servants in India are done with such frequency that fixity of tenure is the exception rather than the rule. Even the Indian Administrative Service, which represents the most powerful group of civil servants in India, is not exempt. The mobility data of the IAS clearly point to the fact that most IAS officers spend less than a year in their postings. While the percentage of IAS officers spending less than a year in their current posting has ranged from 48 to 60 per cent of the total strength of the IAS for the entire country, the percentage of IAS officers who spend more than three years in a current posting has been less than 10 per cent.[37]

Of late, the average tenure of incumbents in posts has tended to decrease even more sharply. In Uttar Pradesh, for example, by December 1990, the average tenure of a district magistrate was only 9.41 months; that of commissioners of divisions 10 months; and secretaries to the government 9.93 months.[38] But that was before Mayawati and Kalyan Singh appeared on the scene, and so, the averages would have plummeted some more.

The decisions of the ruling politicians to transfer a civil servant or even not to transfer him, are taken mostly on the basis of payment of money. As the memorandum of the Indian Police Service Officers Association of Karnataka presented to the Ribeiro Committee on Police Reform states:

It is true that many times transfers are made on caste lines and in most cases for monetary considerations. Elected representatives develop some kind of a contract, fixing the amount to be paid for the officer to remain in a post for a particular period.[39]

In fact, the process of transfers of civil servants is so lucrative that it is euphemistically known as the 'transfer industry'. N.N. Vohra, an ex-civil servant, comments:

Transfers of government functionaries have in many states, virtually assumed the status of an industry. Officials at all levels are repeatedly shifted from station to station in utter disregard of the tenure policies or any concern about the disruption of public services delivery and the adverse effect on the implementation of development programmes.[40]

Robert Wade, in his study of India, has shown how the politicians have used the process of transfers of civil servants to make money. As Wade says:

The transfer is the politicians' basic weapon of control over the bureaucracy, and thus the lever for surplus-extraction from the clients of the bureaucracy. With the transfer weapon not only can the politicians raise money by direct sale; they can also remove someone who is not being responsive enough to their monetary demands or to their request for favours to those from whom they get money and electoral support— in particular, the contractors. One is thus led to visualise a special circuit of transactions, in which the bureaucracy acquires the control of funds... then passes a portion to MLAs and especially Ministers, who in turn use the funds for distributing short-term material inducements in exchange for electoral support. These funds, it should be noticed, do flow through the public domain; but they are neither open to public scrutiny nor available for public expenditure programmes.[41]

In the political vocabulary in India, the authority of a newly-installed political government is considered to be complete only when it is able to transfer civil servants *en masse*. Each change of government in a state, even when the political party in power continues to be the same, results in large-scale transfers of civil servants. Such transfers can run into numbers even exceeding 30,000 at a time.

In Mohsina Begum's case, the Allahabad High Court lamented that 'whenever a new government is formed, there is a tidal wave of transfers of government servants on the basis of caste or community or monetary considerations' leading to 'total demoralisation of the bureaucracy and its division on caste and communal basis, besides spread of corruption' and 'breakdown of all norms of administration'.[42]

Since transfers are made mostly on the basis of monetary considerations, such large-scale transfers can be a veritable source of fortune. Interestingly, the transfer industry takes on the contours of a wholesale market where lucrative posts are literally sold to the highest bidders. After the change of political government in Maharashtra in early 1995, a minister stopped all on-going transfers in his department on the ground that over 10 to 15 crores of rupees had changed hands in these transactions; the minister even quoted the rates charged for the transfers at various levels.[43]

It does not happen only in Maharashtra. The pity is that it happens all over the country and all the time. A recent study of transfer of civil servants in the Delhi Administration, had this to say:

On an average, a bureaucrat lasts less than a year in one Department in the Delhi Government. He or she gets transferred out at a dizzying speed to a whole new office even before he can acquaint himself with the ground realities of his Department. The reason: Bureaucrats do not fall in line with what the Chief Minister and Ministers expect of them.[44]

The study tried to ascertain the reasons for such quick transfers. One of the senior civil servants who was interviewed, gave two reasons:

First, it is done to accommodate favourites among bureaucrats who may sometimes develop an affiliation with a politician in power. Second, it is done to teach a lesson. After being shuffled so often the bureaucrats fall in line and listen to those in power.[45]

The study found that a civil servant who was posted to four departments in the span of one year, including the 'heavy' assignment of the Transport Department, was a typical case. Another civil servant was transferred seven times in her three-year association with the Delhi government and has now been shunted out altogether.

H.D. Shourie of Common Cause filed a Public Interest Litigation in the Supreme Court asking for a direction for framing of rules governing the process of transfer of civil servants. But the Supreme Court refused to do so, on the ground that,

We do not consider it necessary to entertain this writ petition . . . since the guidelines for taking such administrative decisions are well settled and it is obvious that all administrative decisions should satisfy the rule of non-arbitrariness and be honest and fair. Individual cases in which the decision-making process is vitiated for any such reason can always be challenged in a suitable manner.[46]

The Fifth Pay Commission was driven to make some nasty comments about the transfer industry. The commission declared:

there is a definite feeling that the instrument of transfer is widely misused in this country, particularly by politicians in power, to subjugate the government employees. Transfer is also used as an instrument of punishment. . . . Demands have, therefore, been made that any transfer before the expiry of three years in a post, should be made appealable, particularly if it has been made at the behest of politicians.[47]

The Fifth Pay Commission made several recommendations about evolving detailed, clear, and transparent transfer policies.[48] First, the commission recommended that detailed guidelines should be formulated and publicized by each department as part of a comprehensive transfer policy, so that arbitrariness in transfers is eliminated altogether, and transfers are effected in as transparent a manner as possible.

Second, in order to ensure administrative continuity and stability to incumbents, frequent transfers should be discouraged, and a minimum tenure for each posting of officers should be predetermined, and it should normally be three to five years, except in cases where longer tenures are justified on functional grounds, like continued availability of certain specialized skills. In the case of sensitive posts, where opportunities exist for developing vested interests, the tenure should be defined for a shorter period, which may be two to three years.

Third, any premature transfer before the completion of the prescribed tenure should be based on sound administrative grounds, which should be spelt out in the transfer order itself. The civil servant should be given the right to appeal against such an order if he feels aggrieved, and a provision for a summary procedure to deal with such a situation should be made within each department. In case of emergency, when such an order is made in the exigencies of public interest and has to be implemented at once, representation against the transfer order should be dealt with by an authority superior to the officer ordering the transfer after personal discussion, if possible, on the same day.

Fourth, the instrument of transfer should not be allowed to be misused either by bureaucrats themselves or by politicians in power. It should not be used as a means of punishment by circumventing the procedure laid down for disciplinary proceedings.

While the Fifth Pay Commission recognised the right of politicians to have some say in postings to senior assignments in the government, it stressed that certain norms needed be evolved in the matter of transfers. It also recommended the constitution of high-powered civil services boards, both at the level of the central government and the state governments, consisting of (a) a retired judge of the Supreme Court/High court, (b) a prominent person in public life, including a senior bureaucrat, and (c) Cabinet Secretary/Chief Secretary, to look into and regulate cases of premature transfers of senior civil servants.

The commission also enjoined that civil servants should not be permitted to bring political or other extraneous pressure to bear ón the government or on the transferring authorities in the matter of transfers. Any civil servant who brought such pressure should be proceeded against under provisions of the Conduct Rules.

There is a touch of naivete to the recommendations of the commission. It is not as if there is a dearth of institutional mechanisms or rules in the matter of transfers of civil servants. It is just that they are not allowed to operate. In fact, in every department there are rules which carefully prescribe the level of authorities in the departmental hierarchy which is authorized to effect transfers, and even the time period in which transfer should be made is indicated. But politicians have wrested the authorized initiative from the official hierarchy, cocked a snook at the indicated time period, and have chosen to exercise it themselves for reasons which are not far to seek.

Similarly, there are unequivocal rules enjoining that civil servants should not bring political or other extraneous pressure to bear on the government in the matter of their transfers and postings. But they are disregarded. The rules, the prohibitions, and the institutional mechanisms are carefully skirted around so that politicians can provide the necessary opportunities to selected civil servants to make money, and through them, have a share in the proceeds.

The fact remains that the ruling politicians in India have made liberal use of the instrument of transfer of civil servants to make money for themselves. The picture is very clear at the field level. The local legislator has his choice of civil servants manning all the important posts at the constituency level. More often than not, these civil servants extract rent from their clients and pass on a sizable part of it to the legislator, and the official and political superiors in the department concerned. Very much the same thing happens at most levels of the public bureaucracy in India.

EXPERIENCE OF OTHER COUNTRIES

In Japan, recruits to the civil service are chosen by individual agencies out of the list of successful candidates in the civil service entrance examination, and although they may be sent to another agency for special training for a limited period, they work in a particular agency for their entire career. In the matter of recruitment to agencies, the brighter ones among the successful candidates are chosen by the more prestigious agencies.

Once recruited into an agency, the civil servant spends almost his entire official career there. Most civil servants are assigned a variety of positions in the agency during their career. Transfers are made once every two years or so, and the system of transfers is so designed that all senior civil servants become broadly familiar with the agency's complete functions by the time they reach the top. The process of placement within the agencies is free from political considerations. The placements are made on the basis of an internal merit system linked to performance and suitability.

The process of placements in the agency's hierarchy, until the highest levels are reached, is carefully insulated from politics. In order to reach the top in the agency, a civil servant in Japan needs some sensitivity to the factions in the Liberal Democratic Party which has been in power for a long time, but apart from this, there is no political interference in the matter of assignment to jobs within the agency.[49] Matters relating to civil service tenure, discipline and compensation have been insulated from politics. These functions are exercised by the National Personnel Authority, an autonomous and non-political administrative agency.

The National Personnel Authority has ensured that civil service assignments are made on the basis of generally applied standards of merit, competence, and performance rather than personal or political considerations. The autonomous way in which the National Personnel Authority functions, has made sure that the process of placement is open and non-ascriptive.[50]

The National Personnel Authority is autonomous, and as a matter of fact, it happens to be one of the very few autonomous agencies in Japan. Although the idea of setting up a central administrative agency to be in charge of civil service recruitment, compensation, and discipline was proposed as early as 1938 at the time of the first Konoe cabinet, the National Personnel Authority could be created only during the occupation. As described in Articles 3 and 4 of the National Public Employees Law of 1947, the functions of the National Personnel Authority consist of administration of the general public service examinations, recommendations to the Diet on compensation schedules, adjudicatory review by appeal of disciplinary measures against civil servants, training of the civil servants, and administration of benefit programmes for government employees.[51]

It can be said without any exaggeration that the autonomous functioning of the National Personnel Authority has determined civil service behaviour in Japan. The professionalization of Japan's civil service owes much to the National Personnel Authority. Thanks to the authority, civil service positions have been filled on the basis of generally accepted standards of competence. Its authority over recommendations for civil service compensation has ensured that compensation decisions for the civil servants are made in terms of the prevailing private sector standards, and not as a result of political or public pressures.[52]

## NOTES

1. *Report of the First Central Pay Commission*, p. 36. There is a lot of similarity between the pronouncements made by the First Pay Commission and the Lee Commission which had been set up by the British in 1923 to look into emoluments of the civil service in India. The Lee Commission, for example, had commented on the disparity of remuneration between 'a commercial and official career'. While the Lee Commission made a number of recommendations to end the disparity, the First Pay Commission did precious little. See Das (1998), pp. 201–2.

2. *Report of the Second Central Pay Commission*, p. 86.
3. *Report of the Third Central Pay Commission*, p. 30.
4. Ibid., p. 30.
5. Ibid., p. 49.
6. *Report of the Fourth Central Pay Commission, Vol. I*, p. 88.
7. *Report of the Fifth Central Pay Commission, Vol. I*, p. 365.
8. Ibid., p. 365.
9. Ibid., p. 365.
10. Ibid., p. 365.
11. Ibid., p. 439.
12. K.C. Sethi, G. Balaji, and C.P. Shrimali, *Private Sector: Remuneration Structure* (Gurgaon: Management Development Institute, 1985), p. 81.
13. Sethi, Balaji and Shrimali (1995), p. 82.
14. *Report of the First Central Pay Commission*, p. 35.
15. *Report of the Fifth Central Pay Commission, Vol. I*, p. 440.
16. Kamta Prasad, *Report on Determination of a Rational Salary Structure for Senior Functionaries (Joint Secretary and Above) in the Central Government* (Indian Institute of Public Administration, 1996).
17. Jon S.T. Quah, 'Culture Change in the Singapore Civil Service', in *Civil Service Reform in Latin America and the Caribbean* (The World Bank, 1994), p. 210.
18. A.T. Rafique Rahman, 'Legal and Administrative Measures Against Bureaucratic Corruption in Asia', in Carino (ed.), *Bureaucratic Corruption in Asia: Causes, Consequences, and Controls* (Quezon City, The Philippines: NMC Press, 1986), p. 151.
19. T.J. Pempel and Michio Muramatsu, 'The Japanese Bureaucracy and Economic Development: Structuring a Proactive Civil Service' in Kim, Muramatsu, Pempel and Yamamura (1995), p. 50. The civil service compensation in Japan is also a living wage. For example, the average monthly expenditure per household in Japan for food, housing, utilities, clothing, medical care, transportation, education, and recreation was 311,174 yens in 1990. (For Tokyo-Yokohama metropolitan area, it was 354,641 yens; for the Kyoto-Osaka-Kobe metropolitan area, 308,001 yens; for the Tokyo region (Kanto), 346,605 yens; for Okinawa, 234,957 yens; for Shikoku, 268,970 yens; for Kyushu, 277,281 yens; and for Tohuku, 279,792 yens). During the same period, the average section chief in the Japanese government—46 years old, married and with a family of average size— earned a base salary of 534,057 yens per month. See Haley (1995), p. 93.
20. Kim Paul, *Japan's Civil Service System: Its Structure, Personnel and Policies* (Westport: Greenwood Press, 1988), p. 9.
21. *Report of the Fifth Central Pay Commission, Vol. I*, p. 321.

22. Ibid., p. 222

23. Haley (1995), p. 93. In respect of reducing the size of the civil service, Japan has done better than most other industrialized countries. Japan now boasts of one of the lowest cost governments among the industrialized countries as a percentage of GNP. Japan's civil service has been described as 'one of the smallest and least expensive systems in the world'. The result of having a small civil service that is getting even smaller with every passing year, is that Japan has been in a position to pay its civil servants much better than most countries in the world, and at a rate that is only marginally lower than in the private sector.

24. *Report of the Fifth Central Pay Commission, Vol. I*, pp. 190–1.

25. The Fifth Pay Commission had an observation to make on the point. It said, 'Another phenomenon. . . . is the creation of ex-cadre posts with high-sounding titles, which are declared equal to some really powerful posts. For example, the post of Editor-in-Chief of Gazetteer Unit may be declared as of Commissioner's rank; the chairmanship of a Boundary Commission may be equated to the post of Chief Secretary'. *Report of the Fifth Central Pay Commission, Vol. I*, p. 517.

26. *Report of the Fifth Central Pay Commission, Vol. I*, p. 517.

27. Quah (1994), p. 213.

28. Nunberg (1994), p. 39.

29. Pempel and Muramatsu (1995), p. 50.

30. Ibid., p. 50.

31. Peter Hall, 'The Japanese Civil Service and Economic Development in Comparative Perspective', in Kim, Muramatsu, Pempel and Yamamura (1995), p. 488.

32. Hall (1995), p. 488.

33. Michio Muramatsu and T.J. Pempel, 'The Evolution of the Civil Service before World War II', in Kim, Muramatsu, Pempel and Yamamura (1995), p. 186.

34. Madhav Godbole, 'Corruption, Political Interference, and the Civil Service' in S. Guhan and Samuel Paul (eds.), *Corruption in India: Agenda For Action* (New Delhi: Vision Books, 1997), p. 68.

35. Godbole (1997), p. 68.

36. Quoted in Ibid., pp. 68–9.

37. Das (1998), p. 163–4.

38. Godbole (1997), pp. 70–1. In U.P., Chief Minister Mayawati set an all-time record by transferring as many as 270 of the 405 IAS officers and 250 of the 310 IPS officers in the short span of 100 days. Some of these officers were transferred as many as six times during this period.

39. Quoted in *The Times of India* (Bangalore), October 8, 1998.

40. N.N. Vohra, 'The Era of Transfer Raj', *Indian Express*, November 12, 1998.
41. R. Wade, 'The System of Administrative and Political Corruption: Canal Irrigation in South India', *Journal of Development Studies* 18, 3(1982), p. 399.
42. Vohra (1998).
43. Godbole (1997), pp. 68–9.
44. Kota Neelima, 'Bureaucrats' Choices—Plum Inducements or Transfers', *Indian Express*, September 15, 1998.
45. Ibid.
46. Quoted in Godbole (1997), p. 72.
47. *Report of the Fifth Central Pay Commission, Vol. I*, p. 216.
48. Ibid., pp. 218–20.
49. Hall (1995), p. 488.
50. Haley (1995), p. 92.
51. Ibid., pp. 97–8.
52. Ibid., p. 92.

# 7

# Control Systems

The nature and style of public administration in India has not changed very much since the colonial days.[1] In essence, it is a rule-based administration, at least in the way it is designed on paper, and a number of control systems, both internal and external, are in place.

## STATUTORY PENALTY RATE

A number of statutes supplemented by enabling rules and regulations define what constitutes misuse of public office, and such instances are made punishable either by departmental action or in more serious cases, in a court of law. In particular, the Prevention of Corruption Act 1947, as the name of the statute indicates, is an enactment directed at preventing corruption. Section 5 of the act defines the scope of corruption and makes it punishable as acts of criminal misconduct. It extends to (a) habitual acceptance of gratification; (b) obtaining of any valuable thing; (c) misappropriation; (d) abuse of position to secure pecuniary advantage; and (e) possession of property disproportionate to one's source of income.

The Indian Penal Code—enacted by the British in 1860 and still valid today with a few minor amendments—continues to provide the basis of what constitutes use of public office for private gains. Section 161 relates to a public servant taking gratification, other than legal remuneration, in respect of an official act. Section 162 is about gratification by corrupt or illegal means, to influence a public servant. Section 163 relates to gratification for exercise of personal influence with a public servant. Section 164 punishes abetment by a public servant of offenses defined in Section 162 or 163. Section 165 is about a public servant obtaining a valuable thing, from a person concerned in proceeding or business transacted by the public servant. Section 168 prohibits a public servant from unlawfully engaging in trade. Sections 161 and 165 are cross-connected with the relevant provisions in the Prevention of Corruption Act.

In addition, there are several Conduct Rules for employees of the central government and the state governments which define corrupt behaviour and stipulate punishment. There are the Classification, Control and Appeal Rules which prescribe procedures which are to be followed to punish such behaviour within the framework of the safeguards provided to civil servants in the Constitution. At the level of the state governments, there are similar Conduct Rules, and Classification, Control and Appeal Rules. These rules utilize the lines of hierarchy in the governmental apparatus to locate the disciplinary mechanisms. In other words, the disciplinary mechanisms are internal to the department itself.

There are a set of common activities prohibited in these Conduct Rules—using public office to secure employment for any member of the family in any private undertaking, accepting or permitting any member of the family to accept gift or pecuniary advantage, engaging in any trade or business or undertaking any other employment, and speculating in any investment or making an investment which is likely to embarrass or influence discharge of official duties. The Conduct Rules also make it clear that a civil servant holding a supervisory post should take all possible steps to ensure the integrity of all those under his control and authority.

The Prevention of Corruption Act also provides for penalties. Clause (ii) of Section 5 prescribes seven years' term of imprisonment with a minimum of one year, for any civil servant guilty of criminal misconduct. Section 161 of the Indian Penal Code stipulates imprisonment of three years with fine for a civil servant taking gratification. Section 164 prescribes punishment up to three years with fine for abetment by a civil servant. Section 165 provides for punishment up to three years with fine for a civil servant obtaining a valuable thing. Section 168 stipulates simple imprisonment of one year with fine for a civil servant unlawfully engaging in trade.

On the whole, the statutory penalty rate, as prescribed in the statutes, rules, and regulations, is stringent. But as the subsequent discussion makes clear, the regimen of rigorous penalties as enjoined in the book is not implemented for a variety of reasons.

## INTERNAL CONTROL SYSTEM

The public bureaucracy in India is based on the principle of hierarchy, and an internal control system is built into the hierarchy— clean and unequivocally defined—which enable functional supervision of the lower offices by the higher ones. The superior in the hierarchy is invested with adequate authority to monitor, report or even punish corruption by subordinates. Vigilance work in the government is viewed as an integral part of the responsibility of every supervisory officer at each level.

All departments in the central government have a Chief Vigilance Officer (CVO) at the top level assisted by Vigilance Officers (VO) down the line, to handle complaints of corruption and disciplinary proceedings. The CVO, with the help of his VOs, is required to monitor the functioning of the department, review the working procedures and streamline them to eliminate opportunities for corruption, and to ensure that the people who come to transact work with the department are not subjected to corruption.[2]

Provisions exist for superior officers in the hierarchy to comment on the integrity of the subordinates while assessing their work. This is done in an annualized format which contains a specific column for the superior officer to remark upon the integrity of all those working under his supervision.

Although the internal control system, as embedded in the lines of the departmental hierarchy looks impressive on paper, it has not worked as intended. This is because the internal control system is subverted by collusion. Corrupt civil servants routinely buy off their superiors by sharing bribes with them. There is an elaborate sharing mechanism at work, and the mechanism has ensured that the internal control system is undermined.

Departmental proceedings have been taken up only against

a handful of civil servants for contravention of Conduct Rules, although such contravention is very common. Even in those few cases where proceedings are started, they tend to be protracted and generally remain inconclusive for years, because the procedures prescribed in the Classification, Control and Appeal Rules are so demanding that it is difficult to punish even the most glaring lapses. In any case, it so happens that no one in the bureaucratic hierarchy is seriously interested in punishing corruption.

The column in the Annual Confidential Rolls meant for the superior officers to remark on the integrity of their subordinates, gets routinely filled up with non-incriminatory observations such as 'nothing adverse has come to my notice'. Even civil servants known for being corrupt, get away with clean chits because there is an elaborate procedure, daunting to say the least, which has to be followed scrupulously before any remark, even remotely critical, can be entered in the integrity column.[3]

Apart from the departmental hierarchy, the internal control system in India includes anti-corruption commissions such as the Central Vigilance Commission, investigating agencies such as the Central Bureau of Investigation, and Ombudsmen such as the Lok Ayukta.

CENTRAL VIGILANCE COMMISSION

At the level of the central government, the Central Vigilance Commission is the agency charged with the responsibility of dealing with corruption. The commission was set up by way of a Resolution in 1964—in pursuance of the recommendations of the Santhanam Committee on Prevention of Corruption—to advise the central government in respect of all matters pertaining to maintenance of integrity in administration.[4]

Structurally, the commission has been a one-member commission headed by the Central Vigilance Commissioner who is appointed by the Government of India. There are eleven commissioners for Departmental Inquiries in the commission. There is a technical wing attached to the commission with two Chief Technical Examiners of the rank of chief engineer in the Central Public Works Department, assisted by eight Technical Examiners of the rank of executive engineer, and six Assistant Technical Examiners.

Complaints against civil servants are received in the commission either directly or through the departments. After satisfying itself that there is a prima facie case in the complaints, the commission gets them investigated either through the Central Bureau of Investigation (CBI) or the CVOs. Handling of the complaints directly received in the commission is a very small part of its work.

After a complaint including source information is taken up for investigation, it becomes a vigilance case. The departments are required to refer cases to the commission to obtain its advice normally at two stages.[5] After the investigation is completed by the department or the CBI, the commission is consulted as to the further course of action, such as departmental action or prosecution in a court of law or dropping of the case. This is called the first-stage advice.

In cases where departmental action for major penalty is instituted after the first-stage advice, the commission is required to be consulted again for second-stage advice on completion of the enquiry. The commission is consulted for second-stage advice in cases in which departmental action for minor penalty is instituted or the disciplinary authority proposes to close the case. The commission is consulted at other stages of a vigilance case such as consideration by appellate, revising and reviewing authorities.

What has been the performance of the Central Vigilance Commission? As can be seen from Table 7.1, the number of cases received by the commission has varied from year to year, but the fact, and a distressing one at that, remains that the number of cases received by the commission at a level of 3000 to 4000 a year is a very small percentage of the total number of civil servants working in the central government, public sector undertakings and autonomous organizations, and this is so in the context of a country where corruption is admittedly rampant. Interestingly, the number of cases received by the commission seems to be coming down in the recent years. For example, from 3953 cases in 1990, it came down to 3915 in 1991 and 3900 in 1992 (Table 7.1).

TABLE 7.1
*Number of Cases Received by the Central Vigilance Commission*

| Year | Cases |
|------|-------|
| 1985 | 2956 |
| 1986 | 3146 |
| 1987 | 3389 |
| 1988 | 3415 |
| 1989 | 3643 |
| 1990 | 3953 |
| 1991 | 3915 |
| 1992 | 3900 |

*Source:* Annual Report, Central Vigilance Commission (1992)

The rate of disposal of the cases received by the commission appears to be good, as Table 7.2 indicates. But the position becomes clearer as we look at the item-wise disposal of the cases.

TABLE 7.2
*Disposal of Cases by the Central Vigilance Commission*

| Year | Cases received | Cases disposed |
|------|----------------|----------------|
| 1985 | 2956 | 2617 |
| 1986 | 3146 | 3368* |
| 1987 | 3389 | 3092 |
| 1988 | 3415 | 3818* |
| 1989 | 3643 | 3552 |
| 1990 | 3953 | 3814 |
| 1991 | 3915 | 3924* |
| 1992 | 3900 | 4035* |

*Note:* * Includes cases brought forward from previous years

*Source:* Annual Report, Central Vigilance Commission (1992)

The Tables 7.3 to 7.6 provide item-wise details of disposal of cases by the Central Vigilance Commission for the years 1985–92. Table 7.3 gives an analysis of the action recommended by the commission by way of first-stage advice during 1985–92.

TABLE 7.3
*Investigation Reports by the CBI—Number of Cases*

| Year | Advice tendered | Action recommended with percentage | | | |
| --- | --- | --- | --- | --- | --- |
| | | Prosecution | Major penalty | Minor penalty | Others |
| 1985 | 287 | 31 (10.80%) | 120 (41.81%) | 32 (11.15%) | 104 (36.24%) |
| 1986 | 376 | 38 (10.11%) | 185 (49.20%) | 29 (7.71%) | 124 (32.98%) |
| 1987 | 332 | 37 (11.14%) | 164 (49.40%) | 35 (10.54%) | 96 (28.92%) |
| 1988 | 393 | 42 (10.69%) | 201 (51.14%) | 51 (12.98%) | 99 (25.19%) |
| 1989 | 315 | 37 (11.75%) | 134 (42.54%) | 43 (13.65%) | 101 (32.06%) |
| 1990 | 262 | 31 (11.83%) | 116 (44.27%) | 33 (12.60%) | 82 (31.30%) |
| 1991 | 311 | 27 (08.68%) | 125 (40.19%) | 35 (11.26%) | 124 (39.87%) |
| 1992 | 344 | 42 (12.21%) | 171 (49.71%) | 42 (12.21%) | 89 (25.87%) |
| Total | 2620 | 285 (10.88%) | 1216 (46.41%) | 300 (11.45%) | 819 (31.26%) |

*Source:* *Annual Report,* Central Vigilance Commission (1992)

In respect of cases arising out of investigation by the CBI, the advice of the commission for launching prosecution has been a miserable 11 per cent. Even if one were to consider advice for initiating prosecution and departmental action for imposition of major penalty together, the percentage has been just a little more than 57 per cent of the cases received by the commission for advice. The commission has recommended action for minor penalty in about 11 per cent of the cases, and no action in more than 31 per cent of the cases.

The position is much worse in respect of cases which were referred to the commission by way of first-stage advice by the CVOs of departments as the data in Table 7.4 show.

TABLE 7.4

*Investigation Reports by the Chief Vigilance Officers—Number of Cases*

| Year | Advice tendered | Action recommended with percentage | | | |
|------|------|------|------|------|------|
| | | Prosecution | Major penalty | Minor penalty | Others |
| 1985 | 1031 | 3 | 351 | 84 | 593 |
| | | (0.29%) | (34.04%) | (8.15%) | (57.52%) |
| 1986 | 1698 | 8 | 638 | 111 | 941 |
| | | (0.47%) | (37.57%) | (6.54%) | (55.42%) |
| 1987 | 1506 | 7 | 417 | 103 | 979 |
| | | (0.46%) | (27.69%) | (6.84%) | (65.01%) |
| 1988 | 2073 | 3 | 554 | 210 | 1306 |
| | | (0.15%) | (26.72%) | (10.13%) | (63.00%) |
| 1989 | 1634 | 2 | 388 | 139 | 1105 |
| | | (0.12%) | (23.75%) | (8.51%) | (67.62%) |
| 1990 | 1736 | 4 | 478 | 194 | 1060 |
| | | (0.23%) | (27.53%) | (11.18%) | (61.06%) |
| 1991 | 1716 | 16 | 520 | 257 | 923 |
| | | (0.93%) | (30.30%) | (14.98%) | (53.79%) |
| 1992 | 1749 | 6 | 674 | 235 | 834 |
| | | (0.34%) | (38.54%) | (13.43%) | (47.69%) |
| Total | 13,143 | 49 | 4020 | 1333 | 7741 |
| | | (0.37%) | (30.59%) | (10.14%) | (58.90%) |

*Source: Annual Report*, Central Vigilance Commission (1992)

The percentage of cases arising out of the investigation conducted by the CVOs of the departments in which the commission has advised prosecution, is less than 1 per cent. Interestingly, the percentage of cases in respect of which prosecution was recommended by the commission, did not exceed 1 per cent of the cases in any given year. Even if one were to consider cases in which prosecution and action for major penalty was recommended, they constitute less than 31 per cent of the investigated cases in which advice was tendered by the commission. Action for minor penalty was recommended in about 10 per cent of the cases. It means that 59 per cent of the civil servants against whom investigation was conducted by the CVOs and sent to the commission for first-stage advice, were allowed to go scot-free.

The position is as dismal if one analyses the combined picture of the investigation reports of the CBI and the CVOs in which the first-stage advice of the commission was sought and tendered, as can be seen from the Table 7.5.

TABLE 7.5
*Combined CBI/CVO Investigation Reports—Number of Cases*

| Year | Advice tendered | Action recommended with percentage | | | |
|------|------|------|------|------|------|
| | | Prosecution | Major penalty | Minor penalty | Others |
| 1985 | 1313 | 34 (2.58%) | 471 (35.74%) | 116 (8.80%) | 697 (52.88%) |
| 1986 | 2074 | 46 (2.22%) | 823 (39.68%) | 140 (6.75%) | 1065 (51.35%) |
| 1987 | 1838 | 44 (2.39%) | 581 (31.61%) | 138 (7.51%) | 1075 (58.49%) |
| 1988 | 2466 | 45 (1.82%) | 755 (30.62%) | 261 (10.58%) | 1405 (59.98%) |
| 1989 | 1949 | 39 (2.00%) | 522 (26.78%) | 182 (9.34%) | 1206 (61.88%) |
| 1990 | 1998 | 35 (1.75%) | 594 (29.73%) | 227 (11.36%) | 1142 (57.16%) |
| 1991 | 2027 | 43 (2.12%) | 645 (31.82%) | 292 (14.41%) | 1047 (51.65%) |
| 1992 | 2093 | 48 (2.29%) | 845 (40.37%) | 277 (13.24%) | 923 (44.10%) |
| Total | 14,445 | 300 (2.03%) | 4765 (32.99%) | 1517 (10.50%) | 7863 (54.43%) |

*Source*: *Annual Report*, Central Vigilance Commission (1992)

On the whole, the percentage of cases in which civil servants against whom either the CBI or the CVO had investigated allegations of corruption, but who were let off, was as high as 54.43 per cent for the years 1985 to 1992. On the other hand, the percentage of cases in which action for prosecution was recommended was as low as 2 per cent for the same period.

The commission also tenders second-stage advice on punitive action to be taken. This is in cases where departmental action has been instituted on the basis of first-stage advice given by the commission for major penalty, and the enquiry proceedings have been completed by the enquiry officers. The commission also offers second-stage advice in cases in which departmental action was instituted for imposition of minor penalties, and the disciplinary authority proposes to close the case without imposing any penalty. The second-stage advice is, essentially, about imposition of penalties. Table 7.6 indicates the recommendations of the commission in respect of imposition of penalties as second-stage advice.

TABLE 7.6
*Recommendations of the Central Vigilance Commission as Second-Stage Advice*

| Year | Imposition of major penalty | Imposition of minor penalty | Other | Total |
|------|------|------|------|------|
| 1985 | 291 | 54 | 160 | 505 |
|      | (57.63%) | (10.63%) | (31.68%) | |
| 1986 | 282 | 67 | 164 | 513 |
|      | (54.97%) | (13.06%) | (31.97%) | |
| 1987 | 215 | 46 | 217 | 478 |
|      | (44.98%) | (09.62%) | (45.40%) | |
| 1988 | 274 | 83 | 200 | 557 |
|      | (49.19%) | (14.90%) | (35.91%) | |
| 1989 | 287 | 148 | 313 | 748 |
|      | (38.37%) | (19.79%) | (41.84%) | |
| 1990 | 384 | 150 | 281 | 815 |
|      | (47.12%) | (18.40%) | (34.48%) | |
| 1991 | 426 | 162 | 422 | 1010 |
|      | (42.18%) | (16.04%) | (41.78%) | |
| 1992 | 384 | 171 | 380 | 935 |
|      | (41.07%) | (18.29%) | (40.64%) | |
| Total | 2543 | 881 | 2137 | 5561 |
|      | (45.73%) | (15.84%) | (38.43%) | |

*Source: Annual Report,* Central Vigilance Commission (1992)

Table 7.6 makes it clear that the performance of the commission in recommending punishment as second-stage advice has been as unsatisfactory as in its first-stage advice. In about 38 per cent of the cases, the commission did not recommend any positive action although these pertained to cases where the commission itself had recommended action for imposition of penalty in its first-stage advice. Similarly, in almost 16 per cent of the cases, the commission let off civil servants with minor penalties, although it had recommended action for major penalties in its first-stage advice.

It is clear that the commission has been soft in recommending sufficiently deterrent punitive action against corrupt civil servants. It comes across more forcefully when one looks at penalties recommended by the commission which have resulted in loss of government employment. Table 7.7 provides details for the years 1989 to 1992. Such penalties have been imposed on 49 civil servants in 1989, and except for small increases in the intervening years, the number was again 49 in 1992.

TABLE 7.7
*Imposition of Penalties*

| Year | Dismissal | Removal | Compulsory retirement | Total |
|------|-----------|---------|-----------------------|-------|
| 1989 | 20 | 17 | 12 | 49 |
| 1990 | 19 | 22 | 19 | 60 |
| 1991 | 20 | 15 | 26 | 61 |
| 1992 | 13 | 19 | 17 | 49 |

*Source: Annual Report*, Central Vigilance Commission (1992)

Why is it that the performance of the commission has been so dismal as an anti-corruption body? It is often argued that this is because the commission has no statutory status. For example, the Fifth Pay Commission had recommended that the Central Vigilance Commission should be made strictly aloof from the executive, through appropriate constitutional safeguards.

This was confirmed by the Supreme Court in the Jain Hawala case in its judgement delivered on December 18, 1997. The Court directed that 'Central Vigilance Commission shall be given a statutory status', and that the CVC should be selected by a

'Committee comprising the Prime Minister, the Home Minister and the Leader of the Opposition from a panel of outstanding civil servants and others'.

The Government of India, in pursuance of the judgement of the Court, promulgated two ordinances on 25th August and 27th October 1998, conferring statutory status on the commission. In terms of the ordinances, the commission will now consist of a Chief Vigilance Commissioner and four Vigilance Commissioners. Those 'who have held office or are holding office in a corporation established by or under any Central Act or a Government Company owned or controlled by the Central Government and persons who have expertise in finance including insurance and banking, law, vigilance and investigations' are eligible for appointment as the Chief Vigilance Commissioner and other commissioners.

The age of superannuation for the Chief Vigilance Commissioner and the Vigilance Commissioners has been fixed at 65. This, unfortunately, will keep retired judges of the Supreme Court out of the panel of names for the commission.

In terms of the ordinances, the commission will have total control over the CBI with regard to investigation of all corruption-related cases. The commission has been given powers to order *suo motu* enquiries into charges of corruption against civil servants.

With the ordinance of 25th August 1998 as amended by the ordinance of 27th October 1998, an attempt has been made to make the commission a statutory body and ensure a degree of independence in the functioning of the commission. The changes proposed are no doubt transformative, but it remains to be seen whether the changes will have the effect of making the commission truly effective in detecting and punishing corruption.

It may be naive, however, to expect that a multi-member vigilance body would be in a position to ensure greater efficiency in the handling of corruption cases than a single member body. In fact, there is every reason to believe that it may produce the contrary result. The multi-member Election Commission is a case in point. The efficiency of the Election Commission did not particularly improve after it was made a multi-member body. Rather, the way T.N. Seshan and the two Commissioners feuded in the full glare of publicity, prompted the Supreme Court to intervene and chide them for their behaviour. One is not exactly looking forward to similar public displays of unruly behaviour in the multi-member vigilance commission.[6]

## EXPERIENCE OF OTHER COUNTRIES

The most famous anti-corruption body is Hong Kong's Independent Commission Against Corruption. It was established in 1974 when there was a much-publicized corruption scandal involving a top police officer. Corruption was pervasive in Hong Kong in the 1960s and the early 1970s, and how pervasive it was, is captured by expressions popular at the time—people in Hong Kong had the option of 'getting on the bus' (actively participating in corruption) or 'running alongside the bus' (being a bystander who did not interfere with the system). 'Standing in front of the bus' (resisting corruption) was not a viable option.[7]

Bribery and extortions were almost a way of life in Hong Kong in the 1960s and early 1970s. Payment of bribe to civil servants and clandestine commissions in the private sector were considered customary, and in the Police Department, collection and sharing of bribes was institutionalized.

The period also saw the emergence of a new citizenry which was young, educated and civic-minded. The new citizenry was concerned about corruption, and an event in 1973 goaded the new citizenry to demand action from the government. Peter Godber, a Superintendent of Police under investigation for corruption, fled to the United Kingdom. The new citizenry started a campaign for punishing Godber, and also used the opportunity to ask the government to take steps for tackling the larger issue of corruption in Hong Kong.

A Commission of Inquiry under a high court judge was set up in the same year to look into the issue of corruption. The main recommendation of the commission was to establish an independent agency to deal with corruption. As a result, the Independent Commission Against Corruption (ICAC) was set up in February 1974. One year later, Godber was extradited to Hong Kong, convicted and sentenced to four years imprisonment.

While establishing the ICAC, the government realized that the fight against corruption could not be won only by punishing the corrupt. It was necessary for improvements to be made in the way the government functioned. More importantly, fundamental changes had to be brought about in public attitude towards corruption. So, the law establishing the ICAC provided for fighting corruption on three fronts: investigation, prevention, and education. The ICAC has three functional departments—the Operations Department to investigate complaints of corruption, the Corruption Prevention Department to examine systems in government departments and public bodies to identify and reduce opportunities for corruption, and the Community Relations Department to educate the members of the public on the costs and consequences of corruption and seek their support in the fight against corruption.

The ICAC reports directly to the Governor (now the Chief Executive). Its personnel are independent of the police force in Hong Kong and the rest of the civil service. It has a staff strength of about 1200. The majority of the staff serve on a contract basis, the contract being renewable by mutual consent. In terms of remuneration, the staff in ICAC are paid much better than their counterparts in the government. There is a prohibition against transferring the employees of the ICAC to other departments of the government in Hong Kong. They are not permitted to leave the ICAC and work for senior civil servants of the government in Hong Kong, particularly those who have been subjected to investigation by the ICAC.[8]

The ICAC is given adequate powers to deal with corruption offenses. Its powers derive from three specific laws: the Prevention of Bribery Ordinance (PBO), the Independent Commission Against Corruption Ordinance (ICACO), and the Corrupt and Illegal Practices Ordinance (CIPO).

The law governing the offence of bribery is mainly set out in the PBO. Section 3 says, 'Any Government of the Hong Kong Special Administrative Region Servant who, without the general or special permission of the Chief Executive, solicits or accepts any advantage shall be guilty of an offence.' Section 4 makes it an offence for a public servant to solicit or accept any advantage in connection with the performance of his official duty. Conversely, any person offering such an advantage also commits an offence. Section 10 makes it an offence for a civil servant to maintain a standard of living or possess assets which are not commensurate with his official emoluments.

Section 9 of the PBO deals specifically with the private sector.

It safeguards the interests of private companies by protecting employers from employees who are corrupt. It prohibits an agent from soliciting or accepting an advantage without his principal's permission when conducting his principal's affairs or business. Under Section 9, a person who offers the advantage is also guilty.

To ensure that the ICAC functions efficiently, it has been given wide investigative powers. In fact, the powers of the ICAC have great reach; business as well as official corruption falls within its mandate. But there is also an elaborate system of checks and balances to ensure that the ICAC does not use its wide investigative powers arbitrarily. The ICAC only investigates and collects evidence; it has no prosecution powers. The information collected by the ICAC is submitted to the Secretary of Justice who alone can initiate prosecution. The courts in Hong Kong decide on the outcome of the prosecution, and they are empowered to look into how the investigations have been conducted by the ICAC.

The legislature in Hong Kong regularly monitors the work of the ICAC. There are also a number of advisory committees which review the working of the ICAC, and the members of these committees are prominent citizens drawn from all sectors of the community and are appointed by the Chief Executive. All the advisory committees are chaired by non-official members. There are four advisory committees: the Advisory Committee on Corruption, the Operations Review Committee, the Corruption Prevention Advisory Committee, and the Citizens Advisory Committee on Community Relations. The reports of these committees are made public, so that the community in Hong Kong can review and monitor the work of the advisory committees. In addition, there is an independent ICAC Complaints Committee, chaired by a non-official member. The committee monitors and reviews the handling of complaints against the ICAC officers or the ICAC practices and procedures.

The ICAC gets its information on corruption from complaints by the members of the public which flow into the ICAC everyday. The ICAC, in fact, encourages members of the public to identify themselves and make reports in person. Members of the public may lodge complaints at the Report Centre of the ICAC which functions on a 24-hour basis, on the telephone hotline, in the postal box, or at any of the eight ICAC regional offices.

When a complaint is made, it is immediately referred to the Report Centre, a top security area manned round-the-clock by investigators. If the complainant comes to the ICAC in person, he is interviewed within a matter of minutes. If the case is a minor one, it is assigned to the 'Quick Response Team' of investigators which deals speedily with simple cases, thereby leaving the mainstream investigators to concentrate on more complex cases.

Every corruption complaint is listed in a morning report which is studied by the top functionaries in the ICAC. If it is decided to investigate, the investigation is done under conditions of utmost confidentiality. The Prevention of Bribery Ordinance makes it an offence for anyone to warn a suspect that he is under investigation. If, at the conclusion of an investigation, it is found that there is insufficient evidence to conduct a prosecution, the case is tabled before the Operations Review Committee which is chaired by a non-official member appointed by the Chief Executive, and consists of the Secretary for Justice, Commissioner of Police, Director of Administration as well as the Commissioner, ICAC. Other members of the committee are private citizens of civic repute. It is only the Operations Review Committee which can authorize the termination of an investigation.

Table 7.8 provides the statistics of corruption complaints received from members of the public since the inception of the ICAC in 1974. It can be seen that there has been a steady increase in corruption complaints in respect of all categories—government departments, public bodies, and the private sector; but what is striking is that there has been a significant increase in the corruption complaints from the members of the public since 1993. During the six-year period, 1993–8, about 17,000 people have made corruption complaints to the ICAC.

TABLE 7.8
*Corruption Complaints—ICAC, 1974–1998*

| Year | Government department | Public body | Private sector | Total |
|------|------|------|------|------|
| 1974 | 416 | 28 | 2745 | 3189 |
| 1975 | 401 | 117 | 2661 | 3179 |
| 1976 | 474 | 76 | 1883 | 2433 |
| 1977 | 383 | 46 | 1271 | 1700 |
| 1978 | 305 | 42 | 887 | 1234 |

*contd.*

| 1979 | 402  | 81  | 1182 | 1665 |
| 1980 | 534  | 79  | 1159 | 1772 |
| 1981 | 698  | 92  | 1554 | 2344 |
| 1982 | 840  | 88  | 1421 | 2349 |
| 1983 | 881  | 103 | 1542 | 2526 |
| 1984 | 889  | 70  | 1406 | 2365 |
| 1985 | 1009 | 55  | 1486 | 2550 |
| 1986 | 1060 | 150 | 1364 | 2574 |
| 1987 | 1068 | 71  | 1160 | 2299 |
| 1988 | 1046 | 54  | 1062 | 2162 |
| 1989 | 1062 | 64  | 1290 | 2388 |
| 1990 | 1034 | 69  | 1196 | 2390 |
| 1991 | 978  | 64  | 1125 | 2186 |
| 1992 | 1032 | 59  | 1144 | 2257 |
| 1993 | 1166 | 113 | 1798 | 3276 |
| 1994 | 1381 | 101 | 1830 | 3312 |
| 1995 | 1248 | 109 | 1630 | 2987 |
| 1996 | 1304 | 131 | 1651 | 3086 |
| 1997 | 1288 | 198 | 1571 | 3057 |
| 1998 | 1456 | 239 | 1860 | 3555 |

*Source:* *The ICAC*, Hong Kong

Table 7.9 provides the details of corruption complaints from the members of the public for the year 1999 up to the month of July. It can be seen that there has been a continuation of the high plateau of complaint level established in 1993.

TABLE 7.9
*Corruption Complaints—ICAC, 1999*

| Month | Government department | Public bodies | Private sector | Total |
|---|---|---|---|---|
| January  | 96  | 14 | 139 | 249 |
| February | 97  | 7  | 101 | 205 |
| March    | 115 | 31 | 133 | 279 |
| April    | 103 | 21 | 149 | 273 |
| May      | 126 | 23 | 177 | 326 |
| June     | 114 | 17 | 178 | 309 |
| July     | 133 | 11 | 166 | 310 |

*Source:* *The ICAC*, Hong Kong

Interestingly, nearly 70 per cent of the people who reported corruption to the ICAC were sufficiently confident of the integrity of the ICAC to identify themselves. When the ICAC started in 1974, the percentage of people who complained and were prepared to identify themselves, was only 40 per cent. It reached 50 per cent in 1977 itself, and has increased steadily to approximately 70 per cent in 1998. It is evident that the community in Hong Kong has come forward to report corrupt practices, and that too, by taking the risk of identifying themselves.

The credit for raising the consciousness of the community in Hong Kong about fighting corruption, goes largely to the vigorous public education campaigns carried out by the ICAC. The ICAC has used innovative social strategies to combat corruption, but its main emphasis has been to bring about changes in the public attitude to corruption. As we have seen, corruption in Hong Kong was entrenched before the commission started functioning. At that time, people regarded corruption as inevitable and any effort to fight it as futile. But the well-orchestrated public relation campaigns conducted by the ICAC, shattered that conception. The ICAC has, in fact, transformed a passive social environment which condoned corruption and helped sustain it in the process. It has succeeded in inducing a remarkable attitudinal change. For example, the young people in Hong Kong now take a stricter view of corruption than did their parents.

The ICAC has been able to bring about such an attitudinal change by educating the members of public about the costs and consequences of corruption and by rallying their support in fighting corruption. The ICAC has, in fact, taken the anti-corruption message to every corner of the community in a complex operation which has called for the skilful use of every possible avenue open to it.

Mass media has been the most effective channel of spreading the anti-corruption message. Every year, the ICAC produces a series of radio and television advertisements to keep the issue of corruption in the forefront of public consciousness. The advertisements have earned encouraging responses from the public, and they have also won a number of awards in professional advertising competitions locally and overseas.

The ICAC also produces a television drama series called the 'ICAC Investigators', telecast on local television stations. Based on real cases, the series educates the community about corruption by depicting how investigators of the ICAC expose and punish corruption. The print media has also been utilized for spreading the anti-corruption messages. Advertisements, feature articles, and reports in newspapers and magazines, tell people about corruption and the work done by the ICAC.

The ICAC also uses face-to-face contact with the community to spread the anti-corruption message and educate members of the public from all walks of life. Every day, the staff of the ICAC take education services to the door steps of various levels of the community in order to spread the anti-corruption message and enlist public support. To cater to the needs of different groups of people, the ICAC has adopted a 'programme plan approach': each regional officer of the ICAC is also a 'programme coordinator', specializing in communicating with special targets such as the business sector, public servants, youth or conveying specific messages such as reporting corruption.

The ICAC produces specially designed education packages with video and games to appeal to the students in various age groups. These packages inform students of anti-corruption work in Hong Kong. They also seek to promote positive values such as the correct attitude towards money and the importance of fair play. Resource portfolios on business and professional ethics are also developed for use in curricula. Every year, the functionaries of the ICAC conduct talks on anti-bribery law and work ethics to graduating students in secondary and vocational schools as well as technical institutes and universities. The ICAC funds concerts and sporting events which foster social interaction with anti-corruption themes. Corruption is portrayed, in such campaigns, concerts, sporting events and in material distributed to school children, as harmful to families, to the economy, and to the traditional Chinese values.

In order to consolidate community support further, the ICAC Club was established in March 1997. It is one of the initiatives in bringing the ICAC closer to the community. Response to the membership drive has been encouraging. Since the activities are organized regularly, the members of the ICAC Clubs are in a position to internalize the anti-corruption values propagated by the ICAC, to lead by example, and to keep a high degree of vigilance against corruption.

Since the support of the community is considered indispensable to anti-corruption work, a priority area for the ICAC is to keep close contact with district leaders and the members of the public. The eight regional offices of the ICAC regularly hold meet-the-public sessions to establish and sustain contact with different groups, from the CEOs in the private companies to hawkers on the street. The idea is to allay their fear of widespread corruption crawling back and reassure them of the determination of the ICAC to keep Hong Kong corruption-free.

The regional office staff of the ICAC attend regular meetings of district consultation committees such as Fight Crime Committee and Area Committee, to update members on recent developments and seek their views on how best anti-corruption work can be carried out. They also organize publicity activities in large public and private housing estates all over the territory to publicize the work of the ICAC to local residents and encourage them to report corruption.

On the whole, the ICAC has succeeded in taking the anti-corruption message into every corner of the community in Hong Kong. And the strategy seems to have worked. From the evidence available, the ICAC has been successful in combating corruption. As pointed out earlier, corruption was endemic in Hong Kong during the 1960s and early, 1970s, but surveys carried out between 1977 and 1994 reveal that public perception of the incidence of official corruption has fallen significantly. Indirect evidence suggests that active corruption has declined as well.[9]

## CENTRAL BUREAU OF INVESTIGATION

The Central Bureau of Investigation (CBI) is the principal investigating agency of the Government of India in anti-corruption matters. The CBI collects information, conducts checks and searches, and takes necessary action to bring corrupt civil servants to book.[10]

The functioning of the CBI is regulated by the provisions of the Delhi Special Police Establishment Act, 1946. It is headed by a Director who is supported by three Special/Additional Directors, fifteen Joint Directors and other officers, besides a Legal

Adviser and supporting staff. The director is appointed by the Appointments Committee of the Union Cabinet.

What has been the performance of the CBI in detecting and punishing corruption? Table 7.10 provides information about the number of cases examined and investigated by the CBI.

TABLE 7.10
*Number of Cases Examined and Investigated by the CBI*

|  |  | 1972 | 1992 |
|---|---|---|---|
| 1. | Number of complaints examined during the year | 6650 | 6520 |
| 2. | Number which led to regular investigation by the CBI | 477 | 229 |

*Source:* Narsimhan (1997)

A comparison with the ICAC shows how pitifully small the number of cases examined and investigated by the CBI is. The ICAC examined 3189 cases in 1974, and 3312 cases in 1994. And, Hong Kong is ranked 16th in the Corruption Perceptions Index while India is ranked 68th in a sample of 85 countries. Moreover, India is a much larger country with a sizable civil service population.

The small number of cases examined and investigated by the CBI can mean only two things. For one, the staff of the CBI responsible for collecting information and intelligence about corruption are either negligent or are an integral part of the sharing mechanism. Second and even more reprehensible, the members of the public do not obviously regard the CBI as an organization which can be trusted to act on complaints of corruption.

Table 7.11 provides details of the cases handled by the CBI and the action recommended. Interestingly, there has been a fall in the number of cases registered by the CBI over this twenty-year period. But what is really disturbing is the small number of cases which are recommended for action—either by way of prosecution in a court of law or departmental action.

TABLE 7.11

*Cases Handled and Action Recommended by the CBI*

| Items | 1972 | 1992 |
|---|---|---|
| 1. Number of cases registered during the year | 1349 | 1231 |
| 2. Number of cases investigated and finalised during the year (including old cases) | 1790 | 1412 |
| 3. Number of cases prosecuted in the courts | 384 | 505 |
| 4. Number of cases referred for departmental action | 887 | 652 |

*Source:* Narsimhan (1997)

Table 7.12 provides data about the success achieved by the CBI in getting conviction in the courts. The percentage of cases in which the CBI is able to get a conviction is coming down.

TABLE 7.12

*Progress of CBI Cases in the Courts*

| Items | 1972 | 1992 |
|---|---|---|
| 1. Number of cases disposed of in courts during the year | 352 | 237 |
| 2. Number that ended in conviction | 300 | 164 |
| 3. Number that ended in acquittal | 52 | 73 |
| 4. Percentage of conviction in courts | 85.2 | 69.1 |
| 5. Number of cases pending in courts at the end of the year | 1362 | 4148 |

*Source:* Narsimhan (1997)

There has also been a steep deterioration in respect of cases in which prosecution had been filed by the CBI in the courts. In fact, the performance of the CBI has been dismal comprehensively: the pendency has increased, the number of cases which have ended in conviction has come down, and the number of cases ending in acquittal has increased.

What is distressing is that even out of the small number of cases which finally see some kind of punishment, the percentage of cases in which senior civil servants are punished either by the courts or departmentally, is very low. And in the case of senior civil servants who are given some kind of punishment, only a handful have lost their jobs. The details are in Table 7.13.

TABLE 7.13
*Nature of Conviction in CBI Cases*

| Items | 1972 | 1992 |
|-------|------|------|
| 1. Number of civil servants convicted in the courts | 194 | 85 |
| 2. Of gazetted rank out of item (1) | 15 | 44 |
| 3. Number of civil servants punished in departmental action | 806 | 798 |
| 4. Of gazetted rank out of item (3) | 150 | 547 |
| 5. Of item (4), civil servants who lost government employment | 8 | 62 |

*Source:* Narsimhan (1997)

It is clear from Table 7.13 that the number of civil servants who occupy senior ranks and whose punishment would have sent the right kind of signal is negligible. It is also clear that in most cases, the punishment awarded is not exemplary, with the result that the necessary deterrence is not established.

Such an assumption is more than validated by the details of the performance of the CBI in respect of cases of disproportionate assets of civil servants (Table 7.14). Once again, the cases booked by the CBI are so few in number. This is disquieting because it is common knowledge that civil servants in India have stashed away enough and more to last for several generations. Second, the percentage of senior officers in the list is minuscule. This is disturbing because it makes sense to assume that senior civil servants have greater opportunities to make money, and therefore, their presence in the table should have been compellingly larger.

TABLE 7.14

*Cases of Disproportionate Assets*

| | Items | 1972 | 1992 |
|---|---|---|---|
| 1. | Number of cases registered during the year | 89 | 57 |
| 2. | Number of gazetted officers involved in item (1) | 44 | 34 |
| 3. | Number of items investigated and finalised during the year including old cases | 94 | 77 |
| 4. | Number, out of item (3) which were subject to prosecution in the courts | 11 | 24 |
| 5. | Number, out of item (3) which were recommended for departmental action | 58 | 42 |
| 6. | Number of cases disposed in the courts | 6 | 5 |
| 7. | Number, out of the item (4) which ended in conviction | 5 | 2 |
| 8. | Number of gazetted officers involved in item (7) | 2 | – |
| 9. | Number of cases decided in departmental action | 40 | 44 |
| 10. | Number, in item (9) which resulted in punishment | 28 | 24 |
| 11. | Number, of gazetted officers involved in item (10) | 9 | 20 |
| 12. | Number, in item (11) who were dismissed/removed/retired from service | 1 | 2 |

*Source*: Narsimhan (1997)

Table 7.14 makes for depressing reading, but the position regrettably has not changed much in the recent years (Table 7.15). The CBI seems to be the kind of organization which is not easily perturbed by transformative changes in the environment.

TABLE 7.15

*Cases Handled by the CBI*

*(January to August Each Year)*

| | 1994 | 1995 | 1996 |
|---|---|---|---|
| No of cases registered | 975 | 1011 | 1129 |
| No of cases handled by the CBI including cases pending at the beginning of the year | 2078 | 2145 | 2490 |
| No of cases sent up for trial | 314 | 332 | 334 |
| No of cases decided by courts | 199 | 204 | 222 |
| No of cases ended in conviction | 117 | 121 | 122 |
| No of gazetted officers involved | 23 | 34 | 33 |
| No of cases which ended in acquittal, discharge or otherwise disposed of | 82 | 83 | 100 |

*Source*: *Annual Report 1996-97*, Ministry of Personnel, Public Grievances & Pensions, Government of India

Why is it that the functioning of the CBI, the premier investigating agency of the country, has been so dismal? One has to
remember that we are talking about the premier investigating
agency of a country where the civil service numbers have bloated
over the years, and are, at present, around 20 million. And it is
so in the context of a country which ranks as the 68th most corrupt in a sample of 85 countries.

The evidence points to the fact that the CBI has not raised the
stakes for corruption in any visible manner. Could it be that CBI
has been used by the executive as a partisan instrument to shield
and protect acts of corruption, instead of revealing and punishing them as it was intended to?

This is confirmed by the landmark judgement of the Supreme
Court in the Jain Hawala case, which, more than anything else,
addressed the key issue of autonomy for the CBI. The Supreme
Court mandated that the 'Central Government shall take all
measures necessary to ensure that the CBI functions effectively
and efficiently and is viewed as a non-partisan agency'. In essence, the judgement was a mandate to remove superintendence
of the CBI from the executive and hand it over to the Central
Vigilance Commissioner, whose independence from the executive had been ensured in the same judgement by decreeing a
statutory status for the commission.

The mandate of the Supreme Court was unequivocal. The
Court decreed:

While the Government shall remain answerable for the CBI's functioning, to introduce visible objectivity in the mechanism for overviewing
the CBI's functioning, the CVC (Central Vigilance Commissioner) shall
be entrusted with the responsibility of superintendence over the CBI's
functioning. The CBI shall report to the CVC about cases taken up by it
for investigation, progress of investigations, cases in which chargesheets
are filed, and their progress. The CVC shall review the progress of all
cases moved by the CBI for sanction of prosecution of public servants
which are pending with the competent authorities, specially those in
which sanction has been delayed or refused.

The Supreme Court also struck down the executive direction
issued by the central government in 1969—popularly known as
the 'single directive'—which requires the CBI to get the approval
of the central government before investigating civil servants of
the rank of joint secretary to the Government of India and above.

The 'single directive' also covered officers of the Reserve Bank of India of the rank of joint secretary and above, executive directors and above of the Securities and Exchange Board of India, and CMDs and executive directors of nationalized banks. By an amendment effected in February 1997, general managers of nationalized banks were brought under the purview of the 'single directive'.

The Court struck down the 'single directive' on two grounds. First, the 'single directive' was not seen as permissible in exercise of the power of superintendence of the central government. As the court observed, 'The Single Directive cannot . . . be upheld as valid on the ground of it being permissible in exercise of the power of superintendence of the Central Government. In result, the Single Directive is struck down'.

Second, while striking down the 'single directive', the Court observed that it was merely an executive order and not a statutory requirement. In the words of the Court, 'It (the single directive) cannot be made a condition precedent for initiating investigation'.

On the whole, the effect of the order of the Supreme Court in the Jain Hawala case was to rewrite the provisions of Section 4(1) of the Delhi Special Police Establishment Act of 1946, which vests the power of superintendence of the CBI with the Government of India.[11] The Supreme Court even prescribed a procedure by which an impartial director could be chosen. The court laid down that a list of candidates for appointment as the director of the CBI should be compiled by a committee headed by the Central Vigilance Commissioner, and consisting of the Secretary, Ministry of Home Affairs and the Secretary, Department of Personnel. The director is to be chosen out of this list by the Appointments Committee of the Union Cabinet. The director should have a fixed term of two years.

The Supreme Court also mandated a key safeguard against wilful sabotage of investigations by the CBI. It decreed that a panel of lawyers, answering to a body similar to that of the Director of Prosecutions in the United Kingdom, should be created to review the prosecution of cases by the CBI. As the Court observed, this panel of 'competent lawyers of experience and impeccable reputation shall be prepared with the advice of the Attorney General'. According to the judgement of the Court, each case of prosecution by the CBI will have to be reviewed by a lawyer from the panel, and responsibility for unsuccessful prosecution shall be fixed.

In other words, in the event of a prosecution resulting in the discharge or acquittal of the accused, a lawyer on this panel will be asked to prepare a report fixing responsibility for possible dereliction of duty by the investigating officer. In fact, this particular order of the Supreme Court was in response to a demand by *amicus curiae* Anil Divan that the Court create a body similar to the Special Independent Council of the United States to deal with sensitive cases.

How will the Court's order of reviewing prosecution cases by a panel of lawyers work in practice? It is difficult to say, but as a CBI officer puts it,

Most criminal cases in India anyway end in acquittal, and often not because of sloppy investigation but because of legal lacunae, lack of witnesses, and on occasion, sharp practice. The CBI already filters out a high percentage of cases to keep a high success rate. The Court order will simply work as a disincentive against pursuing difficult cases with a low chance of conviction.[12]

There seems to be a measure of agreement on this point. As Praveen Swami says,

The CBI's preferred tactic . . . has been to stonewall investigations endlessly rather than bring prosecutions in the first place . . . . There is no real structural guarantee against stonewalling other than near-complete autonomy, which the court directives do not provide for.[13]

As noted earlier, the government has now promulgated two ordinances in pursuance of the judgement of the Supreme Court. The ordinances amend the provisions of the Delhi Special Police Establishment Act of 1946, particularly those relating to the CBI. The ordinances provide for a minimum tenure of two years for the Director of the CBI. In terms of the ordinances, the selection of the Director of the CBI will be made by an independent committee comprising the Chief Vigilance Commissioner, Secretary of the Home Ministry and Secretary, Department of Personnel of the Government of India. The ordinances also provide that the tenure of the Director of the CBI cannot be extended or curtailed except with the consent of the selection committee.

In terms of the ordinance of 27th October 1998 amending the

earlier ordinance, the provision about the 'single directive' has been dropped. In effect, no prior approval is now necessary to conduct any enquiry or investigation under the Prevention of Corruption Act.

Will the revamped CBI be in a position to work autonomously of the executive? The CBI, which is sought to be liberated now from the shackles of the executive, has shown itself to be extremely pliant in the past. Its credentials in investigating corrupt civil servants have been consistently suspect. The question is: how is an organization peopled by policemen ordinarily in the employment of the executive government going to have the necessary autonomy to investigate and proceed against the high and the mighty of the same government?

That, really, is the crux of the problem. The CBI is to be made truly autonomous of the executive government to function effectively as an anti-corruption body, but this is not likely to happen in spite of the landmark judgement of the Supreme Court and the resultant ordinances. The attempt of the Supreme Court to empower the CBI may, at first sight and given the government's record of unremitting interference in the working of the CBI, be seen as having removed the impediments to the effective functioning of the CBI as an investigative body, but the measures are, at best, a necessary but not sufficient condition to make the CBI a truly autonomous and effective organization. In that sense, the judgement of the Supreme Court is more likely to be viewed as a well-meaning attempt to find solutions which allow a short-cut from the much more demanding and fundamental process of restructuring the political and civil institutions of the country.[14]

Rather, one should ask whether the Supreme Court is addressing a concern that needs to be addressed by the political government. The question is answered by Praveen Swami when he says:

Although its pronouncements (of the Supreme Court) mark a welcome intervention in the debate on the CBI's functioning, the Court cannot fully address issues that the political system must engage with. Even if the CVC is made a statutory body and a truly independent Central Vigilance Commissioner appointed, the CBI will continue to retain an uncomfortably close linkage with the Government. Unlike institutions like the Office of the Comptroller and Auditor-General, which has played a valuable role as whistle blower on more than one occasion, it will not have either the authority or the incentive to monitor regularly the probity of people in public life. . . . Whatever the headlines might have said, the CBI has not gained full autonomy. Setting it free will involve giving concrete shape to the Supreme Court's intentions through sustained people's action.[15]

On the whole, the functioning of the CBI, so far, has not been such as to raise the stakes for corruption. The fact of the matter is that the CBI has developed and nurtured an uncomfortably close linkage with the executive—a linkage close enough to prevent it from being an effective anti-corruption body.

The question, therefore, is: now that the CBI has been given a measure of autonomy under the provisions of the ordinances of 1998, will the picture change? The answer is perhaps no. This is for several reasons. First, the CBI will continue to be manned by policemen who are in the employ of the government. In Hong Kong by contrast, the ICAC, as we have seen, is independent of the local police force. Its officers cannot be transferred to other departments, and are not permitted to leave the ICAC and work for senior officers of the government in Hong Kong who have been investigated by the ICAC. In fact, the officers of the ICAC are forbidden to work in other public agencies for years after leaving it. The result has been that the ICAC is as free from networks of corruption as its architects could make it.

Second, the CBI continues to be, in spite of the ordinances of 1998, a mere investigating agency. In contrast, the ICAC in Hong Kong has used innovative social strategies to produce changes in public attitudes towards corruption. It has undertaken well-orchestrated public relation campaigns to break the belief that corruption is inevitable. The remarkable lesson about the success of the ICAC in fighting corruption has been its unusual focus on the civil society. The CBI, predictably, has no such plans.

Third, the image of the CBI, as far as members of public are concerned, is one of a pliant organization which has, over the years, succeeded in shielding corruption rather than exposing and punishing it. The image has a foundation in facts—the CBI has earned this image on the basis of its past performance. On the other hand, the public image of the ICAC in Hong Kong is that of an organization which has effectively combated corruption. And many people in Hong Kong trust the integrity of the ICAC well enough to report corruption by identifying themselves. The image of the CBI is so irretrievably poor that most people would hesitate to approach the CBI with complaints of corruption. This is because the CBI is seen as an organization which cannot be trusted to take note of people's complaints and act against corruption.

## ANTI-CORRUPTION BODIES OF STATE GOVERNMENTS

At the level of the state governments, similar vigilance and anti-corruption organizations exist, although the nature and staffing of these organizations vary between and across state governments. While some states have vigilance commissions, others have anti-corruption bureaus as a part of the police department.

The state vigilance commissions, wherever they exist, are patterned on the Central Vigilance Commission and headed by a person with the status of a judge of the high court. The state vigilance commissions are empowered to examine complaints against corrupt civil servants. In conducting investigations, state vigilance commissions are assisted by police officers on deputation from the state governments.

Some of the states have anti-corruption departments which, in essence, are extensions of the police department albeit with some degree of autonomy to function as vigilance organizations. In Rajasthan, for example, the Anti-Corruption Department is called the Rajasthan State Bureau of Investigation. The bureau is headed by a Director-General of Police who is on deputation from the Police Department of Rajasthan. He is assisted by an Inspector General of Police, two Deputy Inspector Generals of Police, four Superintendents of Police, six Additional Superintendents of Police, and three Deputy Superintendents of Police, all of whom are on deputation from the Police Department of the state. The bureau reports directly to the chief minister of the state.[16]

The state vigilance commissions or the anti-corruption departments operating at the state level, have typically lacked the autonomy and independence to act effectively as anti-corruption bodies. This is because all the investigating personnel are drawn from the ranks of the state government only. In addition, their anti-corruption efforts are dependent on the caprices of the executive. For example, even in instances in which a prima-facie case exists against a delinquent civil servant, they have to seek the prior sanction of the executive to place the civil servant under suspension or prosecute him in a court of law.

The result is that the functioning of these anti-corruption bodies has not raised the stakes for corruption in any meaningful manner. As Arora and Goyal say of the anti-corruption machinery at the level of the state governments,

It may be noted that the traditional anti-corruption machinery, comprising organizations within the regular executive branch, generally falls short of the requisite effectiveness. There are usual delays and soft actions associated with investigations. The big fish is rarely threatened and what is caught sometimes is only the small fish. Resultantly, only a minuscule minority of the real corrupt elements is brought to book and even they are given belated and mild punishments. Sometimes, suspensions, once ordered, are revoked under pressure and without adequately reasonable grounds. Moreover, what is obvious is that the state anti-corruption machinery, comprising police officials, does not show grit and gumption to catch with required skills and alacrity, suspected police and administrative officials of senior ranks. An administrative will to act with firmness is conspicuous by its gross absence.[17]

Some state governments have set up the institution of Lok Ayukta, an anti-corruption institution which is legally independent of the executive. Although the institution of Lok Ayukta was set up following the recommendation of the Administrative Reforms Commission, there is a great deal of variation in the structure of the institution across states. But one common feature is that the investigating staff generally consist of police officers who are on deputation from the local police department of the state governments. In Karnataka for example, the entire investigating staff of the Lok Ayukta, headed by a Director-General of Police, consist of police personnel on deputation from the state government.

This appears to be the general pattern. As R.L.M. Patil says:

The Lokayukta, in sharp contrast to the 'headless wonder' of the public sector undertakings, is a 'bodiless head', that is, there is no sustainable organization below the Lokayukta himself. . . . For an effective functioning, it is imperative that the Lokayukta gets its own staff in full size and adequate budgetary support. It is understandable why the Lokayukta is not given its own independent staff so far anywhere—because the very existence of the Lokayukta is doubtful! Public servants as well as government servants may indeed have a secret desire not to fatten but starve the holy cow.[18]

In general, there is an impression that the institution of the Lok Ayukta has not been given the degree of independence which is necessary for it to function effectively as an autonomous anti-corruption body. The common refrain in the complaints of the Lok Ayuktas of the various states is that they do not get sufficient information from the government departments which would enable them to function effectively.

The general impression is that the Lok Ayukta is only a recommendatory body. As R.L.M. Patil observes:

The Lokayukta is under the present set up a mere recommendatory body. It has no punitive powers. It is not a court to pronounce judgement on the integrity and efficiency of any officer or a minister. Its annual reports are not properly circulated, or published, or discussed on the floor of the House. Its work is hampered by procedural delays; and even after it is over, the findings of it are not deemed binding. The spirit of providing protection to the honest, and striking terror in the hearts of the dishonest has all but evaporated.[19]

On the whole, the functioning of the Lok Ayukta has not been inspiring. As Arora and Goyal say,

A close look at the performance of the Lok Ayuktas in Indian states does not create a very positive impression. There is much that could have been done and much that should have been avoided. It is paradoxical that half the states have not even adopted the institution so far while the rest seem to be unsure about the status and clout to be granted to this institution.[20]

## DOES THE INTERNAL CONTROL SYSTEM WORK?

The internal control system has not worked in India. This is for several reasons. First, there is collusion at work at all levels of the government and a sharing of the gains from corruption. As a result, there have been very few cases in which corruption is reported, and even in those few cases, there are the usual delays and soft actions which characterize the process of investigation in India. Even civil servants who are not incorporated into the sharing mechanism, are soft on corruption because they visualize serious setbacks to their careers if they take a proactive stand, in view of the comprehensive sharing mechanism which reaches right up to the top.

Second, investigating and prosecuting agencies are not independent of the executive government. In other words, the working of the investigative and prosecuting agencies has not been insulated from possible political interference. A regular vehicle of political interference has been power of the executive government to appoint and transfer key functionaries of the investigative agencies. The result, unenviably, has been lax investigation and prosecution.

This is compounded by the fact that the executive government has been given wide 'supervisory' powers over the functioning of the investigative agencies. For example, the Criminal Procedure Code, the Police Acts, and notably the Delhi Special Police Establishment Act of 1946, the CBI's parent Act, place all investigation under the control of the executive government, and the standard view taken so far was that the government's supervision includes operational interference as well. Such a view had even found favour with the judiciary. For example, this was supported by Justice Desai in the Tata case in 1980, and by Justice Mukharji in the West Bengal Boys case in 1985.

Third, even in the few cases which end up being investigated, there is wilful sabotage of the investigation process. There is no mechanism to monitor the investigation process by a non-partisan, professional body like the Director of Prosecutions in the United Kingdom or the Special Independent Council in the United States.

Fourth, the final decision to proceed against the corrupt civil servant criminally or punish him departmentally, rests with the executive government. Even the autonomous anti-corruption bodies like the Lok Ayukta headed by individuals with judicial background, can only recommend prosecution or departmental action for the consideration of the executive government. And in such cases, the collusive network ensures that the decision goes in favour of the corrupt civil servant.

Fifth, the procedural snarls involved in the proceedings are just too many. For example, there are twelve stages in a departmental action. These stages start with the preparation of a definite chargesheet and end with the imposition of a penalty. The numerous stages are procedurally necessary because of the constitutional safeguards guaranteed to a civil servant. In fact, the safeguards provided to a civil servant in India are more demanding than in most other countries. The constitutional safeguards have generally worked in favour of the corrupt.

On the whole, the internal control system in India, impressive as it is on paper, has not worked. This is essentially because the persons responsible for making the system work are a part of the elaborate sharing mechanism. There is a proverb in Bengali that neatly paraphrases the current health of the internal control system in India. 'If there are ghosts in the mustard seeds, how will the same mustard seeds exorcise the ghosts?'

## EXTERNAL CONTROL SYSTEM

The external control system, as discussed in Chapter 1, acts as a formal mechanism of restraint, and in an administration that provides for separation of powers, checks and balances are exercised by other branches of the government. In India, an external control system is fully in place—it consists of an external audit and an independent judiciary.

### AUDIT

There is a system of audit, represented by the Comptroller and Auditor General (CAG). The CAG is an independent authority created by the Constitution of India. The independence of audit is assured by providing it protection and privileges under the provisions of the Constitution. Its independence is further reinforced by enumerating the powers of the audit in a legislative enactment—the Comptroller and Auditor General of India (Duties, Powers and the Conditions of Service) Act, 1971.

The functions of audit in India are very comprehensive. They consist of audit of all government expenditure incurred from the revenues of the central government and the state governments, audit of stores and stocks, audit of all receipts, audit of appropriation to ensure that government grants are spent for the purpose for which they are provided, audit of classification, administrative audit to ensure that expenditure is supported by requisite administrative authority, audit of propriety to find out improper exercise of discretion and comment on the propriety of sanctions and expenditure, audit of efficiency to ascertain whether the expenditure has achieved the expected results, and audit of accountancy to detect fraud, technical errors and errors of principle in expenditure. The audit by the Comptroller and Auditor General covers public enterprises and autonomous organizations of the central government and the state governments.

Article 151 of the Constitution enjoins the CAG to present audit reports to the President of India and the governors of the states, who lay them before the parliament and the state legislatures respectively. Audit reports are discussed by the public accounts committees of the legislatures, and the discussion include examination of witnesses from the executive. A final report is prepared including action items, and presented to the legislatures.

Chapter 1 had discussed the conditions under which an audit can be effective in tackling corruption. First, audit should be independent of the executive and external to it. An independent and external audit assures expenditure control by exposures and sanctions against corruption. As we have seen, the CAG is independent of the executive and external to it. It has also been given the power, the means, and the resources to scrutinize corrupt practices by civil servants and recommend action.

Second, there should be mechanisms to act on the observations of the audit. In India such mechanisms exist, but in practice, the executive in India has been reluctant to act on the observations of the audit to such an extent that the Fifth Pay Commission was driven to observe,

Government departments have also to develop a high degree of sensitivity to comments by the audit. The approach should not be to close ranks and rush to the defence of the delinquent official. The systematic defects should be removed at once and individual lapses punished with utmost expedition.[21]

Third, no significant lag should be caused between acts of corruption and their exposure in the audit; that is, the audit and action on it should be quick so that erring civil servants are brought to book on the basis of the audit reports well in time. But because of delays in audit and the slow process involved in the consideration of the audit reports by public accounts committees, the impact of audit as an effective instrument of restraint has been only marginal. In fact, as is the common experience, audit reports relate to transactions which are several years old. During the intervening years, it is very likely that civil servants who were involved in questionable practices might have been transferred to other departments, or even worse, might have retired from government service, or even died.

In fairness, the audit does create an impact, but only marginally. For example, the report of the CAG highlighted the Bofors deal, and in that sense, the report of the CAG did a great deal of agenda-setting for a national debate on corruption in high places. But in most cases, the time-lag between the actual act of corruption and reporting about it in audit, is so big that corrupt practices are rarely exposed in time.

The Fifth Pay Commission highlighted this aspect, and it recommended that in order to cut down on the time-lag, audit should be concurrent. In the words of the commission,

Audit should try to be as concurrent as possible. Scandals and scams are known even while they are being planned and executed. If audit draws attention to them forthwith in a well-publicised manner, such scandals can be halted in mid-stride. Post-mortems are useful but can only be conducted while the patient is dead. It is better to cure the patient and try to keep him alive.[22]

THE JUDICIARY

The other external control system, namely an independent judiciary also exists in India. The judiciary in India is called upon to act as an important instrument of restraint, because both the Indian Penal Code and the Prevention of Corruption Act make corrupt practices punishable in a court of law. The judiciary in India is independent—it is independent of the executive.

The judiciary, although independent, has not been able to act as an effective instrument of restraint. There are several reasons. First, not many corruption cases are brought before the courts for trial. This is because of the fact that the power of sanctioning prosecution in corruption cases rests with the executive, and as we have seen, the number of cases that have been sanctioned for prosecution, have been only few and far between.

Second, the prosecutorial system as laid down in the Indian laws and followed in corruption cases, is weak and unprofessional. It has been difficult to obtain evidence, particularly of the kind required under the acts, to prove corruption and obtain conviction.

Third, long delays in obtaining a decision from the courts in corruption cases have been a significant barrier. It is not uncommon to see a corrupt civil servant being convicted long after the crime, and in most cases, only after the civil servant has retired. In other words, there is no judicial effectiveness, and the judiciary in India seems to be incapable of expeditiously disposing off corruption cases.

The number of corruption cases pending before the courts were 1362 in 1972 while in 1992, the number had mounted to 4148. Of these cases, as many as 3000 had been pending for over four years, and some, for over 15 to 20 years.[23] As the Report of the Strategic Management Group points out,

The issue of corruption is also linked to this, as it is extremely difficult to dislodge a civil servant on the grounds of corruption unless the charges are framed and established after going through an elaborate procedure which involves years of trial and litigation.[24]

As a result, only a small minority of civil servants finally get convicted in corruption cases, and that too, after a substantial time-lag. For example, the number of cases prosecuted in courts by the CBI was 384 in 1972, and the number of civil servants convicted was 194. In 1992, the number of cases prosecuted in court was 505, and the number of civil servants convicted was only 85. Interestingly, the percentage of conviction in court declined from 85 to 69 per cent during these twenty years. Cases of civil servants charged with disproportionate assets numbered 89 in 1972 and 57 in 1992, and the number of cases that resulted in conviction was 33 in 1972 and 26 in 1992.

As if to compound matters, the safeguards and procedures prescribed under Article 311 have been so interpreted by the courts in India as if to ensure, unintentionally of course, that the cases go in favour of the corrupt on technical grounds. In fact, as the Santhanam Committee on Prevention of Corruption wryly remarked, 'Article 311 of the Constitution as interpreted by our courts has made it very difficult to deal effectively with corrupt civil servants'.[25] Even after Article 311 was amended, the panoply of safeguards and procedures still available is interpreted in such a manner as to make the proceedings protracted, and therefore, effete in the ultimate analysis.

There is no gainsaying that the provisions of Article 311 have come in the way of bringing the corrupt civil servants to book. The Fifth Pay Commission was driven to observe,

Government could take legal advice as to whether the provisions of Article 311 can be diluted with reference to employees who have either been caught red-handed under the Prevention of Corruption Act or who have been found after due investigation to be in possession of assets disproportionate to their known sources of income. In such cases, suspension could be mandatory.[26]

Of late, there has been a refreshing change. The interpretation of the law by the Supreme Court of India, and following this example, by a few high courts, particularly in corruption-related public interest litigation cases, has been extremely liberal. Public interest litigation have been filed before these courts by concerned citizens, and the subject-matter of many of these public interest litigations has been corruption.

The Supreme Court, through a liberal interpreting of Article 142 of the Indian Constitution (which authorizes the Supreme Court to enforce decrees and orders that it considers necessary for doing 'complete justice in any cause or matter pending before it'), has succeeded in giving a positive direction to corruption cases involving people in high places. Judges of the Supreme Court have gone to the extent of personally supervising the process of investigation if only to ensure that the investigation is not endlessly stonewalled by the investigating agencies at the behest of influential persons.

The proactive stand of the Supreme Court of India has created the desired impact, but, this, even at its best, can only provide a lead. Most corruption cases, however, have to be brought before the ordinary courts as required under the provisions of the Prevention of Corruption Act. So, if the judiciary has to act as an effective instrument of restraint, the necessary burden has to be borne by the entire judicial system, and not merely by the Supreme Court of India.

The point needs to be clarified in the context of the varieties of official corruption which exist in India. Official corruption can, very broadly, be divided into two general categories. One is the corruption of scams, as in the case of large contracts and big favours at the higher levels of the government. This normally involves politicians directly. It is in respect of scams that the

Supreme Court of India has been successful in taking an activist stand.

The other variety is the retail corruption. This is extortionary corruption which touches the lives of most citizens in the country. Retail corruption is more widespread—the Public Affairs Centre's recent studies provide evidence on the extent of retail corruption in India. According to these studies, every fourth person in Chennai ends up paying a bribe in dealing with agencies such as the urban development authority, electricity board, municipal corporation and telephones, while in Bangalore, it is one in eight persons, and in Pune, one in seventeen persons. Clearly, retail corruption is widespread and deserves to be addressed with the same degree of seriousness as scams, if not more, because it touches the lives of citizens in myriad extortionary ways.[27]

For the judiciary to act as an effective instrument of restraint, four conditions should be met. The four conditions are: judicial independence, judicial enforcement, free access to the judiciary, and judicial effectiveness. The judiciary in India is independent. There is judicial enforcement—the judiciary in India is capable of enforcing its decisions. There is access to the judiciary. But in respect of the most important condition, the judiciary in India has been remiss: there is no organizational efficiency in the judiciary in disposing off cases without soft, long delays.

## SOCIAL CONTROL

A strong and vigilant civil society can be a check on corruption and form the basis for countervailing action. Corrupt states abound in anti-corruption bodies and watchdog organizations which eventually end up concealing and protecting corruption instead of punishing it, because no one outside the state structure is in a position to demand accountability if the results are unsatisfactory. Even the most comprehensive set of formal democratic institutions may not be in a position to produce the needed accountability in the absence of a strong and vigilant civil society to energize them.

For the civil society to act as a check on corruption and form the basis for countervailing action, two core conditions have to be met. First, the community should have social capital—informal rules, norms and long-term relationships which facilitate coordinated action and enable people to undertake cooperative ventures for mutual advantage. The presence of social capital can improve the collective efficiency of the community. Second, there should be a widely-shared popular conception of right and wrong by which civil servants need to be judged.

A caveat is in order at this stage. As Sunil Khilnani observes,[28] the relationship of state and society in India, at least historically, has been an uneasy one. The state in India has been, for the most part, external to the society. It has not touched the lives of its citizens as deeply as it did in other social formations. Society in India has made its own laws. It has also enforced its laws and interpreted them, and even more importantly, society has laid down the vision of a moral order—a vision which can be achieved only by following the laws that society has made, enforced, and interpreted.

The state has been external to the society not merely because it was denied a role in the making and enforcing of the societal laws, but also because it had no role in the conception and realization of that moral order. The state has been given no voice in things which have mattered—in changing the belief system or in altering economic relations.

Since the state was not given the capacity over or the responsibility for society, rulers in India have represented only themselves, and not society or the people. It is also accepted in India that state exists only to extract rent, and that rent is to be used for the personal aggrandizement of those who man the state apparatus. In other words, the society in India has not generally questioned how the resources of the state are deployed, and it has been left to those who man the state to expend the resources of the state in any manner they like.

Things have not changed all that much in modern, democratic India. Although a full set of formal democratic institutions is now in place, and people are called upon to participate in periodic elections to elect a government to power, the hiatus between state and society continues to divide, and society's access to look into how the state functions, exists only in borrowed theory. So we have a piquant situation in which a full set of democratic institutions has not been able to produce accountability, because civil society in India has not energized these democratic institutions.

As far as civil society is concerned, the hangover of old attitudes and inhibitions continues to persist. This has been in two ways. First, civil society in India is not too keen to look into the actual processes of the state, reinforcing in the process as it were, the view of state functionaries that the operations of the state are in the nature of a black box. Second, there is a shared belief—an inheritance from the past, once again—that it is perfectly alright for those occupying public offices to use the state, its structure, and resources, in a manner that they choose i.e., in furtherance of their private interest.

Does it mean that our social capital is weak? We have any number of horizontal associations in India, but they are all organized along the lines of caste, religion or ethnicity. We also have associations organized on the lines of trade and profession. But these horizontal associations, organized along lines of caste, ethnicity, religion, trade or profession, have fought shy of tackling corruption. Anti-corruption efforts by these associations have been conspicuous only by their absence.

The main dimension, of course, is that the civil society in India does not share a common vision or values so far as corruption is concerned. It has not developed strong and legitimate norms about what is right and wrong, and as a result, it is not in a position to promulgate codes of good practice. Since there is no widely-shared popular conception of right and wrong, which can be used as a benchmark to judge the behaviour of civil servants, there has been no judgement at all. This perhaps explains the fact that although quite a few groups are working in the area of civil liberties and human rights, there are not many groups working in the area of fighting corruption. H.D. Shouri of Common Cause has put up a brave but solitary fight, mainly through the courts, against corruption. The only other group—Samuel Paul's Public Affairs Centre in Bangalore—is better known abroad than in India.[29]

There have been instances of citizens organizing themselves and imposing modest anti-corruption sanctions. For example, some years ago, the villagers in remote villages in Rajasthan organized themselves and were able to impose anti-corruption sanctions against corrupt village-level government functionaries.

Oldenburg cites the instance of beneficiaries coming together to fight corruption in the process of land consolidation in Uttar Pradesh in the 1980s.[30] But the instances of citizens organizing themselves and imposing anti-corruption sanctions are so few and far between that they become newsworthy.

## INFORMATION

Information about the government is a precondition for any meaningful anti-corruption effort by civil society. In India, a citizen is entitled to have access to government information only if he can satisfy the authorities that his life is affected by such information.

India has a very comprehensive Official Secrets Act. Like most of our other vital enactments, it was enacted by the British government. Britain passed its Official Secrets Act in 1889. The Indian Official Secrets Act was passed in the same year by the Imperial Legislative Assembly. In 1911, British parliament passed the Official Secrets Act, and some amendments were introduced later in the light of the experience gained during World War I. The Indian Official Secrets Act, 1923 is a replica of the British Act of 1911 as amended in 1920. The Indian Official Secrets Act, 1923 continues to be in force even today.[31]

The provisions of Section 5 of the Act are so comprehensive that almost all information about the government can qualify to be classified as an official secret.[32] Sir Hari Singh Gour made a telling point when he told the Legislative Assembly,

Your provisions are so wide that you will have no difficulty whatever in running in anybody who peeps into an office for the purpose of making some, it may be entirely innocent, enquiry as to when there is going to be the next meeting of the Assembly or whether a certain report on the Census of India has come out and what is the population of India recorded in that period.[33]

To make matters worse, nowhere have the words 'secret' or 'official secret' been defined precisely in the Act. In terms of the provisions of Section 5, any kind of information can attract prosecution under the provisions of the Act, whatever the purpose or impact. Communication of information to the members of public does not constitute an exception.

There have been repeated demands for amending the Act, but such demands have gone unheeded. This is all the more disquieting because the provisions of the parent British Official Secrets Act of 1911 have been amended comprehensively in 1988 to enable free flow of information to the members of the public.

All civil servants in India fervently swear by the provisions of the Official Secrets Act. Public bureaucracies have traditionally been closed shops—their stranglehold over information and refusal to part with it, has been, in a true sense, the real source of their power. Such bureaucratic self-enclosure is usually sustained under the rubric of security and confidentiality, but in the hands of the Indian civil servants, such self-enclosure has been made into a veritable art form.[34]

Civil servants in India can be exasperatingly sticky about following the provisions of the Official Secrets Act, both in letter and spirit. Even minor deviations are not easily tolerated. A recent occurrence is an example. In October 1998, Ram Jethmalani, the then Union Minister for Urban Affairs, decided to give members of the public access to the files of his ministry on demand and payment of a token fee. It was a well-publicized move and widely reported in the media. Civil servants, however, did not take kindly to the move on the ground that it was violative of the provisions of the Official Secrets Act. Ultimately, the Cabinet Secretary put on hold Jethmalani's initiative, and the age-old confidentiality of government information has now been happily restored.

The Official Secrets Act is a convenient smokescreen to deny members of the public access to government information. The bottom line is that knowledge is power, and therefore, the Official Secrets Act is a handy weapon in the hands of civil servants to hold on to as much of it close to their chest as possible. It has the blessings of ruling politicians who, in any case, would scarcely wish to account for their dubious decisions.[35]

Whatever may be the provocation, the government in India has been particularly parsimonious in the matter of making information available to the public. Even in cases where a citizen is entitled to information under the current laws because his life is affected by such information, it is a tortuous process to get the information although one pays for it. There are the usual long delays, and the citizen is subjected to customary caprices of the government functionaries. At the lower levels of the government, officials part with information only in exchange for a bribe, and that too, in cases where the person seeking information is entitled to it. It is not surprising, therefore, that when *jan sunway*is in Ajmer, Pali, and Rajasmand districts in Rajasthan demanded access to information from the local government on public works, it created quite a stir.

Statutes and rules get to be published in the Official Gazette only to satisfy requirement, but not enough copies are printed, and it requires superhuman effort and sizable bribes for members of the public to get hold of them. The proceedings of the legislative bodies and details of the revenue collections of the government are not made available to the members of the public easily. Accurate documents about the basic operations of the government are not published, and therefore, information about government is effectively outside the reach of the members of the public.

As regards making information available to people, the practice in India contrasts very sharply with the position in other countries. For example, Canada has an Access to Information Act which gives all Canadian citizens the right to have access to Federal government records which are not of a personal nature. The Canadian government has taken steps to ensure that information about the activities of the government is broadly available to the citizens, with exceptions being limited and narrowly defined, and provisions for resolving any disputes over the application of such exceptions independently of the government. An Information Commissioner has been appointed to investigate complaints from the members of the public arising from the provisions of the Access to Information Act.

In the United Kingdom, several amendments were effected in 1988 to the provisions of the Official Secrets Act of 1911 to narrow the scope of official information falling within the ambit of the Act, and thus made possible much greater volume of official information available to members of the public. In addition, a White Paper guaranteeing a statutory right of access to personal records held by the government has been implemented in April 1994. The Citizen's Charter contains a number of specific provisions for promoting increased openness about reasons for decisions taken by the government.

The Freedom of Information Act in the United States and similar measures in a number of European countries have been specifically enacted to increase the flow of official information to members of the public, and in that sense, to supplement the process of effective overseeing of governmental processes by civil society. The important thing about such freedom of information laws is that they enable citizens to obtain government information without having to prove that their lives are affected by such information. In addition, steps have been taken by most countries to ensure that information about the activities of the government is broadly available to the members of the public.

There is no comparable system in India which assures freedom of information to the citizens. Under the existing dispensation, a citizen has to prove that the information which he requires from the government, affects his life. There have been suggestions from several quarters that India should enact a Freedom of Information Act, and take steps for dissemination of information about the government to the members of the public.

## CITIZENS' VOICE

The citizens' voice can be used to expose, denounce, and restrain corrupt behaviour of civil servants. It has been done in other countries with spectacular results. Japan is a good example. Social disapproval has been the principal means of regulating civil service behaviour in Japan.

Social disapproval in Japan is expressed in several ways. One is social shaming. The other is political embarrassment, and as most Japanese civil servants admit, political embarrassment can be a very effective way of regulating official conduct.

Social disapproval has been particularly effective as an instrument of restraint in Japan in the context of its hierarchical public bureaucracy. Senior civil servants in Japan are held accountable for the acts of omission and commission of their subordinates. Social disapproval in Japan is as much directed at the corrupt civil servant as at the senior civil servants supervising his work. So, when corruption is exposed in the courts, the media, or the Diet, the impact of the exposure is felt throughout, as senior civil servants of the department including the minister in charge, suffer the social consequences of the resulting public disapproval. In cases where social disapproval is particularly trenchant, the shamed civil servant chooses to take his life, unable to bear the social disgrace.

Social disapproval has been effective in regulating civil service behaviour in Japan largely because the civil servants see themselves as guardians of public interest.[36] The civil service in Japan is extremely proud of its image as the guardian of public interest. It is in this context that society's approval and endorsement of their behaviour become so critically important to civil servants.

How important such an image is to the civil servants in Japan, is evident from the way civil servants respond to pronouncements of the Japanese courts. In general, the judiciary in Japan has been reluctant to sit in judgement over administrative actions of civil servants. This is because restrictive doctrines derived from German administrative law continue to dominate the interpretation of the judiciary's authority to adjudicate direct appeals from formal administrative actions of civil servants.[37]

Limited judicial relief from the administrative actions of civil servants is available by way of private damage action under the National Compensation Law of 1947. The relief is very limited: the National Compensation Law only provides for after-the-fact compensatory damages, and even then, the law does not empower the courts to take preventive measures or order civil servants to act in a particular manner. But within the context in which the Japanese civil servants see themselves as guardians of public interest, the mere threat of judicial condemnation brings about social disgrace, and to that extent, even the limited judicial relief provided under the National Compensation Law has the wholesome effect of disciplining civil service behaviour.

In that sense, any judicial action or even the threat of such an action is considered disgraceful, because it undermines the image of civil servants as guardians of public interest. Litigation, under the circumstances, becomes more important as a catalyst for social penalty rather than the process through which the formal, legal remedy is obtained.

Japan has succeeded in creating and sustaining a bureaucratic culture in the context of which social disapproval of civil service behaviour has played a desirable role as an instrument of restraint. Such a bureaucratic culture has evolved because civil servants themselves have valued the opinion of society greatly.

But it is also important to note that such a bureaucratic culture is the result of the process of state–society integration in Japan, an on-going process since at least the time of the Meiji Restoration. The institutional and legal framework of the Japanese civil service has been the product of such a process of integration—a process in which the voice of the key stakeholders of Japanese society has been embedded in transparent, consultative ways of public decision-making.

The lack of coercive powers of civil servants is an example. The institutional and legal framework of the Japanese civil service allows very little coercive powers to the Japanese civil servant in the matter of implementation of public policy. Although responsibilities given to civil servants are broad and comprehensive, they are not accompanied by matching coercive powers, and therefore, the responsibilities of civil servants are merely promotional in nature. Typically, civil servants in Japan are granted broad mandates to supervise and issue directions, but they lack legal powers to issue sanctions in case there is failure to comply with the directions.

Such a situation, one that Haley describes as 'broad mandates with limited powers of enforcement'[38] has interesting ramifications. The statutory mandate of responsibility which is given to Japanese civil servants is truly enormous. Civil servants, in a succession of legislative enactments, have been made responsible for activities as broad and diverse as the performance of the private sector, adequate levels of growth in the economy, efficient allocation of resources, and promotion of strategic industries. In other words, civil servants have been given responsibility for the success of many of the tasks which are carried out in the private sector, but without the powers to compel anybody to move in a particular direction.

The Ministry of International Trade and Industry (MITI) is an example. MITI was given the responsibility 'to adjust' energy supply in the context of national energy policy, but such responsibility did not include coercive powers to regulate energy prices or to allocate output. In other words, MITI was given the responsibility to adjust energy supply, but minus any powers to enforce its decisions in the matter.[39]

This is also the case with all ministries and agencies in Japan. The statutes outlining the responsibilities of civil servants give them no formal power in the matter of enforcement. In fact, if the broad mandates of Japanese civil servants had been matched with commensurate coercive powers of enforcement, the public bureaucracy in Japan would have been a command and control bureaucracy.

The combination of broad mandates with limited powers of enforcement has led to substantial administrative weakness, and an appreciation of such a weakness is the key to one's understanding how state–society integration takes place in Japan. In the absence of powers of enforcement, civil servants are forced to negotiate the consent of the concerned parties; that is, the system requires that the consent of the parties affected by the operation of a particular public policy should be negotiated before the policy can be enforced.

The process of negotiating the consent of the parties in the matter of formulating and implementing public policy has moved the Japanese civil service away from degenerating into a command and control bureaucracy. More wholesomely, it has moved the behaviour of civil servants away from corruption; the absence of formal, coercive powers combined with the compulsion of negotiating the consent of those regulated to the regulation itself, has ensured that bureaucratic discretion is not used for seeking bribes.

The combination of broad mandates with limited powers of enforcement has also led to the creation of institutions connecting the civil service to civil society. Compelled to negotiate the consent of the regulated to the regulation, civil servants have sought to maintain a close working relationship with key stakeholders in civil society for whose performance they have been made responsible, and in the process, build the credibility necessary to negotiate consent and enlist voluntary compliance of governmental measures. This has resulted in the creation of 'nodes of policy network' in the civil society, that is, institutions connecting the civil service and civil society.[40]

What is important, however, is whether these nodes are embedded in the policy network in transparent, consultative processes. In order that these organizations in civil society become institutions connecting state and society, it is essential that civil servants, while framing and implementing public policies, should have transparent links to stakeholders in civil society for feedback and accountability.[41]

Japan has institutionalized civil service–private sector collaboration through the establishment of deliberation councils. Deliberation councils are formal organizations and are established by ministries in the government. The deliberation councils are generally associated with a specific bureau within the establishing ministry. The councils are of two types. One is organized along functional or thematic lines, such as pollution or finance; and the second type is organized according to industry, for example, automobile or chemicals.

According to a survey undertaken by Nikkei Business in September 1994, there are 215 deliberation councils, involving some 4700 persons serving on these councils.[42] Some of the important ones are the Economic Reconstruction Planning Council (consisting of 377 members), the Industrial Rationalization Deliberation Council, the Economic Council, and the Administrative Reform Council. Almost all the ministries have deliberation councils. For example, the Ministry of Agriculture, Forestry and Fisheries has about twenty deliberation councils. There are thirty-three deliberation councils in MITI alone, including the Industrial Structure Council, the largest and the most famous, which consists of several divisions such as the Iron Division and the Chemical Industry Division.

The deliberation council provides the forum for the civil servants and stakeholders of civil society—business, labour, consumers, academia, and press—to discuss current trends, exchange information and more importantly, evolve blueprints for public policy through mutual, transparent consultations. Consensus is encouraged. The background material for deliberation on a proposed policy is prepared by the research group of the concerned ministry and placed before the council. On the basis of the discussions in the deliberation council, a report on the proposed policy is prepared and released to the public to explain the objectives of the new policy. In cases where the policy blueprint has been deliberated in the council, the Diet routinely approves the policy proposal.

The merits of such a public–private deliberation mechanism are obviously many, but what is important is that the repeated game feature of the deliberations in the council creates incentives for participants to work together. In that case, the deliberation council works as a credible commitment mechanism. In other words, corruption by civil servants is more or less constrained by the repeated nature of the collaboration. Because the rules are effectively established within the council by a transparent and collaborative process, every participant including the civil servant knows that the rules cannot be changed arbitrarily, and there will be no cheating and reneging.

The position in India is very different. There has been no attempt to develop a bureaucratic culture which is responsive to the opinion of civil society. Worse still, India has succeeded in creating and sustaining a culture, enduring it would seem, which is inhospitable to the evolution of any 'nodes of policy network'. To top it all, the institutional and legal framework of the civil service in India has been such as to effectively preclude any consultative, transparent link with stakeholders of civil society.

The institutional and legal framework of the civil service has clothed civil servants in India with a comprehensive array of formal, coercive powers. The coercive powers have been so comprehensive that civil servants, armed with them, have been in a position to control almost all aspects of human endeavour, and no interlocutor in civil society has been free from such control.

In the context of such an institutional and legal framework, public policies that require extensive direct compulsion have been encouraged, with the result that civil servants have not found it necessary to negotiate the consent of the regulated to the regulation. Consequently, a process of negotiating the consent of the parties and the resulting collaboration of the civil service with the stakeholders in civil society has not evolved in India.

In any case, the process of policy formulation in India is a closed and intransparent activity. The process does not contemplate any consultation with stakeholders in civil society. This has meant that stakeholders are in a position to influence the process only at the stage of policy implementation, and that too, by paying huge bribes to civil servants. It is as if the processes of policy formulation and implementation in India are expressly designed to provide limitless opportunities for corruption.

Because the policy-making process is so closed and opaque, a system of public–private consultation has not evolved. Although there are a large number of associations and community groups in India in critical areas which have the potential for being used as 'nodes of policy network' and thus, providing the locus for state–society integration. But these associations and community groups have not been associated with governmental processes in any informal or institutional ways of consultation.

This does not mean that there is no collaboration at all between civil servants and stakeholders in the private sector; what is suggested is that the kind of collaboration which exists in India between civil servants and the stakeholders in the private sector, is not institutional or systemic. For example, a great deal of collaboration takes place between individual civil servants and individual industrialists. There have been several instances in which top industrialists have managed to instal their favourite civil servants—their nominees and understandably, faithful protectors of their individualized interests—in top slots in the ministries of the government.

Such collaboration as it exists in India between individual civil servants and individual industrialists, can be characterized by way of what Cardoso and Falletto call the 'bureaucratic rings'[43]— only a few civil servants may be privately connected to a few individual industrialists. But the personalized nature of such a relationship in India contrasts sharply from the institutional ties in Japan which have discouraged corruption. On the contrary, the very personalized character of the individual relationship, as it exists in India, lends itself admirably to corrupt practices.[44]

On the whole, public bureaucracy in India has succeeded in creating and nurturing a culture which encourages the civil servants to distance themselves from civil society. In fact, it has been a continuing exercise, historically blessed it would seem, in maintaining an arms-length culture—in typical civil service vocabulary, it takes on the contours of 'us' and 'them', and the boundaries are very zealously protected. As a result, the institutional and legal framework of the civil service has not exactly encouraged the process of state–society integration. Small wonder, then, that the public bureaucracy in India is a command and control bureaucracy which governs only by issuing orders.

As if to oblige the civil service, civil society, on its part, has not been too keen on getting involved. Neither has it evinced any interest in taking a stand on corruption. Rather, there is a high degree of social acceptance of corruption. There is no mistaking the fact that civil society in India has capitulated to corruption; in fact, the capitulation has been so total that some chief ministers have advised people to pay bribes and get their work done.[45]

Interestingly, there is no social stigma attached to corruption. Corrupt civil servants are not subject to social shaming as in Japan. On the contrary, corrupt civil servants, because of the wealth they accumulate, have become social role models, and most others, not so fortunate because of lack of opportunity, have desperately wanted to emulate them. It is in this context that Kaushik Basu, the economist, talks of the sanskritization of corruption, a process currently fashionable in India—corruption gets sanskritized when others start becoming corrupt because it is a badge of belonging to the elite class.

Social acceptance of corruption in India is evident from the way the term bribe is denoted colloquially in day-to-day parlance. The word commonly used for bribes, particularly in the area of retail corruption, is *Chai-Pani*. In India, practically in every area of interaction between the members of the public and the government, Chai-Pani becomes as important as the actual cup that cheers or the glass that quenches.[46]

The use of the word Chai-Pani to denote petty bribes is significant. It evokes the image of a kind of subsidy by the society to support the life-style of a civil servant who gets paid poorly. There is no stigma attached to Chai-Pani. Although the process involves paying and taking a bribe, it is done quite openly—there is not even an attempt to hide it. In fact, the way it is done, the bribes almost take on the contours of an entitlement, and they are acknowledged as such both by the giver and the taker. Social acceptance of corruption could not have been more complete.

Social acceptance of corruption is also evident from the way a civil servant is adjudged as a potential bridegroom in the arranged marriage market. A civil servant who works in a department in which there are greater opportunities for corruption, is considered more eligible and merits a higher dowry. The bride's side normally uses a ready reckoner for the purpose of evaluating the worth of the bridegroom—the computation being what the bridegroom gets as legitimate salary from the government and the estimated amount he can extract as bribes by using his public office. As the Report of the Strategic Management

Group points out, 'It is an open secret that there is an unwritten schedule for dowry levels for officers of different Group A Services in the marriage market.'[47]

Another indicator of the social acceptance of corruption is the fact that corruption is not even considered newsworthy unless it concerns new, innovative ways of making money or involves people in high places. As Kuldip Nayar, a veteran journalist, says:

The fact is that corruption has ceased to be news in India. Nor does it make people sit up. It is one of those things India cannot live with but knows no way to live without. These past few years, the country has been a land of scams and scandals: political chicanery, diary entries, defence weapon kickbacks and mysterious bank accounts. Leaving aside two or three state chief ministers, the rest have fingers in the till.[48]

In general, there is a high degree of social acceptance of corruption. There are several explanations for this. First, paying bribe works. Bribes serve several purposes in India. They act as an incentive bonus. They lower costs for those who pay them. They clear the market. They can facilitate bending of rules and seeking exceptions to the generalized prescriptions. In other words, bribes can override legal norms. On the whole, paying bribes gets one's work done.

Second, policy-making in India is a closed activity. An overwhelmingly large part of the population is excluded from it even though the resultant policy has direct impact on their lives. It is only during the process of its implementation that the people get an opportunity to access civil servants in charge of implementation and get their work done—by paying bribes, of course. In that sense, paying bribes and getting their work done is a kind of surrogate participation in the working of the government, a participation which is otherwise denied to them because of the closed nature of government processes.

Third, allocation of government resources, as it happens in India, is an interaction between favour-seeking individuals and rent-seeking civil servants. The only way citizens can get access to what government has to offer is by paying bribes. Citizens do not have access to what the government has to offer because they lack information. This is what Dhrubjyoti Bhaumik calls the process of mystification, a process in which civil servants withhold information, even the information which citizens have a right to know. Information and the consequential access to what government has to offer, can only be bought by paying bribes.

But above all else, there is the widely-shared impression about the inevitability of corruption—that there is no option to corruption. Since official corruption is sanctioned by politicians in India, concerted corruption has closed off people's alternatives, giving the entire administration a more corrupt leverage. The institutional monopolies of services by the government have resulted in a shortage of economic alternatives, and such a shortage has meant that people have to deal with corrupt civil servants and satisfy them, if they have to get any service from the government at all. Under the circumstances, people see corruption as inevitable, and in that sense, the social acceptance of corruption in India is merely an expression of social capitulation.

## POLITICS AND CONTROL SYSTEMS

Politicians in power can weaken the control systems in two ways. First, by making the public bureaucracy the instrument by which they extract rent. Second, by layering in the public bureaucracy with loyalist civil servants.

In India, politicians in power have weakened the control systems in both the ways. First, the public bureaucracy has been used as the instrument by which ruling politicians have extracted rent from the clients of the civil service both to buy political support and enrich themselves. Second, politicians have layered in the bureaucracy with loyalist civil servants and have created a patronage system in which public office has been used as a form of currency, and the loyalty of civil servants has been exchanged for parcels of patronage or privileges of public office.

Both these aspects—using the bureaucracy as an instrument for seeking rent, and layering in the bureaucracy with loyalist officers—has been artfully blended into a single, efficient system in India. Robert Wade has shown how exactly this is done in his study of canal irrigation in India. The transfer of the civil servants has been the politician's basic weapon of control over the bureaucracy, and thus, the lever for surplus-extraction from clients of the bureaucracy. There is a special circuit of transactions in which civil servants extract money from contractors, pass a

portion to MLAs, and especially the ministers, who, in turn, use
the funds for distributing short-term material inducements in exchange for electoral support.[49]

What Wade describes with reference to the Irrigation Department, happens with all other departments in India. The Police
Department is an example. The Indian Police Service Officers Association of Karnataka complained to the Rebeiro Committee on
Police Reforms against 'constant political interference in transfers
and postings' in the state. The memorandum submitted by the
association went on to add:

Politicians and influential persons have hijacked the system to their advantage and rendered it helpless . . . . It is true that many times transfers
are made on caste lines and most cases for monetary considerations.
Elected representatives develop some kind of a contract, fixing the
amount to be paid for the officer to remain in a post for a particular
period.

The result, the memorandum states, has been, 'devastating
corruption of a serious nature'.[50] It is the politician's power to
transfer civil servants from one post to another which has
enabled politicians to use the public bureaucracy as a vehicle to
extract rent from the system.

While describing how the ill-gotten money is spent, Wade was
being charitable to politicians. Politicians in India have used the
money not merely to meet the cost of electoral competition, but
also to enrich themselves. In fact, if the priorities of Indian
politicians is anything to go by, using the money to enrich themselves has a much higher priority than meeting the costs of
electoral competition. In any case, the take is so substantial that
it can be used to fund both activities optimally.

Civil servants have also benefitted enormously. The system
has enabled them to share the bribe, and still retain a sizable part
of it for themselves. The system has the added merit that it has
helped the civil servant to buy immunity from the control systems by sharing the bribe. The sharing mechanism has made sure
that the probability of detection is almost non-existent. In effect,
the sharing mechanism has produced an enviable degree of system coordination which has facilitated a trouble-free vertical
exchange of the proceeds, and collusive behaviour all around.

The corruption network in India is so perfectly orchestrated that there is a thriving internal economy linking principals and agents. The principals (ruling politicians) provide the opportunity and protection, while the agents (civil servants) pay for their spoils by sharing the bribe. The corruption network with its experienced operatives resembles a well-oiled, well-coordinated collection machine which is organized almost professionally, and like any professional organization, it is focused on what it does.

The client in India who consumes the services that civil servants provide, has absolutely no relief from the corrupt network. Concerted corruption has closed off all his political, economic and bureaucratic alternatives. This has given the administration all the leverage it needs for its predation. The administration in India has, in fact, created an efficient network of operatives sharing not only the bribes but also the risks. All the actors involved—ministers, civil servants, anti-corruption functionaries— have a stake in protecting corruption and increasing its proceeds, and also, in freezing out the critics of corruption.

Not that there are many critics to worry about. Even the political opposition is very often coopted into the sharing mechanism and incorporated into the collusive network. The few critics of corruption, typically from civil society, have not been given voice, and in any case, they have found it difficult to demand accountability in the degraded environment.

Such concerted corruption as it exists in India, thrives in the syndrome of poor institutions linked to reduced growth. The prolonged slow growth in India has perpetuated the scarcity of economic alternatives, inhibiting the development of new economic activities and political interests, while continuing to preserve the dependency on corrupt civil servants and politicians.

Some commentators feel that political corruption may be the reason for bureaucratic corruption. As Kuldip Nayar says,

Corruption at political level may well be the reason why the bureaucracy is steeped in dishonesty. Clean officers, both at the Centre and in the states, can be counted on the fingers. At the lower level, corruption is so prevalent that it is difficult to spot any one who is above board.[51]

Whatever may be the cause and effect, political corruption and official corruption in India are interlinked. And the interlinked system has worked efficiently—bureaucratic rents have been coordinated and shared across both the realms, while power over the state structure has allowed politicians to preempt any anti-corruption initiative. In India, the functional distinction between bureaucratic and political corruption has all but disappeared.

Steps have been suggested from time to time to limit political corruption. These steps relate to three areas. The first is the enactment of a new legislation which will eradicate corrupt electoral practices. Since a part of the rents is deployed to meet the cost of electoral competition, proposing the idea of eradicating corrupt electoral practices makes good rhetoric.

The second is the setting up of a National Electoral Fund to provide funds to the political parties for fighting elections. It is suggested that contribution to the fund could be open to companies in the private sector and appropriate tax relief could be offered by way of incentives. The third is the enactment of the Lok Pal Bill at the earliest. The Lok Pal, it is proposed, should be provided support in the form of an investigative machinery.

It is not as if we lack legal provisions to limit corruption. The pity is that we are not even inclined to make use of the existing laws in an optimal fashion. The Representation of the People Act has enough provisions in it to take care of corrupt electoral practices. In any case, for a variety of reasons, the proposed legislation to eradicate corrupt electoral practices has not seen the light of the day.

The same is the case with the National Electoral Fund. No progress has been made in the matter of setting up the National Electoral Fund although a leading industrial house, in a particularly well-publicized move, set apart money for the non-existent fund. In any case, it is common knowledge that the bulk of the funding for the elections comes from these companies for services rendered, the only rider being that such fundings are not publicly acknowledged either by the giver or the taker.

Action on the Lok Pal Bill represents the worst kind of dithering ever imaginable. The Lok Pal Bill was introduced in the Lok Sabha in May 1968, and passed in August 1968. It was sent to the Rajya Sabha for consideration. With the premature dissolution of the Lok Sabha in December 1970, the bill lapsed. The bill was reintroduced in the Lok Sabha in April 1971, but it was not passed till 1977, when the Lok Sabha was dissolved and the bill lapsed once again. A new bill was introduced in the Lok Sabha in July 1977, but it lapsed in 1979 when the Lok Sabha was dissolved. A fresh bill was introduced in 1985, but it lapsed when the Lok Sabha was dissolved. It was reintroduced in the Lok Sabha in 1990, but it lapsed in November 1990 when the National Front Government collapsed.

EXPERIENCE OF OTHER COUNTRIES

The control systems in Singapore have not been undermined by politics. The civil service has not been used by ruling politicians as an instrument for extracting rent from the system. For that matter, politicians in Singapore have not layered in the civil service with loyalists.

On the other hand, ruling politicians in Singapore, working with a vision and singlemindedness, have, through sustained effort, transformed a civil service which was once very corrupt, to one of the world's most honest, in a matter of three decades. When it assumed office in June 1959, the PAP government had inherited a civil service which was notoriously corrupt and totally insensitive to the needs of the people. PAP leaders realized at the time of assuming power that the colonial bureaucracy they had inherited, needed to be transformed to ensure that the socio-economic development programmes of the PAP could be efficiently implemented. For the purpose, the PAP government brought about changes in the structure and functioning of the civil service.

As a result, the civil service in Singapore has changed in four important ways. It is no longer plagued by corruption, it attracts and retains the best and brightest of the country's educational system, it is lean and compact, and it is people-friendly and committed to improving the quality of services to the public. This was possible because the PAP wanted an honest and capable civil service, and not a civil service which was to be used as a vehicle for extracting rent from the system.

In Japan, politicians have refrained from using the bureaucracy as an instrument to seek rent. Neither have the politicians layered in the bureaucracy with loyalist civil servants. In that sense, the control systems in Japan have not been undermined by politicians.

This is not to suggest that politicians in Japan are paragons of virtue. On the contrary, corruption has been embarrassingly pervasive during the long rule of the Liberal Democratic Party in Japan. Corruption has been such an integral part of the functioning of the Japanese political system that scandals involving political corruption have caused the untimely exit of several political governments. Admittedly, corruption scandals have been the staple of electoral politics in Japan.

The point to note is that while the politicians in Japan have been so unfailingly corrupt, political corruption has taken place outside the civil service. In fact, the civil service has been very carefully insulated from partisan politics. Such insulation goes back to the days of the Meiji Restoration. During the Meiji period, the civil service was explicitly designed to carry out the technical aspects of the country's industrialization and modernization. The Meiji founding fathers took a conscious decision to insulate the civil service from partisan politics, so that the civil service could be used only to promote national goals—industrialization and modernization of the country. Japan's civil service was designed to minimize the kinds of patronage which permeated the civil services of the United States and parts of Western Europe at the time.[52]

But the process also demanded a commitment from the Japanese politicians that they will not use the civil service in the service of partisan politics, and that the civil service will be used only to promote national goals. For the political leaders of Meiji Japan, there was only one overriding ideology—Japan had to increase its economic capabilities as rapidly as possible in order to become a 'first-rate' nation, an industrial power capable of participating in the international political arena on equal terms with western countries.[53]

Japan's desire to become a first-rate nation remained unchanged into the period between the two world wars, and the desire to catch up with the West was no less strong in the years following World War II. Defeated and demoralized, Japan's national goal well into the 1960s was to wage a 'total war' for rapid economic recovery and growth. In that sense, rapid growth became a 'war to be won, the first total war in Japanese history for which all of the nation's resources were mobilized voluntarily'.[54] There was a national consensus in adopting pro-growth policies so that the country's economic capabilities could be increased as rapidly as possible. In other words, pro-growth goals transcended all other public and private interests.

It is important to note that the ideology of catching up with the West by pursuing a pro-growth agenda was a shared one.[55] Inherent in the sharing of the catch-up ideology was the acceptance of the premise that civil service was the agency to achieve this agenda, and that civil servants should be left free to implement it. So far as politicians were concerned, this meant a commitment that the civil service would not be used for any other purpose.[56] The insulation of the civil service in Japan from partisan politics has, by and large, continued to the present day.

## NOTES

1. The general administrative pattern which prevails in India can be traced to practices set in motion in 1756 when the President and the Council of the East India Company at Fort William transacted all their business in one general department with the help of a secretary and a handful of assistants. On the arrival of the 'packets' from England, the secretary laid them before the council for orders, and the instructions were conveyed for execution to the authorities concerned.

2. The scheme of having the chief vigilance officers and the vigilance officers was introduced in 1955, as a result of the recommendations of the Santhanam Committee. A fundamental principle projected by the committee was that the primary responsibility for maintaining integrity in a department was that of the head of the department. In other words, the preventive aspect of anti-corruption work had to be done by the head of the department and his staff. It was the considered opinion of Santhanam Committee that vigilance work should be viewed as an integral part of the responsibility of any supervisory officer at every level. See C.V. Narsimhan, 'Prevention of Corruption: Towards Effective Enforcement', in Guhan and Paul (1997), p. 264.

3. The confidential report for the Indian Administrative Service officers which has a column on integrity, prescribes the procedure to be followed while filling up the column relating to integrity. It reads,

'The following procedure should be followed in filling up the column relating to integrity:
   (i) If the officer's integrity is beyond doubt, it may be so stated.
   (ii) If there is any doubt or suspicion, the column should be left blank and action taken as under:

(a) A separate secret note should be recorded and followed up. A copy of the note should also be sent together with the Confidential Report to the next superior officer who will ensure that the follow up action is taken expeditiously. Where it is not possible either to certify the integrity or to record the secret note, the Reporting Officer should state either that he had not watched the officer's work for sufficient time to form a definite judgement or that he has heard nothing against the officer, as the case may be.

(b) If, as a result of the follow up action, the doubts or suspicions are cleared, the officer's integrity should be certified and an entry made accordingly in the Confidential Report.

(c) If the doubts or suspicions are confirmed, this fact should also be recorded and duly communicated to the officer concerned.

(d) If as a result of the follow up action, the doubts or suspicions are neither cleared nor confirmed, the officer's conduct should be watched for a further period and thereafter action taken as indicated at (b) and (c) above.

(Ministry of Home Affairs O.M. No. 5114164—Estt(a), dated 21.6.1965.)

4. The resolution of 1964 makes it clear that the commission has been given, in the exercise of its powers and functions, the same measure of independence and autonomy as the Union Public Service Commission. But the Union Public Service Commission is independent and autonomous because of the statutory provisions while the independence and autonomy of the Central Vigilance Commission is provided for by a mere resolution.

5. The jurisdiction of the Central Vigilance Commission extends to all civil servants working in the central government as well as employees of organizations under the administrative control of the central government including public sector undertakings and nationalized banks. However, for the sake of practical considerations, the commission advises only on those individual vigilance cases where the following categories of civil servants are involved:

(a) Gazetted civil servants;

(b) Board-level appointees in the public sector undertakings;

(c) Officers of the rank of Scale III and above in the nationalized banks;

(d) Officers of the rank of assistant manager and above in the insurance sector (covered by LIC and GIC);

(e) Officers in the autonomous bodies or local authorities or societies etc., comparable in status to the gazetted civil servants in the central government.

This, however, does not mean that the civil servants of other categories are excluded from the purview of the commission. The commission is fully within its powers to call for any individual case in respect of any civil servant other than the ones mentioned above and tender advice as to the appropriate course of action in such cases.

6. Editorial, 'Costly Vigilance: One More Case of Judicial Activism Going Haywire', *Indian Express*, August 27, 1998.

7. The *World Development Report, 1997*, p. 107.

8. See Johnston (1997). Also see, Klitgaard (1988).

9. The *World Development Report, 1997*, p. 107. For more information on the ICAC, visit ICAC's site on the internet.

10. As an investigating agency, the CBI has a hoary past. Even before the country became independent, the colonial government had thought of establishing an exclusive organization to investigate cases of corruption involving civil servants, and the Special Police Establishment was created in 1941. Originally its jurisdiction extended to cases of corruption in the War and Supply Department, and later, to the Railways. In 1946, its jurisdiction was further expanded and it became a part of the Ministry of Home Affairs. In 1963, it became the present CBI, still attached to the Ministry of Home Affairs. Subsequently, it came under the administrative purview of the Department of Personnel.

11. The bulk of the court's instructions on the structure of the autonomy of the CBI derives from the recommendations of the Independent Review Committee set up by the Government of India in September 1997 to look into the future of anti-corruption investigations. B.G. Deshmukh, former Cabinet Secretary, N.N. Vora, the former Principal Secretary to the Prime Minister, and S.V. Giri, the Central Vigilance Commissioner were members of this review committee. The committee addressed the structural issues arising from the evidence of interference in the investigation of corruption. The key recommendation of the Independent Review Committee, now endorsed by the Supreme Court, was that the CBI should operate under the superintendence of the Central Vigilance Commission and that the CVC be given statutory status.

12. Quoted in Sudha Mahalingam and Praveen Swami, 'Empowering Investigative Agencies', *Frontline*, January 9, 1998, p. 27.

13. Praveen Swami, 'A Step Towards Autonomy', *Frontline*, January 9, 1998, p. 28.

14. Editorial, 'Restoring Sanity: Reign of Inquisition is No Answer to Corruption', *Indian Express*, August 29, 1998.

15. Swami (1998), p. 29.

16. Arora and Goyal (1995), pp. 606–7.

17. Ibid., p. 607.

18. R.L.M. Patil, 'How To Make Lokayukta Effective?', A Paper presented in the National Seminar on Administrative Reforms for Good Governance, November 2, 1998.

19. Patil (1998).

20. Arora and Goyal (1998), p. 616.

21. *Report of the Fifth Central Pay Commission, Vol. I*, p. 208.

22. Ibid.

23. Narsimhan (1997), p. 261.

24. *Report of the Strategic Management Group* (1995), p. 190.

25. *Santhanam Committee Report*, pp. 10–11.

26. *Report of the Fifth Central Pay Commission, Vol. I*, p. 210.

27. Samuel Paul, 'Corruption: Who Will Bell the Cat'? *Economic and Political Weekly*, June 7, 1997, pp. 1351–2.

28. Sunil Khilnani, *Idea of India* (London: Hamish Hamilton, 1997), pp. 19–20.

29. The Public Affairs Centre in Bangalore produces report cards on services to the urban poor in five cities. The report cards show that about one-third of the slum dwellers needed to bribe to obtain services.

30. Philip Oldenburg, 'Middlemen in Third World Corruption: Implications of an Indian Case', *World Politics* 39(4), 1987, pp. 508–35.

31. There have been some minor changes in Official Secrets Act brought about by the amending Act 24 of 1967.

32. Section 5 reads,

    (1) If any person having in his possession or control any secret official code or password or any sketch, plan, model, article, note, document or information which relates to or is used in a prohibited place or relates to anything in such a place, or which is likely to assist, directly or indirectly, an enemy or which relates to a matter the disclosure of which is likely to affect the sovereignty and integrity of India, the security of the State or friendly relations with foreign states or which has been made or obtained in contravention of this Act; or which has been entrusted in confidence to him by any person holding Government office, or which he has obtained or to which he has had access owing to his position as a person who holds or has held office under Government or as a person who holds or has held a contract made on behalf of Government, or as a person who is or has been employed under a person who holds or has held such an office on contract:

       (a) wilfully communicates the code or password, sketch, plan, model, article, note, document or information to any person other than a person to whom he is authorised to communicate it, or a Court of Justice or a person to whom, it is, in the interests of the State, his duty to communicate it; or

(b) uses the information in his possession for the benefit of any foreign power or in any other manner prejudicial to the safety of the State; or

(c) retains the sketch, plan, model, article, note or document in his possession or control when he has no right to retain it, or when it is contrary to his duty to retain it, or wilfully fails to comply with all directions issued by lawful authority with regard to the return or disposal thereof; or

(d) fails to take reasonable care of, or so conducts himself as to endanger the safety of, the sketch, plan, model, article, note, document, secret official code or password or information; he shall be guilty of an offence under this section.

(2) If any person voluntarily receives any secret official code or password or any sketch, plan, model, article, note, document, or information knowing or having reasonable ground to believe, at the time when he receives it, that the code, password, sketch, plan, model, article, note, document or information is communicated in contravention of this Act, he shall be guilty of an offence under this section.

(3) If any person having in his possession or control any sketch, plan, model, article, note, document or information which relates to munitions of war, communicates it directly or indirectly to any foreign power or in any manner prejudicial to safety or interests of the State, he shall be guilty of an offence under this section.

(4) A person guilty of an offence under this section shall be punishable with imprisonment for a term which may extend to three years, or with fine, or with both.

33. Quoted in A.G. Noorani, 'The Right to Information', in Guhan and Paul (1997).

34. Das (1998), p. 21.

35. Editorial in *Indian Express*, October 13, 1998.

36. Hall (1995), p. 488.

37. Haley (1995), p. 98. In a Grand Bench decision in 1992, the Japanese Supreme Court held that the due process provision of Article 31 of Japan's constitution was not applicable to administrative proceedings in general.

38. John O. Haley, *Authority Without Power: Law and the Japanese Paradox* (New York: Oxford University Press, 1991). Also see, Haley (1995), pp. 94–5.

39. Haley (1995), pp. 94–5.

40. Peter Katzenstein, *Policy and Politics in West Germany: The Growth of a Semisovereign State* (Philadelphia: Temple University Press, 1987), p. 35.

41. Japan has had a long history of embedding the voice of the important stakeholders of the civil society in the processes of the government. The local trade associations (*dogyo kumiai*), working in

tandem with civil servants regulated prices, fixed market shares, prices and wages, and settled disputes between member-firms before World War I. *Boren,* the All-Japan Cotton Spinners Association in collaboration with civil servants allocated its members' quota of raw cotton whose import it controlled. At the time of the Second World War, these industry group associations came to be known as *tosekai* or control associations. They were authorized to act as surrogates of government agencies in matters such as formulation of plans to expand production capacity, allocation of resources (particularly foreign exchange), management of distribution of materials and the allocation of production quotas.

42. Hyung-Ki Kim, 'The Japanese Civil Service and Economic Development: Lessons for Policymakers from Other Countries', in Kim, Muramatsu, Pempel and Yamamura (1995), p. 518n.

43. Fernando Henrique Cardoso and Enzo Falletto, *Dependency and Development in Latin America* (Berkeley: University of California Press, 1979), p. 215.

44. Das (1998), pp. 173–4.

45. For example, a group of villagers from the Hissar district of Haryana drove to the Chandigarh residence of their chief minister and local MLA, Bhajan Lal, to complain against the *patwari*—the local village accountant. They said,

    'The patwari is not helping us. He probably expects us to pay him something'.
    They requested Bhajan Lal to intervene and set things right.
    The Chief Minister asked,

    'How much does he want'?

    The group told him that the patwari was asking for five hundred rupees. Bhajan Lal put his hand into his pocket and fished out the money. He said,

    'Here, take this money and give it to him. You people must have spent at least Rs 200 on taxi to come here, and you have wasted your time, too. You should have given the money to the patwari at the very outset.'
    The common belief is that Bhajan Lal got a share of what the patwari collected. See *The Week*, May 25, 1997, p. 35.

46. *The Week*, May 25, 1997, p. 36.

47. *Report of the Strategic Management Group* (1995), p. 190.

48. Kuldip Nayar, 'Corruption and Complacency', *Indian Express*, October 13, 1998.

49. Wade (1982), p. 399.

50. *The Times of India* (Bangalore), October 8, 1998.

51. Nayar (1998).

52. Pempel and Muramatsu (1995), pp. 34–5.

53. Kozo Yamamura, 'The Role of Government in Japan's 'Catch-up' Industrialization: A Neoinstitutionalist Perspective', in Kim, Muramatsu, Pempel and Yamamura (1995), p. 111.

54. Ibid., p. 112.

55. Interestingly, the Japanese left is fragmented and Japan is the only industrialized democracy never to have had an independent left-of-centre government in its entire history. Consequently, it has never had a government committed to the establishment of a welfare state and to massive economic redistribution. Therefore, the national ideological climate has been extremely conducive to pro-growth policies.

56. Pempel and Muramatsu (1995), p. 34.

# 8

# Identification with the Organization

For a meaningful discussion on organizational loyalty of civil servants in India, a distinction has to be made between two categories of civil servants. One is the group of civil servants belonging to the all-India services. The other category consists of civil servants who are recruited to a particular department, who are insiders to that organization, and who work in the same organization throughout their official career.

## OFFICERS OF THE ALL-INDIA SERVICES

Civil servants belonging to the all-India services are a class apart. Patterned on their colonial predecessors, they occupy positions of control in the state structure. They staff strategic posts specially reserved for them in the districts, as heads of departments and in the secretariats both at the centre and in the state governments.

Posting of civil servants belonging to the all-India services to control posts in the state structure is made possible by incorporating these posts in the respective cadre of the all-India services. For example, in a typical state government, the posts of all the important heads of the executive departments are encadred in the IAS. So are all the important posts at the field level such as the collector and the executive head of the developmental administration in the district. The posts of all the important secretaries in the state secretariat are also included in the IAS cadre. Much the same thing happens in the central government, though to a lesser degree.

In effect, the heads of most organizations in the state structure whether at the centre or in the state governments, and in most cases, even the joint or the deputy heads of the organizations, are encadred in the all-India services. Although the civil servants from the all-India services are supposed to have a fixed tenure in these posts, in practice they move very quickly between these posts. The movement data relating to the IAS officers (Table 8.1) establish the fact that most IAS officers spend less than a year in their respective posting in an organization.

TABLE 8.1
*IAS Post Tenures 1977–1996*

| IAS as of 1 January | Number | Length of time in post (% of IAS) | | | |
|---|---|---|---|---|---|
| | | Less than 1 year | 1–2 years | 2–3 years | More than 3 years |
| 1978 | 3084 | 58 | 26 | 10 | 6 |
| 1979 | 3236 | 55 | 30 | 10 | 5 |
| 1981 | 3373 | 60 | 22 | 11 | 7 |
| 1982 | 3539 | 52 | 31 | 9 | 8 |
| 1983 | 3734 | 51 | 29 | 13 | 7 |
| 1984 | 3797 | 56 | 26 | 12 | 7 |
| 1985 | 3910 | 51 | 31 | 11 | 7 |
| 1986 | 3970 | 58 | 25 | 12 | 6 |
| 1991 | 4497 | 58 | 25 | 10 | 6 |
| 1992 | 3951 | 56 | 27 | 11 | 6 |
| 1993 | 3991 | 49 | 31 | 13 | 8 |
| 1996 | 4621 | 48 | 28 | 13 | 11 |

*Source:* Das (1998)

The number of officers spending less than a year in their respective postings, has ranged from 48 to 60 per cent of the total strength of the IAS over the years. Interestingly, the number of IAS officers who spend more than three years in their respective postings is consistently less than 10 per cent of the total strength of the IAS. In fact, the solitary year for which it has been marginally higher than 10 per cent, is 1996.

So, it is clear that a large percentage of IAS officers who work as heads, joint heads or deputy heads in different organizations, spend less than a year in their current postings. A study of the civil servants working in the Delhi Administration found that on an average, these officers lasted less than a year in one department in the Delhi government.[1] According to the study, in less than five years there were seven postings of Principal Secretaries in the Departments of Finance and Urban Development, and five postings each of Commissioners of Excise, Transport, and Food and Civil Supplies in the Government of Delhi.

The study tried to assess the impact of such quick transfers. One of the senior civil servants who was interviewed, said,

Every time we go to a new Department, it takes six months to get to know the staff properly. Then it takes another six months to develop a working understanding. Only then can a Department look beyond the procedure and take decisions.

He went on to add that, 'We do not even get the names of the staff right.' Another senior civil servant who was interviewed, compared such abbreviated tenures with the norm of keeping a post with a civil servant for three years. He said, 'It helps the officer in getting committed to the job. Any government interested in improvement cannot entertain a floating administration.'

Studies of the functioning of different departments have also clearly brought out this fact. For example, M.C.Purohit, in his study of the Sales Tax Department, points out how IAS officers posted to head the Department of Sales Tax have not been able to provide effective leadership because of their brief tenures in the department.

Since the officers of the all-India services have gallivanted from the headship of one organization to another so quickly, they do not identify with any of the organizations they work in. Such rapid transfers from one organization to another has discouraged what Chester Barnard calls 'the process of inculcating points of view, fundamental attitudes, loyalty to the organization . . . that will result in subordinating individual interest to the good of the cooperative whole'.[2] On the whole, conditions which would have induced officers from the all-India services to identify their personal and private interest with the interests of the organization, have not been created.

In the case of officers belonging to the all-India services, the identification is perhaps expected to be with the service cadre to which civil servants belong. In the case of the IAS officers, for example, such identification is expected to be with the IAS as a service. Such an identification with the civil service, presupposes the existence of a system of shared values, norms, and differential role expectations which serves as a definitive standard for official conduct and binds the individual civil servant to forms of behaviour that are acceptable to the entire civil service. It also becomes the basis of determining whether the individual civil servant is straying from what the service is committed to.

In other words, the civil service develops *esprit de corps* which binds its members to acceptable forms of behaviour and disapproves of those who stray. This raises an important question for our subsequent discussion: is there a system of shared values, norms, and differential role expectations in the all-India services which binds their members to acceptable forms of behaviour?

There are certain conditions which have to be met in order to create and nurture *esprit de corps*. First, *esprit de corps* is fostered to the extent to which the recruitment and the reward system is merit-based. Second, the group should have a corporate identity. Third, it should have internal coherence. Fourth, it should be bound together by a sense of shared vision. Fifth, it should preferably be small and compact, a sort of *corps d' elite*.

In colonial India, the Indian Civil Service (ICS) was the perfect example of a civil service group which had built and nurtured *esprit de corps*. The recruitment to the ICS was merit-based and so was the reward system. The ICS was lean and compact. At no point of time, did its strength exceed a little more than a thousand. The ICS had a corporate identity as a group, and it gave all its members a strong sense of purpose and belonging. There was a high degree of internal coherence among the members of the ICS. The members of the ICS were bound together by a shared vision, but it was also nurtured by informal networks among the civil servants.

Small wonder, then, that the ICS had developed and nurtured *esprit de corps*. It had created a system of shared belief and orientation which served as a definitive standard for the official conduct of its members. The ICS had created and sustained values, norms, and differential role expectations that bound individual members to forms of behaviour which were acceptable to the entire ICS as a collectivity. These also became the basis of determining whether an individual ICS officer was straying from what the collectivity was committed to.

One acceptable form of behaviour which developed as a part of the ICS ethos was that ICS officers were not to indulge in corruption. Better still was the unwritten injunction of the ICS collectivity that no individual ICS officer shall accept presents—all the ICS officers were guided by the *Phal–Phul* principle which enjoined that they should not accept presents other than fruits and flowers.[3]

Predictably, the ICS had a reputation for incorruptibility. Its administration was 'probably the most incorruptible ever known'.[4] John Morris, a fierce critic of the British Raj otherwise, had this to say, 'I would have no hesitation in saying that during the years I was in India, bribery and corruption were unknown.'[5]

What about the IAS, the successor to the ICS? The IAS today is not the kind of meritocratic entity which one would associate with the premier civil service of a country. Over-recruitment to the IAS in the 1970s and 1980s has resulted in massive cadre congestion. There has been unnecessary creation of posts to accommodate civil servants. And, as if to complete the picture, inadequate compensation compounded by a sharp fall in living standards relative to the private sector and in real terms, has seriously undermined the reward structure. There is growing political interference in transfers and postings.

The IAS is not the lean and compact organization which it was when it took over as the anointed successor to the ICS. In 1951, the IAS, with a strength of 1115, looked very much like the ICS size-wise. By 1996, the IAS had bloated, with 5047 officers. It had increased in number by almost a factor of five in as many decades. The IAS with its bloated size can no longer qualify to count as a *corps d' elite*.

There is no shared vision for the IAS. Each officer in this once-elite service is on his or her own, and this has not been conducive to promoting internal coherence of the IAS as a service. The great heterogeneity of educational and social background of civil servants does not exactly make the IAS a homogeneous entity. As a serving IAS officer comments,

The civil service is not a homogeneous body any more. Its members are drawn from several sources—apart from the young recruits who are picked through a prestigious examination, there are lateral entrants from other services and promotions. Overall, it is a mixed group which makes cohesion and a common value system difficult to attain. Within the association, entrants of different origins are also not fully assimilated. This is a signal organisational flaw that marginalises individuals who could make useful contributions to group integrity.[6]

Since a large number of civil servants are inducted on the basis of reservation made on caste and communal lines, they owe allegiance to alignments based on caste and community. In addition, there are the usual political alignments in an increasingly politicized civil service like the IAS. It is now customary for IAS officers to attach themselves to sub-goals linked to caste, communal or political alignments. In other words, the internal coherence of the IAS as a service is seriously impaired by civil servants attaching themselves to such sectarian or political sub-goals.

IAS officers have no sense of corporate identity either. The sprawl of the IAS combined with the its lack of shared vision has compounded the problem of internal coordination and impeded its corporate coherence. There is no sense of belonging to the IAS as a collectivity except for the minor comfort which the individual IAS officers derive by appending the initials 'IAS' to their name, as if the repeated use of the acronym alone can help retrieve the lost *esprit de corps*.

It was not always like that. The IAS, at the time it succeeded the ICS, had inherited the values, the norms, and the differential role expectations of the ICS, or the *esprit de corps* which had characterized the ICS as a collectivity. But as the IAS began to bloat and lose its shared vision, it became increasingly difficult to sustain that *esprit de corps*, particularly in the absence of homogenization in the service.

For the most part of the five decades that the IAS has functioned as the premier civil service of the country, the system of shared values that the ICS had bequeathed to the IAS and which had originally served as a definitive standard for official conduct, has atrophied because it is no longer shared. The norms of conduct which had been passed on to the IAS in a set of common expectations decreeing how IAS officers should behave, have become irrelevant, because individual IAS officers no longer use them as a benchmark to separate legitimate behaviour from the illegitimate.

In other words, the individual IAS officers no longer identify with the civil service as a collectivity. The IAS boasts of no self-discipline that could possibly wean its members away from undesirable behaviour. It is, therefore, not altogether surprising that IAS associations of most state cadres do not have prevention of corruption as an issue on their agenda. But it raises an interesting question. Does it mean that if IAS associations had corruption as an issue on their collective agenda, things would have been different?

The answer, one hates to admit, will still remain the same. The experience of the IAS association in Uttar Pradesh has a story to tell. The association identified six IAS officers who were voted as the 'most corrupt' in a process of secret ballot in 1996 and 1997. It furnished the names of these six officers to the U.P. government with a request that action should be taken against the identified civil servants. The association even furnished evidence of corruption against these officers to the government, but instead of taking action against the six officers, the political leadership ended up rewarding these officers with influential posts where they could make even more money.[7]

Small wonder, then, that IAS associations have been largely ineffectual in setting standards for their members. The service associations are commonly seen as 'defunct, inactive and docile'.[8] The common perception of these service associations is that the association is more of a club than anything else. The meetings of these associations are considered fun-times where, one is 'even allowed to drink and get drunk'.[9]

On the whole, IAS officers who occupy control positions in almost all the important organizations in the state structure, identify neither with the organizations they work in because of the brevity of their tenures, nor with the civil service organization they belong to. The result is that these officers have not inculcated, as in Chester Barnard's memorable metaphors, the points of view, the fundamental attitudes and the loyalties to the organization which would have resulted in subordinating their individual interests to the good of the cooperative whole.

## ALL OTHERS

In respect of the second category of civil servants—the ones who work in a particular department throughout their official career—identification with the organization has been difficult to achieve. This is for several reasons.

First, the reward structure which the departments provide is pitifully inadequate. The compensation that these civil servants receive, is less than a living wage and not enough, in most cases, to meet their current consumption requirements and reasonable commitments.

Second, upward mobility in the departments is slow and not assured. As we have seen, most of these civil servants do not even get more than two promotions in their entire official career. The problem is compounded by the fact that there has been a tremendous increase in civil service numbers at all levels of the government, and overcrowding has resulted in unrelieved stagnation.

Third, it has not helped that all the top posts in the organization have been taken away by the officers belonging to the all-India services. This has only meant that top posts in the organization are not available to insider civil servants. They have very little hope to reach the top slots in the organization where they have to spend their entire official career.

Fourth, there is no sense of a shared mission which can bind civil servants together in a bond and form the basis of all their actions. Civil servants who head these departments are birds of passage from the all-India services, lasting, for the most part, less than a year, and who, because of their abbreviated tenures, do not identify with the departments. Under such circumstances, the department does not develop a mission, let alone share it with its permanent civil servants.

The result is a high degree of frustration, and very often, an overwhelming disenchantment with the organization. The predominant ethos is a kind of fundamental alienation from the organization that Michel Crozier found so pervasive in bureaucratic structures.[10] The combination of frustration, sense of dissatisfaction with the organization and fundamental alienation is the exact opposite of identification with the organization.

## EXPERIENCE OF OTHER COUNTRIES

The civil service in Singapore is now well-known for its 'coherence and sense of purpose'.[11] This is all the more impressive because it was not too long ago when Singapore did not have much of a civil service to speak of. Within a little more than two decades, the country's civil service has evolved from what was at best a corrupt and mediocre bureaucracy to one of world's most reputable and honest.

Singapore has been able to achieve this by taking the right steps. First, the recruits to the civil service are the best and brightest of the country's educational system. They come from the top performers of the graduating class at the National University of Singapore and the Nanyang Technological University. There is no system of reservation of jobs in the civil service. The sheer meritocracy of the recruitment procedure has secured the foundation for creating *esprit de corps*. Their common educational background has brought the recruits towards a common understanding of what is expected of them as civil servants and has created the basis for building trust amongst them.

Second, the meritocratic promotion system has given civil servants in Singapore a stake in achieving the goals of the organization in which they work. Third and above all else, the single-mindedness of the leadership and its continuous efforts at imbuing the civil service with its desired values have helped strengthen the bond among civil servants. Together, all these factors have created *esprit de corps* in Singapore's civil service.[12]

In Japan, the identification of civil servants with the organization in which they work, has been total. This is because of a combination of factors: recruitment policies, the reward structure, and the personnel practices of the organizations in which civil servants work.

Candidates who appear for the civil service examination in Japan, are screened through three levels of competitive examination and evaluation, administered by the National Personnel Authority. Based on the results of the examinations and evaluation, the authority compiles rosters of successful candidates by fields of specialization and ranks them in order of the scores earned. The agencies, then, select candidates from these lists after conducting interviews.

After being recruited individually by the agencies, civil servants remain within the agency for their entire official career. This means that a civil servant in Japan enters a specific agency in his early twenties, and once in that agency, his entire governmental career is spent there. The agencies are staffed only by civil servants recruited on the basis of the civil service examination. The agencies are prohibited from inducting outsiders.

Such a practice of limiting entry into higher offices in the agency to only those who are recruited early in their career on the basis of the entrance examination, serves two important purposes. First, it provides for a good deal of cohesiveness within each agency, and the cohesiveness contributes to the process of identification of the civil servant with the agency. Second, it assures the civil servant that all the high offices in the agency are open to him, and in that sense, it becomes an incentive for the civil servant to identify his career fortunes with that of the agency. This also makes for loyalty of the civil servant to his agency.

Civil servants who are recruited into the agencies are highly homogenous. There are no significant ethnic, religious, and linguistic differences in Japan, and therefore, such considerations are irrelevant so far as recruitment is concerned. The process of homogenization is largely the result of common educational background, but the process is intensified by the fact that most recruits are male, although by the beginning of the 1990s, a small but increasing number of women were being recruited.

The effective meritocracy of recruitment and the total absence of personalism and patronage in the process of induction to the agencies, is an essential attribute for building *esprit de corps*. The common educational background, sharing the triumph of having been successful in the rigorous civil service examination ('victory after a trial by educational fire'),[13] and a commonality in what to expect of a career in the civil service, bring the new recruits towards a common understanding of what is expected of them as civil servants and prepare the basis for building trust among civil servants in an agency.

The uninterrupted tenure of the civil servant in a single agency throughout his career provides the ideal environment for his identification with the agency. Throughout the career of the civil servant, loyalty to the agency is inculcated very sedulously. Loyalty to the agency takes priority and far outweighs all other considerations. Since the civil servant spends his entire career there, the process of inculcating loyalty to the agency becomes a life-long process.

Personnel practices in Japan are conducive to the creation of conditions which help the civil servant to identify with the agency. These personnel practices enable the recruitment of the best and brightest of the Japanese educational system who are then inducted into the agencies and formed into a highly capable group owing allegiance to a particular agency. This is made possible by the fact that the process of the civil service examination is separated from the actual appointment of the applicant into an agency. As a result, the loyalty of the civil servant remains, not to the civil service as a whole, but to a particular agency.

The personnel practice of each agency is designed to ensure that the process of identification of the civil servant with the agency is made as complete as possible. Individual efforts congruent with the goals of the agency are rewarded, and incentive towards any kind of deviation from such goals is discouraged. The agencies try their best to ensure that the more successful civil servants are rewarded with the most lucrative post-retirement *amakudari* placements that the agency can manage.[14] In any case, it is made abundantly clear that continued dedication to the goals of the agency will be rewarded, and ultimately, the post-retirement careers of the civil servants will be a function of such dedication.

The reward system in the agency, therefore, ensures that those civil servants who serve the agency loyally for 25 to 30 years, can expect to be rewarded with the most attractive post-retirement placements. Personal interest thus dictates that civil servants identify with the agency throughout their careers in order to make sure of their post-retirement positions. A major consequence of such a practice is to establish an effective link between civil service careers and long-standing identification with the agency.

Even for those civil servants who lose out in the race for promotions, the agency ensures that their future is protected. In the long term, the agency makes sure that even the less successful civil servants are helped to achieve social as well as financial positions much better than other individuals of their age group who go directly from college to private corporations and who have successfully climbed the corporate ladder. In other words, attractive post-career job opportunities await even those who lose out in the race for promotions in the agency. That way, agencies are able to secure the loyalty of the less successful civil servants.

The personnel practice of each agency in Japan is geared towards ensuring that the identification of the civil servant with the agency is not allowed to flag. The reward system operates in such a manner that no one in the agency, not even the civil servant who loses in the race for promotions, gets frustrated. In essence, the agency treats all civil servants as elite, and takes steps to see that while the more successful civil servants maintain a high degree of motivation, the less successful ones are not allowed to lose their motivation.

The system also creates a sense of mission for civil servants working in the agency. This is largely through the fierce competition generated between the agencies for access to the scarce resources which the government in Japan as a whole has to offer to the agencies. The mandates given to the agencies are very broad while the resources, such as extra manpower, new programmes or budgetary allocations are limited and reduced progressively with every passing year. The result is fierce competition among the agencies for increased access to the limited resources of the government.

Competition between the agencies is, indeed, intense. In fact, most researchers looking at how the government in Japan functions, have commented on how fierce the competition is between the agencies. The intense competition heightens the sense of mission of each agency, and the sense of mission, in turn, intensifies the process of identification of the civil servant with the agency.

There is an enviable degree of coherence among civil servants working in an agency. The effective meritocracy of induction into the select membership of the agency, the common educational background, the ties among the alumni of the few but elite universities from which civil servants are recruited, the shared values, and the ideology and the mission of the agency, have all contributed to the building and sustaining of internal coherence. Obversely, the factors which generally detract from internal coherence such as ethnic, religious, and linguistic differences, do not exist in Japan.

The agencies also have their own corporate identities. With clear missions and mandate, an agency acquires a distinct corporate personality, and the higher the ranking of the agency in public esteem, the more distinct is its corporate identity. In popular perception, the corporate identity of each agency is symbolically cued—the Ministry of Finance, at the top of the heap, is the 'Mount Fuji'; the Ministry of International Trade and Industry, the builder of modern industrial Japan, is the headquarters of 'Japan Inc.'; and so on with other agencies. Civil servants working in the agencies partake of the corporate character of the agency, and it gives them the necessary sense of belonging to a corporate organization with an avowed mission.

The corporate character of the agencies is also partly the result of the autonomy which the agencies enjoy in the matter of formulating their own goals and implementing them. In fact, if the individual agencies in Japan had not been autonomous in the sense of their being capable of independently formulating their own goals and being able to count on the civil servants working in the agencies to see implementation of these goals as part of the agency's corporate mission, the agencies would not have been able to sustain their corporate character and also the strong sense of purpose and belonging of their civil servants.[15]

On the whole, all these factors have in tandem created the conditions in which the identification of the civil servant with the agency has been made possible. The identification of the Japanese civil servant with the organization and his overwhelming loyalty to it, has been responsible for discouraging corruption.

The practice in Singapore and Japan provides the perfect contrast to that in India. In Singapore and Japan, conditions have been created, which have induced the civil servants to identify their personal and private interests with the interests of the organization. As a result, the identification has produced a shared commitment to the objectives of the organization, and more enviably, a common understanding among the civil servants about what is desirable and undesirable behaviour. In India, on the other hand, civil servants identify neither with the civil service as a collectivity nor with the organization in which they work.

## NOTES

1. Neelima (1998).
2. Chester Barnard, *The Functions of the Executive* (Cambridge, Mass: Harvard University Press, 1942), p. 179.
3. Charles Allen (ed.), *Plain Tales from the Raj* (London: Futura Publications, 1979), p. 226.
4. Navnit Sinha, 'Role and Rationale of All India Services', *Indian Journal of Public Administration*, Vol. xxxvii, No. 1, January–March 1991, p. 98.
5. Allen (1979), p. 225.
6. Renuka Viswanathan, 'Service Associations and Civil Service Integrity', Paper Presented at the National Seminar on Administrative Reforms for Good Governance, November 2, 1998.
7. *The Asian Age*, September 15, 1998.
8. Godbole (1997).
9. Statement attributed to Sri Akhand Pratap Singh, who was voted the most corrupt IAS officer. See *The Week*, May 25, 1997.
10. Michel Crozier, *The Bureaucratic Phenomenon* (Chicago: University of Chicago Press, 1964), p. 3.
11. *World Development Report, 1997*, p. 96.
12. Ibid., p. 96.
13. Pempel and Muramatsu (1995), p. 45.
14. For example, the Ministry of Finance gets for its more successful civil servants, the position of the president of the Bank of Japan or head of the Tokyo Securities Exchange. The Ministry of Transport gets for its civil servants the president of the Japan Airlines or any of the six Japan Railways. The Ministry of International Trade and Industry strives hard to get for its civil servants the position of presidents or vice-presidents of major private companies. The Ministry of Home Affairs gets for its civil servants the governorships of Tokyo Prefecture and other big prefectures. See Muramatsu and Pempel, 'The Civil Service before World War II', in Kim, Muramatsu, Pempel and Yamamura (1995), p. 185–6.
15. See Peter Evans, 'Predatory, Developmental, and Other Apparatus: A Comparative Political Economy Perspective on the Third World State', in Douglas Kincaid and Alejandro Portes (eds.), *Society and Economy in the New Global Order* (Chapel Hill: University of North Carolina Press, 1994).

# 9

# Conclusion

The nineteenth century paradigm had assumed that if the four sources of motivation—meritocracy, rewards, control systems, and organizational identification—are put in place and sustained over time optimally, the stakes for corruption would be raised. What is striking about our analysis is how weak India's civil service system has been along all the dimensions of the four sources of motivation.

On the whole, the sources of motivation have failed to motivate. The civil service in India now looks remarkably similar, at least in the manner of its functioning, to the ones which existed before the public bureaucracy was rationalized in the nineteenth century. From the evidence available, it is clear that the present bureaucracy in India is used as the personal instrument of ruling politicians. In the functioning of today's bureaucracy, the distinction between public and private has almost disappeared in actual practice, although such a distinction continues to be made conceptually. Does that mean that the rationalization which was attempted in the nineteenth century failed in India?

One is tempted to answer the question in the affirmative, although the process of rationalization did succeed, at least in its initial years. On the whole, the basic premises of rationalization have been seriously compromised. In essence, the sources of motivation have been progressively trifled with, and, therefore, they no longer motivate.

It can be argued that this does not mean that the paradigm has failed. All that one has to do is put the sources of motivation in place and allow them to function optimally, and one will have an honest civil service. The issue, unfortunately, is not as simple. Part of the reason lies in politics. Ruling politicians have preferences on how to treat a public bureaucracy, and these preferences translate into an incentive structure which governs the behaviour of civil servants. Depending on the nature of political dynamics, political preferences can translate into public bureaucracies with very different standards of integrity.[1]

## POLITICS AND CIVIL SERVICE

It is the nature of politics in India which has determined what should be the nature of the civil service and to what end it would be used. This is not only true of India, but equally true of other countries. In Singapore, for example, the PAP, the political party which came to power in 1959, when Singapore stopped being a British colony, decided that the corrupt civil service it had inherited would not be in a position to implement the socio-economic development programmes which the PAP had on its agenda. The PAP government set out to reform the corrupt civil service in a number of ways, and in the process it built a capable and honest civil service. The point to note is the conscious decision of the PAP to use the civil service as an agency to build a modern and prosperous Singapore rather than use it to serve the narrow ends of partisan politics.

Singapore's civil servants are recruited on merit and compensated well. Singapore is in a position to pay its civil servants well, primarily because it has a lean and compact civil service. Unlike in Malaysia, the Philippines, Indonesia and Thailand where the civil service has grown considerably over the years, the civil service in Singapore has grown only 2.2 times since 1959—the numbers in the civil service have increased from 28,253 in 1959 to 61,340 in 1992.[2] Since 1986, Singapore has a zero-growth manpower policy. Ruling politicians in Singapore have not resorted to the expediency of making the government the employer of the last resort—the political populism of overstaffing and underpaying.

There has been no political interference of any kind in the matter of promotions in the civil service. Promotions have been internal and merit-based: merit and not seniority has been the basis. As Prime Minister Lee Kuan Yew said in 1961, 'I am in favour of an efficient service. The brighter chap goes up and I don't care how many years he's been in or he hasn't been in.'[3] Politicians have not used the transfer of civil servants as an instrument of control. Transfers are entirely based on merit and performance. As Lee Kuan Yew declared, 'If he's the best man for the job, put him here.'[4]

The PAP has not undermined the control systems. The Prevention of Corruption Act which was enacted in June 1960 almost immediately after the PAP came to power, has been implemented strictly without any political interference or collusion. The Corrupt Practices Investigation Bureau which is the anti-corruption agency responsible for enforcing the provisions of the Prevention of Corruption Act, has been given the necessary clout, authority and autonomy to function. Although it is located in the office of the Prime Minister and reports directly to the Prime Minister, there has been no political interference in its working.[5] Small wonder, then, that Singapore's civil service is now considered one of the world's most reputable and honest.

Last but not the least, Singapore's civil service is well-known for its coherence and sense of purpose. The recruitment process, meritorious internal promotion and focused efforts of the leadership have helped create *esprit de corps* in Singapore's civil service and turn it into the civilian equivalent of a well-oiled, highly focused fighting machine.[6]

Likewise, Japanese politicians did not resort to any partisan, self-serving measure which would detract from the effectiveness of the civil service in attaining the goal of developmental parity with the West. Japanese politicians, for instance, have not interfered with the system of merit-based selection of civil servants. There has been no reservation of jobs of any sort. The politicians of the long-ruling Liberal Democratic Party have followed a conscious policy of limiting public employment and making the compensation package very attractive. They have also not interfered with the process of promotions and placements of the civil servants. On the whole, the politicians in Japan have not interfered with matters relating to civil service tenure, discipline, and compensation.

In the ultimate analysis, the marked preference of ruling

politicians in Japan to have a civil service which is to be used as an agency to implement pro-growth goals rather than in the service of partisan politics, has translated into an incentive structure which governs the behaviour of the civil servants. The result is a public bureaucracy which is both capable and honest, and it is not surprising that such a bureaucracy was able to oversee the most amazing transformation of the country's economy in the troubled years following World War II.

The lesson is clear. It is politicians who decide what should be the nature of the civil service, and to what end it will be used. They may well decide that the nature of the civil service should be patrimonial so that it can be used to promote narrow ends of politics—like in India. Or, they may decide on a capable and honest civil service and use it for achieving broader goals of public good—as in Singapore and Japan. So, the fact remains that the ruling politicians have preferences on how to treat the civil service and these preferences ultimately translate into an incentive structure which governs the behaviour of civil servants.

This is where the nineteenth-century paradigm went wrong. It assumed that the installation of a merit-based civil service was sufficient by itself to insulate the civil service from politics. Use of merit to select civil servants, it was assumed, would keep politics out of the selection process. Reliance on expertise, it was assumed, would remove political considerations from administration. In other words, merit and expertise were expected to be the means by which administration would have been depoliticized.

The assumptions have clearly gone awry, but the peculiar circumstances which prevailed in the nineteenth century and were responsible for such assumptions to be made, need to be put in perspective. At the time the assumptions were made, the administration was colonized by patrimonial politics. Merit and expertise were, therefore, viewed as the basis for good government as opposed to the one provided by politics. In fact, politics was the very evil which was sought to be exorcised from administration.

Politics, obviously, had to be kept out. But where the paradigm fails, is in its refusal to see that mere installation of merit and expertise is not sufficient to depoliticize the administration. The process of keeping politics out involves a lot more than putting in place a merit-based civil service system. At a minimum, it calls for a restructuring of the relations between a public bureaucracy and ruling politicians, ·and ironically, a restructuring that needs to have the consent of politicians themselves.

This, as stated earlier, is the essence of the puzzle. Merit and expertise are expected to respond to the legitimate authority of the patrimonial politics and at the same time offset its evil. The problem is that politics, even if patrimonial, means popular participation in government through elections, and therefore, the civil service has to be responsive to political direction. However given the unrelenting urge of patrimonial politics to be self-serving, the problem is: how to include politics in the system of administration so that there is popular participation in government, and yet, exclude politics so that it does not use the administration for its narrow ends?[7]

## THE NEW PARADIGM

The new paradigm addresses this puzzle. The new paradigm separates, very deliberately, the roles and functions of both politicians and civil servants. The areas of functioning are thus delimited, fenced off, and made distinct through contractual arrangement, to which both the politicians and civil servants agree. The new paradigm is the 'new public management' or 'new managerialism'. It has already been tried out in New Zealand, Australia, the United Kingdom, and Sweden with success.

The new paradigm borrows the conventional distinction between output and outcome from financial management literature, and uses the distinction to limit the area of functioning of politicians and civil servants, and construct boundaries. Outputs are specific services that civil servants produce and deliver, and therefore, civil servants are held to account for the provision of outputs. Outcome is the success in achieving social goals, and it is politicians who decide what outputs should be included so that the outcomes or the desired social goals can be achieved.

The civil servant enters into a performance agreement with the minister every year, and the agreement details the services to be provided by the civil servant. These services are described as outputs, and the assessment of the civil servant's performance is based on production and delivery of outputs as described in the performance agreement.

In return, the civil servant gets total autonomy for managing his organization. He is freed from control by the minister in personnel, financial, and other matters. In other words, such autonomy gives the civil servant the power and flexibility to determine the most effective means of carrying out his responsibility—the production and delivery of outputs as stipulated in the performance agreement.

The new paradigm thus provides a solution to the puzzle that we had talked about earlier. The new paradigm includes politics to the extent that politicians decide policy goals or the outcome. Ruling politicians decide what outputs shall be included in the annual performance agreement so that the outcome or the desired social goals can be achieved. The control over what outputs are included to produce a particular outcome, arms the politicians with the necessary means of determining the policy outcome. The politicians remain accountable to the legislature and the electorate for the outcome, and they are judged on the basis of whether they have chosen the right outputs to achieve the desired social goals.

The new paradigm excludes politics from the administration to the extent that once the outputs are specified by ruling politicians in the annual performance agreement for producing a particular outcome, the politicians are given no further say in how the outputs are realized. In other words, civil servants are given the necessary autonomy and flexibility to manage their departments, and are held accountable for the realization of the outputs.

What it means is that the politicians make policies, and the civil servants implement them. Boundaries are constructed between these two areas (policy-making and policy-implementation) by the signing of contracts between politicians and civil servants. Once the annual performance contract, detailing the outputs to be realized during a year, is signed, the minister has no further role in how the outputs are realized. The civil servant is given the power and the resources to realize the outputs, and he remains responsible for delivering the outputs as described in the annual performance contract.

The question, then, arises: what about civil servants? Would it now mean that the civil servants, freed from the liability of sharing bribes with politicians, can keep all the bribes for themselves? As a matter of fact, with the autonomy and the flexibility which the new paradigm gives them to manage their departments, the civil servants will now have limitless opportunities for rent-seeking. How does the new paradigm deal with such a contingency?

DEFINING OF JOBS

The first thing that the new paradigm does is to define the jobs which civil servants are required to perform. In defining them, the following question is to be asked of all activities to be performed by civil servants:

(a) Does the job need to be done at all?

(b) If the activity has to be carried out, does the government have to be responsible for it?

(c) Where the government needs to remain responsible for an activity, do civil servants have to carry out the task themselves?

(d) Where the job must be carried out by civil servants, is the organization properly structured and focused on the job to be done?

The process of defining jobs calls for a review, primarily to see whether they should be abolished, privatized, contracted out, or, if absolutely necessary, retained in the government to be performed by the civil servants. The general idea is to expose public services to competitive forces so that the choices for the public are increased and the scope for corruption is reduced. The prescription is to identify areas for intervention in terms of the more corruption-prone public agencies which have the most interaction with the people.

The other step is to clarify and streamline laws in ways which reduce areas of official discretion, and thereby, limit corruption. What the new paradigm calls for is discipline in these areas through an explicit adoption of guidelines for the use of discretion, and documentation of the specific reasons for discretionary decisions, which is to be made available to the affected parties. In fact, the idea is to reduce official discretion as far as possible. Sometimes, a certain risk of corruption is tolerated because the benefits of a discretionary approach to programme administration exceed the costs of corruption. But even in such cases, transparency is expected to blunt the incentive to corruption.

EMPOWERMENT OF PEOPLE

The new paradigm gives the people the leading role in anti-corruption efforts. It emphasizes that citizens should come forward to monitor and denounce corruption. What is stressed is that corruption can be most effectively tackled when systematic efforts are made to inform the citizens about their rights and entitlements, and in the process, enable them to monitor and challenge corruption. In other words, citizens are empowered to raise the stakes for corruption.

In order to empower people and enable them to fight corruption, the new paradigm recognizes the crucial role that information plays in the process. It notes that the aura of secrecy which envelopes the functioning of the government must be smashed so that citizens have access to information which they need to understand, assess, and challenge the ways of functioning of civil servants. In fact, the new paradigm makes it clear that the right to information is fundamental, and information is the only real deterrent to corruption.

The new paradigm recognizes that in respect of services which civil servants provide, opportunities for corruption arise because people do not know what they can expect in terms of service delivery. To this end, it is stressed that civil servants who provide services, should be called upon to specify and announce the standards and norms which they intend to meet in their areas of responsibility. The remedies which are available to the public when the assured standards of service are not met, should also be indicated. The new paradigm stresses that dissemination of such information will bring about transparency in the working of the government, and in the process, empower people to fight corruption.

On the whole, the new paradigm differs from the old paradigm in several ways. First, the new paradigm separates the role of policy-making from that of implementation of such policies. In that way, the role of ruling politicians becomes limited to making of policy while civil servants are responsible for its implementation. Second, while in the old system, anti-corruption efforts consisted of mechanisms of punishment using formal institutions and criminal law, the new paradigm also uses overseeing by ordinary citizens who are given the leading role in anti-corruption efforts. Third, it seeks to reduce opportunities for civil servants to be corrupt, by limiting the activities of the government, and also by cutting back on the discretionary authority of individual civil servants.

There is much to commend the new paradigm. But what is particularly commendable is that it has already found acceptance in a number of countries. New Zealand has restructured its public bureaucracy and operationalized the new paradigm, and the process has paid rich dividends. A similar process is under way in the United Kingdom, Sweden, and Australia.

## WHAT ABOUT INDIA?

We have seen that the civil service system in India has not worked as intended. It has been corrupt, and it has served the narrow ends of patrimonial politics. It is clear, therefore, that in India, the older paradigm has failed to solve the paradigmatic puzzle. It is in a state of ferment. So, the question is: how does the change occur so that the older paradigm is replaced by the new paradigm?

The greatest barrier to such a change are the powerful groups who stand to lose by it—politicians and  civil servants. The present system in India has worked well in coordinating rents and getting them shared across both the official and political realms. Politicians and civil servants stand to lose by any change in the system. Understandably, they have a vital stake in protecting corruption and the present system.

The acceptance of the new paradigm by politicians can only be by way of a self-denying act. Successful politics in India is an expensive proposition. The costs of electoral competition, keeping the flock together, and sustaining a winning coalition in fragile situations all add up to a pretty penny. In addition, politics, by definition, is a precarious profession with uncertain prospects. A politician in India tries to mobilize as much personal wealth as possible not merely to look after the expensive present, but also the uncertain future. In other words, politics in India is all about making as much money out of public office as possible, so long as the opportunity lasts.

Accepting the new paradigm would necessarily mean limiting politics to the realm of policy making. Policy making may be portrayed as important in conventional literature, but it offers only limited prospects of making immediate money. On the other hand, there are limitless opportunities for making money in day-to-day administration: transfers and postings of civil servants, awarding of major contracts and concessions, provision of goods and services free or below the market prices—the list seems to be endless. So, being denied a voice in day-to-day administration will essentially mean lack of access to highly lucrative areas, and, in that sense, accepting the new paradigm can only mean killing of the golden goose.

Politicians in India do not take kindly to changes which seek to limit opportunities for making money. The on-going economic liberalization is a case in point. The process of liberalization which India was forced to accept in the early 1990s under sheer duress, was essentially an exercise to create alternatives and introduce competition. A limited degree of deregulation and debureaucratization was introduced in the early years of liberalization, and the process has now slowed down. Understandably, politicians are not too keen to shackle themselves with what they perceive as unnecessary restraints.

If politicians do not come forward to operationalize the new paradigm, the initiative can only come from civil society. Civil society can demand, and thereby, force politicians to accept the change. If the demand is persistent and there is a groundswell of support, politicians have to sit up and take note.

But this is easier said than done. Admittedly, India provides the most degraded terrain for the mobilization of civil society. There is a high social acceptance of corruption. Civil society has capitulated to corruption, and most citizens see corruption as inevitable and efforts to fight it as futile. One does not expect such a quiescent civil society to take the initiative in clamouring for change.

The few citizens, educated and enlightened, and therefore expected, by definition, to provide leadership to civil society in such efforts, have a certain ambivalence in their attitude toward corruption. To them, bribes have desirable incentive properties. A common though self-serving view among these privileged citizens is that corruption greases the wheels of commerce, and that, without it, there would be no transactions, and hence, no growth.

As if to confirm this, community groups fighting corruption have not exactly been popular in India. As we have noted earlier, there are not too many of them in the anti-corruption field. The only groups which come to mind are Common Cause of H.D. Shourie and Samuel Paul's Public Affairs Centre in Bangalore. Common Cause has been waging a lonely if valiant battle against corruption and has won several court cases involving corruption, but it is a sad comment that not many people have come forward to make common cause with it. The Public Affairs Centre is better known abroad than in its own country.

Instances of citizens organizing themselves to fight corruption are very rare. Some villagers in Rajasthan organized themselves to rally against the corruption of local government functionaries. Oldenburg cites the instance of beneficiaries organizing themselves to control corruption in the process of land consolidation in certain villages of Uttar Pradesh in the 1980s. Admittedly, these are isolated instances which seem to come to life only once in a while, but what is heartening is that every time the citizens have organized themselves to fight corruption, they have been in a position to impose anti-corruption sanctions, however modest, relatively quickly, and on a lesser burden of proof than what is needed for criminal penalties.

What is really required but sorely lacking is information about the government. The system of administration in India is such that it is difficult for anybody outside the state structure to access information about what goes on in the government. Perverse processes and procedures, combined with an exasperating and often unhelpful lack of openness has mystified the ways of the government. It is in the dark and obscure recesses of such mystification that bureaucratic corruption has nestled so comfortably.

Things are looking up, though. There is already a right-to-information campaign which is under way in some states in India. The right-to-information campaign which began as a need for information about government programmes in the rural areas, has now snowballed into a mass movement. The campaign started in Rajasthan and later spread to Madhya Pradesh and Uttar Pradesh. The noteworthy point about the campaign was that it was spearheaded by ordinary and illiterate rural folk.[8]

The campaign had its genesis in the backward Bhim Tehsil, along the borders of Ajmer, Pali, and Rajasmand districts of

Rajasthan, where a mass organization of workers and peasants, Mazdoor Kisan Shakti Sangathan, began to focus on the right of common people to information in order to break the various circles of corruption.

Interestingly, the right-to-information campaign started in drought-prone areas where the poor people rely on the employment schemes of the government such as Jawahar Rozgar Yojana and Employment Assurance Scheme for seasonal employment during the lean season. These people found that although they had not been provided with employment, they figured in the muster rolls of the employment schemes of the government.

Enraged, these people demanded that they should be given the right to inspect and scrutinize the muster rolls, bills and vouchers for the works taken up in their villages. They also demanded that the details of specific development projects taken up in their area should be shown to them for scrutiny. Public hearings (Jan sunwayis) were started for demanding such information and unearthing the corrupt practices of local officials.

The Jan sunwayis are generally held under a big tree in the village. There, the villagers describe their experiences with corrupt local officials, and they make the officials read out the details of the bills, vouchers, and muster rolls which list them as employed in schemes in which they had never worked. The villagers make charges of corruption against the local officials openly. In many cases, local officials have had to endure public humiliation and even return the money to villagers. But the main success of Jan sunwayis has been that people have been able to get information about the government, and in the process, they are empowered to fight corruption.

The proactive stand taken by the judiciary in corruption cases, particularly by the Supreme Court of India, has come as breath of fresh air. Public interest litigations by vigilant groups has been a path-breaking initiative, and the fact that the courts have entertained them and are so positively inclined to issue directions in such litigation, is heartening. Under directions from the courts, somnolent investigative agencies have been goaded to some action in corruption cases. But what is really remarkable is the constructive role which the Supreme Court has played in raising the consciousness of people about corruption.

The press and electronic media in India is already playing a major role in exposing corruption, and in the process, it has made information about corruption available to people. At a minimum, public exposure in the print and electronic media has increased public awareness about corruption. If this continues, its impact on public opinion and values is going to be immeasurably immense.

The process of economic liberalization in India might not have been as comprehensive as one would have liked it to be, but even the limited gain has been of tremendous significance for civil society. It has unleashed an information revolution in the country spearheaded by the print and electronic media. Thanks to the enthusiasm of the media in reporting the progress of corruption cases before the courts, information about corruption in high places in government, the pathologies, and the utter sordidness of it all, is now a part of the nation's folklore.

What should have been a part of the nation's folklore, but regrettably is not, is the harm that corruption does to the country's growth agenda, its economy, and the polity. Information about the harm caused by corruption is not known because data on corruption is difficult to obtain. Luckily for us, research is now possible because of compilation of data by private firms in the form of multinational corruption index. This is to provide information to international companies trying to decide which countries to invest in. These data sets are based on the impressions of people knowledgeable about the countries concerned such as investors, bankers, and financial analysts.

The most comprehensive multinational corruption index is prepared by the Transparency International. The Corruption Perceptions Index (CPI) for the year 1998,[9] prepared by the Transparency International is an example. The CPI which ranks 85 countries, is a 'poll of polls', drawing upon numerous distinct surveys of expert and general public views of the extent of corruption in these countries, and to that extent, it reflects the perceptions of business people who participated in these surveys. Such data may not perhaps be as well-documented or replicable as social scientists would like them to be, but they are the best macrolevel data available in a difficult area such as corruption.[10]

Using data sets of such multinational corruption index, a number of recent cross-country studies are now in a position to establish the macroeconomic impact of corruption. For example,

Paolo Mauro's study indicates that high levels of corruption are associated with lower levels of investment as a share of the GDP in a cross-section of the countries studied.[11] Mauro demonstrates that countries with high levels of corruption invest very little in human capital and in particular, investment in education is only minimal. This is because education provides fewer opportunities for corruption when compared to other types of more capital-intensive public spending such as infrastructure and defence.[12]

Knack and Keefer's study shows that high levels of corruption mean reduced investment, a lack of credible guarantees of property and contract rights, and poor institutionalization of the government. Knack and Keefer demonstrate how prolonged, slow and negative growth perpetuates the scarcity of economic alternatives, inhibiting the development of new economic activities and political interests, while preserving dependency on corrupt civil servants. In essence, corruption then becomes an integral part of a syndrome of poor public institutions linked to reduced growth.[13]

A study by Ades and Tella corroborates the point made by Knack and Keefer—the link between scarcity of economic alternatives and corruption. Ades and Tella show that the degree of competition has a significant effect on corruption. Corruption occurs through the rents which absence of competition creates, and which the civil servants and politicians, then, extract. In other words, high levels of corruption are closely correlated to poor economic competitiveness. That is why, Ades and Tella argue, more competitive economies are less corrupt because they have fewer economic rents available for capture by the corrupt. Kimberly Elliott's study also makes the same point—corruption leads to relatively closed economic and political systems.[14]

A study by Shang-Jin Wei linking corruption to international investment[15] proves that corruption acts like a tax on foreign direct investment. While a one point increase in the tax rate reduces FDI by 5 per cent, an increase in the corruption level from that of corruption-free Singapore to corrupt Mexico is the equivalent of 32 per cent percentage point increase in the tax rate. In another study, a one standard deviation (2.4) improvement in the corruption index is associated with over a 4 percentage point increase in the investment rate and half a percentage increase in the annual growth rate of per capita GDP.[16]

There are also a number of studies which tell us about the health of a society which experiences high levels of corruption. Robert Cooter's study shows that a society with high levels of corruption, has low levels of social interaction and weaknesses of the rule of law.[17] Cooter, using game theory, shows that where people freely interact on a repeated basis, they are more likely to form strong and legitimate norms. According to Cooter, survey and interview research on popular conceptions of right and wrong suggests that most citizens judge civil servants by social norms learned in these everyday interactions. Cooter also points out that in advanced countries, a range of social groups—trade and professional associations, or community groups—have functioned as 'law merchants', and they have succeeded in promulgating codes of good practice and have been in a position to impose anti-corruption sanctions.

Mauro's study suggests that people in societies plagued by corruption have low educational attainments because not enough investment is made in education.[18] Two studies by Isham, Kaufmann, and Pritchett demonstrate that societies with high levels of corruption have low levels of mass participation in politics and weak protection of civil liberties.[19] The study by Easterly and Levine establishes that a society with large incidence of corruption is characterized by deep ethnic divisions and conflicts.[20]

In other words, these studies establish how corruption is closely correlated to reduced growth, reduced investment, and poor economic competitiveness. In essence, corruption hurts the economy. The studies also tell us how in the longer run, societies with high levels of corruption have low levels of social interaction and weaknesses of the rule of law, low educational attainment, low levels of participation in politics, weak protection of civil liberties, and deep ethnic divisions and conflicts.

On the whole, corruption, apart from being worrisome for those who have to pay bribes, has more fundamental implications for the economy and the society. High levels of corruption hurt the economy and make the society very sick. These cross-country studies provide these sickness metaphors, and they need to be taken seriously.

People need to be educated on how corruption is not merely irritating in the experiential short run, but also harmful in the longer run, especially as it relates to the larger perspective of the country's economy and society, and in that sense, it affects the lives of people who do not otherwise experience corruption. It is in this context that the passivity of the people in their attitude towards corruption needs to be changed. So far, most people in India have viewed corruption as inevitable, and therefore, any effort to fight it as futile. Such passivity, more than anything else, has been responsible for the failure of civil society to act as a check on corruption and form the basis for countervailing action. Such an attitude has to change.

The experience of Hong Kong is an object lesson in how such an attitude can be changed. Corruption was endemic in Hong Kong in the 1960s and the early 1970s, and worse still, most citizens saw it as inevitable and resistance to it as futile. But, public surveys carried out between 1977 and 1994 indicate that public perception of corruption has changed. By the 1980s, young people in Hong Kong took a stricter view of corruption than did their elders. In other words, there was a change in the public perception about the inevitability of corruption.

The reason for such a change is the commendable initiatives by the ICAC by way of vigorous public education campaigns. The ICAC has taken the anti-corruption message into every corner of the community in a complex operation which has called for a skilful use of every possible means available to it. Public education programmes, sporting events and public concerts funded by the ICAC have fostered social interaction with anti-corruption themes. These well-orchestrated campaigns have succeeded in breaking the belief that corruption is inevitable. Corruption was portrayed in such campaigns and public events as harmful to families, to the economy and to the traditional Chinese values.

The clearest lesson that Hong Kong's experience has to offer is that the attitudes of people can be changed through focused efforts. In Hong Kong, it is the ICAC, an institution of the government which has been the catalyst of change. It may be naive to expect a government body to take similar initiative in changing people's perception in India. In any case, the government here does not have the right credentials. As Kuldip Nayar says, 'There have to be exposures and loud public protests. A people's movement has to be built, not by political parties but by those who are outside the system and enjoy credibility.'[21] So, it can only be committed groups in civil society who can take up the task.

· No doubt, the social capital of the community in India is weak. But, then, one should remember that it is not necessarily a permanent condition. Social capital can be generated by participation itself, and here, committed groups in civil society can play a very positive role. If people can be educated about the costs and consequences of corruption, and goaded to freely interact with each other on a repeated basis, they would have been persuaded to clamour for change, and a day will soon come when the government of the day will find it difficult to resist the demand for change.

On the whole, people need to be exposed to information about incentives to have a corruption-free government. Change will come when the incentives to throw out a corrupt system becomes stronger than the incentives to retain such a system.

## NOTES

1. Campos and Pradhan (1996), p. 1.
2. Das (1998), p. 59.
3. Quah (1994), p. 208.
4. Ibid., p. 208.
5. Das (1998), p. 58.
6. *World Development Report, 1997*, p. 96.
7. Ingraham (1995).
8. Kiran Ramachandran Nair, 'Social Movements for Development: Emerging Communication Strategies', *Man & Development*, June 1999, pp. 34–5.
9.

TABLE 9.1

*The Corruption Perceptions Index, 1998*

| Country rank | Country | 1998 CPI score | Standard deviation | Surveys used |
|---|---|---|---|---|
| 1 | Denmark | 10.0 | 0.7 | 9 |
| 2 | Finland | 9.6 | 0.5 | 9 |
| 3 | Sweden | 9.5 | 0.5 | 9 |
| 4 | New Zealand | 9.4 | 0.7 | 8 |
| 5 | Iceland | 9.3 | 0.9 | 6 |
| 6 | Canada | 9.2 | 0.5 | 9 |
| 7 | Singapore | 9.1 | 1.0 | 10 |
| 8 | Netherlands | 9.0 | 0.7 | 9 |
| 9 | Norway | 9.0 | 0.7 | 9 |

*contd.*

| *Country rank* | *Country* | *1998 CPI score* | *Standard deviation* | *Surveys used* |
|---|---|---|---|---|
| 10 | Switzerland | 8.9 | 0.6 | 10 |
| 11 | Australia | 8.7 | 0.7 | 8 |
| 12 | Luxembourg | 8.7 | 0.9 | 7 |
| 13 | United Kingdom | 8.7 | 0.5 | 10 |
| 14 | Ireland | 8.2 | 1.4 | 10 |
| 15 | Germany | 7.9 | 0.4 | 10 |
| 16 | Hong Kong | 7.8 | 1.1 | 12 |
| 17 | Austria | 7.5 | 0.8 | 9 |
| 18 | United States | 7.5 | 0.9 | 8 |
| 19 | Israel | 7.1 | 1.4 | 9 |
| 20 | Chile | 6.8 | 0.9 | 9 |
| 21 | France | 6.7 | 0.6 | 9 |
| 22 | Portugal | 6.5 | 1.0 | 10 |
| 23 | Botswana | 6.1 | 2.2 | 3 |
| 24 | Spain | 6.1 | 1.3 | 10 |
| 25 | Japan | 5.8 | 1.6 | 11 |
| 26 | Estonia | 5.7 | 0.5 | 3 |
| 27 | Costa Rica | 5.6 | 1.6 | 5 |
| 28 | Belgium | 5.4 | 1.4 | 9 |
| 29 | Malaysia | 5.3 | 0.4 | 11 |
| 30 | Namibia | 5.3 | 1.0 | 3 |
| 31 | Taiwan | 5.3 | 0.7 | 11 |
| 32 | South Africa | 5.2 | 0.8 | 10 |
| 33 | Hungary | 5.0 | 1.2 | 9 |
| 34 | Mauritius | 5.0 | 0.8 | 3 |
| 35 | Tunisia | 5.0 | 2.1 | 3 |
| 36 | Greece | 4.9 | 1.7 | 9 |
| 37 | Czech Republic | 4.8 | 0.8 | 9 |
| 38 | Jordan | 4.7 | 1.1 | 6 |
| 39 | Italy | 4.6 | 0.8 | 10 |
| 40 | Poland | 4.6 | 1.6 | 8 |
| 41 | Peru | 4.5 | 0.8 | 6 |
| 42 | Uruguay | 4.3 | 0.9 | 3 |
| 43 | South Korea | 4.2 | 1.2 | 12 |
| 44 | Zimbabwe | 4.2 | 2.2 | 6 |
| 45 | Malawi | 4.1 | 0.6 | 4 |

*contd.*

| Country rank | Country | 1998 CPI score | Standard deviation | Surveys used |
|---|---|---|---|---|
| 46 | Brazil | 4.0 | 0.4 | 9 |
| 47 | Belarus | 3.9 | 1.9 | 3 |
| 48 | Slovak Republic | 3.9 | 1.6 | 5 |
| 49 | Jamaica | 3.8 | 0.4 | 3 |
| 50 | Morocco | 3.7 | 1.8 | 3 |
| 51 | El Salvador | 3.6 | 2.3 | 3 |
| 52 | China | 3.5 | 0.7 | 10 |
| 53 | Zambia | 3.5 | 1.6 | 4 |
| 54 | Turkey | 3.4 | 1.0 | 10 |
| 55 | Ghana | 3.3 | 1.0 | 4 |
| 56 | Mexico | 3.3 | 0.6 | 9 |
| 57 | Philippines | 3.3 | 1.1 | 10 |
| 58 | Senegal | 3.3 | 0.8 | 3 |
| 59 | Ivory Coast | 3.1 | 1.7 | 4 |
| 60 | Guatemala | 3.1 | 2.5 | 3 |
| 61 | Argentina | 3.0 | 0.6 | 9 |
| 62 | Nicaragua | 3.0 | 2.5 | 3 |
| 63 | Romania | 3.0 | 1.5 | 3 |
| 64 | Thailand | 3.0 | 0.7 | 11 |
| 65 | Yugoslavia | 3.0 | 1.5 | 3 |
| 66 | Bulgaria | 2.9 | 2.3 | 4 |
| 67 | Egypt | 2.9 | 0.6 | 3 |
| 68 | India | 2.9 | 0.6 | 12 |
| 69 | Bolivia | 2.8 | 1.2 | 4 |
| 70 | Ukraine | 2.8 | 1.6 | 6 |
| 71 | Latvia | 2.7 | 1.9 | 3 |
| 72 | Pakistan | 2.7 | 1.4 | 3 |
| 73 | Uganda | 2.6 | 0.8 | 4 |
| 74 | Kenya | 2.5 | 0.6 | 4 |
| 75 | Vietnam | 2.5 | 0.5 | 6 |
| 76 | Russia | 2.4 | 0.9 | 10 |
| 77 | Ecuador | 2.3 | 1.5 | 3 |
| 78 | Venezuela | 2.3 | 0.8 | 9 |
| 79 | Colombia | 2.2 | 0.8 | 9 |
| 80 | Indonesia | 2.0 | 0.9 | 10 |
| 81 | Nigeria | 1.9 | 0.5 | 5 |

contd.

| Country rank | Country | 1998 CPI score | Standard deviation | Surveys used |
|---|---|---|---|---|
| 82 | Tanzania | 1.9 | 1.1 | 4 |
| 83 | Honduras | 1.7 | 0.5 | 3 |
| 84 | Paraguay | 1.5 | 0.5 | 3 |
| 85 | Cameroon | 1.4 | 0.5 | 4 |

*Source:* The Transparency International.

The column '1998 CPI Score' relates to perceptions of the degree of which corruption is seen by business people. A perfect score of 10.00 would mean a totally corruption-free country. 'Standard Deviation' indicates differences in the values of the sources for the 1998 index—the greater the variance, the greater the differences of perceptions of a country among the sources. The number of surveys used had to be at least 3 for a country to be included in the CPI.

10. Susan Rose-Ackerman, 'The Costs and Causes of Corruption', Paper Prepared for Panel Discussion on Corruption (Washington D.C.: International Monetary Fund, 1997), p. 2.
11. Paolo Mauro, 'The Effects of Corruption on Growth, Investment and Government Expenditure: A Cross-Country Analysis', in Kimberly A. Elliott (ed.), *Corruption in the World Economy* (Washington D.C.: Institute for International Economics, 1997).
12. Mauro (1997). Also see Paolo Mauro, 'Corruption and Growth', *Quarterly Journal of Economics* 109, 1995, pp. 681–712.
13. Knack and Keefer (1995), pp. 207–27.
14. Kimberly A. Elliott, 'Corruption as a Global Policy Problem: Overview and Recommendations', in Kimberly A. Elliott (ed.), *Corruption in the World Economy* (Washington D.C.: Institute for International Economics, 1997).
15. Wei Shang-Jin, *How Taxing is Corruption on International Investors?* (Cambridge, Mass: Harvard University, Kennedy School of Government, 1997).
16. Rose-Ackerman (1997).
17. Cooter (1996).
18. Mauro (1997).
19. Isham Jonathan, Daniel Kaufmann and Lant Pritchett, *Governance and Returns on Investment: An Empirical Investigation* (Washington D.C.: The World Bank, Policy Research Working Paper 1550, 1995), and *Civil Liberties, Democracy, and the Performance of Government Projects* (Washington D.C.: The World Bank, 1996).
20. William Easterly and Ross Levine, *Africa's Growth Tragedy: Policies and Ethnic Divisions* (Washington D.C.: The World Bank, 1996).
21. Nayar (1998).

# Bibliography

Aberbach, Joel. D., and Bert A. Rockman, 'Political and Bureaucratic Roles in Public Service Reorganization', in S.J. Colin Campbell and B. Guy Peters (eds.), *Organizing Governance: Governing Organizations*, Pittsburgh: University of Pittsburgh Press (1988).

Ades, Alberto, and Rafael di Tella, 'Competition and Corruption', Working Paper, Institute of Economics and Statistics, Oxford University, United Kingdom, (1994).

Akerlof, George. A., and Janet Yellen, 'Gang Behaviour, Law Enforcement and Community Values', in Henry J. Aaron, Thomas E. Mann, and Timothy Taylor (eds.), *Values in Public Policy*, Washington D.C.: Brookings (1994).

Allen, Charles (ed.), *Plain Tales from the Raj*, London: Futura Publications (1979).

Aravind, Vibha, 'Role Of Professional Associations and Peer Groups to Maintain Integrity in Civil Services', Paper presented at the National Seminar on Administrative Reforms for Good Governance, November 2, 1998.

Arora, Ramesh. K., and Rajni Goyal, *Indian Public Administration: Institutions and Issues*, New Delhi: Wishwa Prakashan (1995).

Athar, Ali. M., 'Towards an Interpretation of the Mughal Empire', in Herman Kulke (ed.), *The State in India 1000–1700*, Delhi: Oxford University Press (1997).

Aylmer, G.E., *The King's Servants: The Civil Service of Charles I, 1625–1642*, London (1973).

Ball, V. (transl. and ed.), *Jean Baptiste Tavernier: Travels in India*, London (1889).

Barnard, Chester, *The Functions of the Executive*, Cambridge, Mass: Harvard University Press (1942).

Besley, Timothy, and John McLaren, 'Taxes and Bribery: The Role of Wage Incentives', *Economic Journal* V. 103 (1993).

Bidwai, Praful, 'Reforming the Bureaucracy: Recruitment, Training must Change', *Times of India*, September 8, 1994.

———'Are we Killing the IAS'?, *The Tribune*, August 2, 1995.

Blake, Stephen. P., 'The Patrimonial-Bureaucratic Empire of the Mughals', in H. Kulke (ed.), *The State in India 1000–1700*, Delhi: Oxford University Press (1997).

Braibanti, R., 'Reflections on Bureaucratic Reforms in India', in R. Braibanti and J. Spengler (eds.), *Administration and Economic Development in India*, Duke University Press (1963).

Braithwaite, John, *Crime, Shame and Reintegration*, Cambridge: Cambridge University Press (1989).

Campos, Ed, and Sanjaya Pradhan, 'Building Institutions for a More Effective Public Sector' (1996), Background Paper for World Development Report, 1997.

Campos, Ed, and Hilton L. Root, *The Key to the Asian Miracle: Making Shared Growth Credible*, Washington D.C.: Brookings Institution (1996).

Cardoso, Fernando. Henrique, and Enzo Falletto, *Dependency and Development in Latin America*, Berkeley: University of California Press (1979).

Central Vigilance Commission, *Annual Report*, (1992).

Constable, A. (ed.), *Francois Bernier: Travels in the Mogul Empire, 1656–68*, London: Constable (1891).

Cooter, Robert D., 'The Rule of State Law Versus the Rule-of-Law State: Economic Analysis of the Legal Foundations of Development', in *Proceedings of the Annual World Bank Conference on Development Economics* (1996).

Cox, Eva, *A Truly Civil Society*, Sydney: ABC Books (1995).

Crozier, Michel, *The Bureaucratic Phenomenon*, Chicago: University of Chicago Press (1964).

Das, S.K., *Civil Service Reform and Structural Adjustment*, Delhi: Oxford University Press (1998).

Dia, Mamadou, *A Governance Approach to Civil Service Reform in Sub-Saharan Africa*, Technical Paper 225, Africa Technical Department Series, Washington D.C.: The World Bank (1993).

D'sousa, J.B., 'Selection for the Civil Services, Change in the System Vital', *Economic Times*, May 9, 1981.

Easterly, William, and Ross Levine, *Africa's Growth Tragedy: Policies and Ethnic Divisions*, Washington D.C.: The World Bank (1996).

Elliott, Kimberly A., 'Corruption as a Global Policy Problem: Overview and Recommendations', in Kimberly A. Elliott (ed.), *Corruption in the World Economy*, Washington D. C.: Institute for International Economics (1997).

Evans, Peter, 'Predatory, Developmental, and Other Apparatus: A Comparative Political Economy Perspective on the Third World State', in Douglas Kincaid and Alejandro Portes (eds.), *Society and Economy in the New Global Order*, Chapel Hill: University of North Carolina Press (1994).

Evans, Peter. B., and James Rauch, *Bureaucratic Structure and Economic Growth: Some Preliminary Analysis of Data on 35 Developing Countries*, Berkeley: University of California (1996).

Flatters, Frank, and W. Bentley McLeod, 'Administrative Corruption and Taxation', *International Tax and Public Finance*, V. 2: 397–417 (1995).

Fukuyama, Francis, *Trust: The Social Virtues and the Creation of Prosperity*, New York: The Free Press (1995).

Fulton Committee, *The Civil Service, Vol. I*, London: HMSO (1975).

Ghosal, U.N, *Contributions to the History of Hindu Revenue System*, Calcutta (1929).

*Global Competitiveness Report* (1996), World Economic Forum.

Godbole, Madhav, 'Corruption, Political Interference, and the Civil Service', in S. Guhan and Samuel Paul (eds.), *Corruption in India: Agenda for Action*, New Delhi: Vision Books (1997).

Gupta, Dipankar, 'The Question of Quotas: Reservation Versus Affirmative Action', *The Times of India*, September 26, 1998.

Habib, Irfan, *The Agrarian System of Mughal India, 1556–1707*, Bombay (1963).

———'The Mansab System, 1595–1637', *PIHC*, Patiala (1967).

Haley, John O., *Authority Without Power: Law and the Japanese Paradox*, New York: Oxford University Press (1991).

———'Japan's Postwar Civil Service: the Legal Framework', in Hyung-Ki Kim, Michio Muramatsu, T.J. Pempel, and Kozo Yamamura (eds.), *The Japanese Civil Service and Economic Development*, Oxford: Clarendon Press (1995).

Hall, Peter A., 'The Japanese Civil Service and Economic Development in Comparative Perspective', in Kim, Muramatsu, Pempel and Yamamura (1995).

Hazarkla, Niru, *Public Service Commissions*, New Delhi: Leela Devi Publications (1979).

Hutton, W., *The State We're In*, U.K.: Vintage Books (1996).

Ingraham, Patricia Wallace, *The Foundations of Merit: Public Service in American Democracy*, Baltimore: The Johns Hopkins University Press (1995).

Isham, Jonathan, Daniel Kaufmann, and Lant Pritchett, *Governance and Returns on Investment: An Empirical Investigation*, Policy Research Working Paper 1550, Washington D.C.: The World Bank (1995).

——*Civil Liberties, Democracy, and the Performance of Government Projects*, Washington D.C.: The World Bank (1996).

Johnson, Chalmers, *MITI and The Japanese Miracle*, Stanford: Stanford University Press (1982).

Johnston, Michael, *What Can Be Done About Entrenched Corruption?*, Paper for Annual Bank Conference on Development Economics, 1997, Washington D.C.: The World Bank (1997).

Kangle, R.P, *The Kautiliya Arthasastra*, Parts I, II and III, Delhi: Motilal Banarsidass Publishers (1992).

Katyal, K.K, 'How Autonomous are the Public Service Commissions'? *The Hindu*, December 1, 1990.

Katzenstein, Peter, *Policy and Politics in West Germany: The Growth of a Semisovereign State*, Philadelphia: Temple University Press (1987).

Khan, Sakina Yusuf, 'Fatal Attraction' *Sunday Times*, July 23, 1995.

Khilnani, Sunil, *Idea of India*, London: Hamish Hamilton (1997).

Kim, Hyung-Ki, 'The Japanese Civil Service and Economic Development: Lessons for Policymakers from Other Countries' in Kim, Muramatsu, Pempel, and Yamamura (1995).

Kim Hyung-Ki, Michio Muramatsu, T.J. Pempel, and Kozo Yamamura (eds.), *The Japanese Civil Service and Economic Development: Catalysts of Change*, Oxford: Clarendon Press (1995).

Kim, Paul, *Japan's Civil Service System: Its Structure, Personnel and Policies*, Westport: Greenwood Press (1988).

Klitgaard, R, *Controlling Corruption*, Berkeley: University of California Press (1988).

Knack, Stephen, and Philip Keefer, 'Institutions and Economic Performance: Cross-Country Tests Using Alternative Institutional Measures', *Economics and Politics* 7, 3 (1995).

Kuhn, Thomas S., *The Structure of Scientific Revolutions*, Chicago: University of Chicago Press, Phoenix Edition (1964).

Kulke, Hermann, 'Introduction: The Study of the State in Pre-modern India', in Kulke (1997).

Lindauer, David, and Barbara Nunberg (eds.), *Rehabilitating Government: Pay and Employment Reform in Africa*, Regional and Sectoral Studies Series, Washington D.C.: The World Bank (1994).

Mahalingam, Sudha, 'One More Ordinance', *Frontline*, November 20, 1998.

Mahalingam, Sudha, and Praveen Swami, 'Empowering Investigative Agencies', *Frontline*, January 9, 1998.

Mauro, Paolo, 'Corruption and Growth'. *Quarterly Journal of Economics*, 109 (1995).

——'The Effects of Corruption on Growth, Investment and Government Expenditure: A Cross-Country Analysis', in Kimberly A. Elliott, (ed.), *Corruption in the World Economy*, Washington D.C.: Institute for International Economics (1997).

Ministry of Personnel, Public Grievances and Pensions, Government of India, *Annual Report*, 1996–97.

Misra, B.B., *The Central Administration of the East India Company, 1773– 1834*, Manchester (1959).

——*The Bureaucracy in India, An Historical Analysis of Development up to 1947*, Delhi: Oxford University Press (1977).

——*The Indian Middle Classes: Their Growth in Modern Times*, Delhi: Oxford University Press (1978).

Moreland, W.H., *From Akbar to Aurangzeb*, London (1923).

Muramatsu, Michio and T.J. Pempel, 'The Evolution of the Civil Service before World War II', in Kim, Muramatsu, Pempel and Yamamura (1995).

Nair, Kiran Ramachandran., 'Social Movements for Development: Emerging Communication Strategies', *Man & Development*, June 1999.

Narsimhan, C.V., 'Prevention of Corruption: Towards Effective Enforcement', in Guhan and Paul (1997).

Nayar, Kuldip, 'Corruption and Complacency', *Indian Express*, October 13, 1998.

Neelima, Kota, 'Bureaucrats' Choices—Plum Inducements or Transfers', *Indian Express*, September 15, 1998.

Noonan, John T., *Bribes: The Intellectual History of a Moral Idea*, Berkeley: University of California Press (1987).

Noorani, A.G., 'The Right to Information', in Guhan and Paul (1997).

Nunberg, Barbara, *Managing the Civil Service: Reform Lessons from Advanced Industrial Countries*, World Bank Discussion Paper 254, Washington D.C.: The World Bank (1995).

Oldenburg, Philip, 'Middlemen in Third-World Corruption: Implications of an Indian Case', *World Politics*, 39, 4 (1987).

O'Malley, L.S.S., *The Indian Civil Service 1601–1930*, London: John Murray (1931).

Patil, R.L.M., 'How To make Lokayukta More Effective?', a Paper presented at the National Seminar on Administrative Reforms for Good Governance, November 2, 1998.

Paul, Samuel, 'Corruption: Who will Bell the Cat'? *Economic and Political Weekly*, June 7, 1997.

Paul, Sumita, 'A Bureaucracy in Need of Servicing', *Sunday Times*, July 23, 1995.

Pelsaert, F., W.H. Moreland, and P. Geyl, (trans), *Jahangir's India*, Cambridge (1925).

Pempel, T.J., and Michio Muramatsu, 'The Japanese Bureaucracy and

Economic development: Structuring a Proactive Civil Service', in Kim, Muramatsu, Pempel, and Yamamura (1995).

Prasad, Kamta, *Report on Determination of a Rational Salary Structure for Senior Functionaries (Joint Secretary and Above) in the Central Government*, New Delhi: Indian Institute of Public Administration, (1996).

Putnam, Robert, Robert Leonardi, and Rafaella Y. Nanetti, *Making Democracy Work: Civic Traditions in Modern Italy*, Princeton, N.J.: Princeton University Press (1993).

Quah, Jon. S.T., 'Culture Change in the Singapore Civil Service', in *Civil Service Reform in Latin America and the Caribbean*, Washington D.C.: The World Bank (1994).

Rahman, A.T. Rafique, 'Legal and Administrative Measures Against Bureaucratic Corruption in Asia', in Carino (ed.), *Bureaucratic Corruption in Asia: Causes, Consequences, and Controls*, Quezon City, The Phillipines: NMC Press (1986).

*Report of the Committee on Prevention of Corruption* (Santhanam Committee), Ministry of Home Affairs, New Delhi (1964).

*Report of the First Central Pay Commission*, Government of India, (1950).

*Report of the Second Central Pay Commission*, Government of India (1959).

*Report of the Third Central Pay Commission*, Government of India, (1973).

*Report of the Fourth Central Pay Commission*, Government of India, (1986).

*Report of the Fifth Central Pay Commission*, Government of India, (1997).

Rijckeghem, Caroline and Beatrice Weder, *Corruption and the Rate of Temptation: Do Low Wages in the Civil Service Cause Corruption?* (1996), Background Paper for the *World Development Report, 1997*.

Rose-Ackerman, Susan, 'Corruption and Development', Paper presented at the Annual Bank Conference on Development Economics, April 30 and May 1, 1997, Washington D.C.: The World Bank.

———'The Costs and Causes of Corruption', Paper presented for Panel Discussion on Corruption, 1997, Washington D.C.: International Monetary Fund.

Saran, P., *The Provincial Government of the Mughals 1526–1658*, Allahabad (1941).

Saxena, Pradeep, *Public Policy and Administration and Development*, Jaipur: Print Well (1988).

Schiavo-Campo, Rino, 'Civil Service and Economic Development—A Selective Synthesis of International Facts and Experience, (1996)', Background Paper for *World Development Report, 1997*.

Sen, Atindra (ed.), *Civil Service Reforms*, Mussoorie: Lal Bahadur Shastri National Academy of Administration (1995).

Sethi, K.C., G. Balaji, and C.P. Shrimali, *Private Sector: Remuneration Structure*, Gurgaon: Management Development Institute (1995).

Sewell, R., *A Forgotten Empire*, London (1900).

Silberman, Bernard S., *Cages of Reason: The Rise of the Rational State in*

*France, Japan, the United States, and Great Britain,* Chicago: University of Chicago Press (1993).

——'The Structure of Bureaucratic Rationality and Economic Development in Japan', in Kim, Muramatsu, Pempel, and Yamamura (1995).

Singh, Raj, 'Indian Bureaucracy and Development', *Indian Journal of Public Administration,* Vol. xxxiv, No. 2 (1985).

Sinha, Navnit, 'Role and Rationale of All India Services', *Indian Journal of Public Administration,* Vol. xxxvii, No. I, Jan–March 1991.

Spear, Percival, *A History of India, Vol Two, From the Sixteenth Century to Twentieth Century,* New Delhi: Penguin Books (1990).

Srinivasavardan, T.C.A., 'Some Aspects of Indian Administrative Service', *Indian Journal of Public Administration,* Vol. vii, No. I (1961).

Srivastva, L.P., *Public Personnel System in India,* Patna: Janaki Prakashan (1987).

Stein, Burton, 'Reapproaching Vijayanagara', in R. Frykenberg and P. Kolenda (eds.), *Studies in South India: An Anthology of Recent Research and Scholarship,* Madras/New Delhi, (1985).

Strategic Management Group, *Governance and Government: Emerging Scenarios in the 21st Century—From Administrative Bureaucracy to Service-Driven Result-Oriented Management by Government in India,* A Study Commissioned by the Fifth Central Pay Commission, (1995).

Subramaniam, V., *Social Background to India's Administration: A Social Economic Study of the Higher Civil Services in India,* Publications Division, Government of India (1961).

Swami, Praveen, 'A Step towards Autonomy', *Frontline,* January 9, 1998.

Tanzi, Vito, and Parthasarathi Shome, *A Primer on Tax Evasion,* IMF Working Papers, 93/21 (1993).

Thapar, Romila, *A History of India, Vol. One,* Penguin Books (1990).

*The East Asian Miracle: Economic Growth and Public Policy,* A World Bank Policy Research Report, Oxford University Press (1993).

Union Public Service Commission, *Thirty-Fifth Report,* 1984-5.

——*Thirty-Seventh Report,* 1986–7.

——*Thirty-Ninth Report,* 1988–9.

——*Fortieth Report,* 1989–90.

——*Forty-First Report,* 1990–91.

——*Forty-Second Report,* 1991–2.

——*Forty-Fifth Report,* 1994–5.

——*Forty-Seventh Report,* 1996–7.

Viswanathan, Renuka, 'Service Associations and Civil Service Integrity', Paper presented at the National Seminar on Administrative Reforms for Good Governance, November 2, 1998.

Vohra, N.N., 'The Era of Transfer Raj', *Indian Express,* November 12, 1998.

Wade, Robert, 'The System of Administrative and Political Corruption:

Canal Irrigation in South India', *Journal of Development Studies*, Vol. 18, No. 3 (1982).

——'Recruitment, Appointment and Promotions to Public Office in India', *World Development*, Vol. 13, No. 4 (1985).

——*The Governance of Infrastructure: Organizational Issues in the Operation and Maintenance of Irrigation Canals*, Washington D.C.: The World Bank (1994).

Weber, Max, 'Bureaucracy' in H.H. Gerth and C. Wright Mills (ed.), *From Max Weber: Essays in Sociology*, New York: Oxford University Press (1946).

——Guenther Roth and Claus Witich (eds.), *Economy and Society: An Outline of Interpretative Sociology*, Vols 1–3, Berkeley (1978).

Wei, Shang-Jin, *How Taxing is Corruption on International Investors?* Cambridge, Mass: Harvard University, Kennedy School of Government (1997).

Wolferen, K., *The Enigma of Japanese Power*, New York: Vintage Books (1990).

Woo-Cumings, Meredith, 'Developmental Bureaucracy in Comparative Perspective: The Evolution of the Korean Civil Service', in Kim, Muramatsu, Pempel, and Yamamura (1995).

*World Development Report, 1997*, Washington D.C.: The World Bank (1997).

Yamamura, Kozo, 'The Role of the Government in Japan's 'Catch-up' Industrialization: A Neoinstitutionalist Perspective', in Kim, Muramatsu, Pempel, and Yamamura (1995).

# Index